THE COLLEGE BOARD
GUIDE TO
Jobs and Career Planning

THE COLLEGE BOARD GUIDE TO

GUIDE TO

Jobs and Career Planning

Second edition

Joyce Slayton Mitchell

COLLEGE ENTRANCE EXAMINATION BOARD, NEW YORK

Copies of this book may be ordered from College Board Publications, Box 886, New York, New York 10101-0886. Enclose a check for $14.00 plus $3.95 handling.

Editorial inquiries concerning this book should be directed to Editorial Office, The College Board, 45 Columbus Avenue, New York, New York 10023-6992.

Library of Congress Catalog Number: 90-082324

ISBN: 0-87447-467-1

Printed in the United States of America

9 8 7 6 5 4 3 2 1

Contents

To my Hardwick, Vermont, tennis team:

A model for young women, these professional women have learned well how to balance marriage, young children, and a professional career, and yet each finds time for sport and encouragement of others. With love and much admiration to Deborah Aschenbach, Sara Behrsing, Cheryl Crytzer, Sue Hudson, Jocelyne Lussier, and Kathleen Sampson.

Sources and Acknowledgments

The primary sources of information for *The College Board Guide to Jobs and Career Planning* are the 1994–95 *Occupational Outlook Handbook, Career Guide to Industries*, 1992, and the *Occupational Projections and Training Data*, 1992, published by the United States Department of Labor. Other primary sources were young men and women in the first five years of their career, and the many Career Planning Offices on college campuses from every part of America. Many career stories were cited from *Forbes, Fortune, Working Woman, The New York Times*, and *The Wall Street Journal*, as well as from many trade and professional magazines and newsletters. It is a pleasure to thank the many young men and women who told what life is like in their careers. Enthusiastic thanks too, to my colleagues at The College Board for this new edition, especially to Associate Director of Publications Carolyn Trager, and Senior Editor Renée Gernand.

Joyce Slayton Mitchell
New York City
January 1994

Introduction

THE MID-1990s WORLD OF WORK

It's tough to read that Sears is cutting 50,000 jobs, IBM 25,000, Boeing 20,000, United Technologies 10,500, and McDonnell Douglas 8,700. But the truth is that these large firms have not been major contributors to the labor force for some years. Nearly 75 percent of the 1.5 million new jobs created in 1992 were in companies with fewer than 20 employees. Dun & Bradstreet points out that more than 500,000 new businesses started up in the first nine months of 1992.

The *National Business Employment Weekly* reports that the top 10 job opportunities for the mid-1990s are in areas of the economy that will be called upon to help resolve our most pressing national problems. These growth areas are:

1. Career counseling
2. Computer services
3. Day care
4. Educational services and products
5. Financial planning
6. Home health care
7. Marketing and promotion services
8. Senior fitness and recreation
9. Environmental protection
10. Business services

More jobs were created in health care in 1992 than in any other field. Next among the areas of growth were education, followed by business and management services and securities and investments.

Future job patterns are best described as mobile, with people moving from company to company to self-employment and back again to a company. In other words, there will be more job hopping than job climbing. To fit into this new pattern, you will need portable health insurance and pension plans that go with you as you move. Many of you will be self-employed for some part of your lives. You will create your own careers, and that's new for the 1990s. Creating your own job pattern is an opportunity for you to develop your career as you want it, when and where you want it. You can alter your career pattern to suit different phases of your life. The work world of the 1990s has changed. Be ready to change with it!

PART 1

High School Planning

Curriculum and College Choices Are Career Choices

It's true. Many students can find a full life in high school with sports, clubs, publications, music, cafeteria, and each other. But most educators and parents like to think that your classes are the core, or center, of your education. Whether you like your classes or not, most of you will agree that high school courses are here to stay. The question is, how do you choose which classes to take? Which subjects to study? Which curriculum to sign up for?

Some students choose by what they want to be when they get out of school. Others choose according to college admission requirements. Still others take the minimum courses they need to graduate from high school. The problem with making curriculum decisions based on your future career plans is that chances are you will change your mind many times. And if you take only the minimum science, math, and foreign language requirements, you'll never know how good you are and how much depth you can handle. The best way to choose—the only way you can't go wrong— is to always select *the strongest curriculum you can handle well regardless of what you want to be or where you want to go after high school*. In that way, you are keeping all doors open. Like all choices in education, your future options depend on your past record. Every course you take determines what selections you can make next.

You can't choose Advanced Placement (AP) French in your senior year if you haven't had a B or better in French IV. The same is true for mathematics and science. Keep in mind that nothing, not even an SAT total score of 1400, is as important for getting into college as is a strong curriculum. And the only way to show your strength is to succeed in, for example, mathematics and foreign language. Calculus and AP Latin or AP Spanish can separate top scholars from ordinary students.

When you graduate from high school, you should be able to look at your academic record and ask yourself, "What do I do best? What do I like best? Am I strong in science? In history? In mathematics? If so, what choices should I make for college?" It's no good to say, "I want to study premed," when you have C's in biology and chemistry. It doesn't make sense to talk about a law degree when English and history are your worst subjects. Keep an open mind about your career choice, and do your best in high school so that you will know where your interests and abilities lie on the basis of the curriculum you have studied. It's too late to tell yourself, "I could have done better if I had studied harder." What you should have learned about yourself if you haven't studied hard is that you don't put studying very high on your list of priorities even when studying harder means better grades.

When you think about it, curriculum choices in the eighth and ninth and tenth grades are career choices. For example, just think of the career implications if you choose general math over algebra I in the eighth grade. Or if you decide not to take a foreign language. These are both clear career decisions, or at least have career implications. You began to make basic career decisions way back then, in the eighth grade. And curriculum choices lead to college choices, which in turn build the foundation from which career options and directions are selected. For example, if you can meet a rigorous curriculum challenge with calculus, French V, and AP Physics, you've got one set of college options, but quite another set of choices if you select *down* in your senior year to probability and statistics or change from foreign language to a humanities elective. Or fill in a fifth course with a fine arts or computer science selection. Subjects that you can learn while watching TV are not competitive enough to get you into the most selective colleges. The point to be made here is that high school curriculum choices add up to college choices, and college choices lead to career possibilities.

Reading *The College Board Guide to Jobs and Career Planning* will help you raise your level of career awareness as you think about college choices. You can ask more than "Can I get in? What's it like? How much will it cost?" You can add a career dimension to your questions: "What will become of me if I go to Grinnell, to Carolina, to Penn?" You can ask the admission officers at the colleges where you are thinking of applying what becomes of their graduates. If 60 percent go to graduate school, ask if they go to law school or business school or for an education degree or a social work degree or a Ph.D. The college environment will be different if most graduates go to graduate school rather than directly into a job. It will be different if most go into engineering or into fine arts.

The career descriptions in this book will raise your awareness of your job possibilities. To get a sense of the range and complexity of careers, read whatever areas interest you. Don't end up in college with narrow views of jobs that you picked up through hearsay, through TV versions of trial lawyers, cops, and docs, or through parental pressure on you to go into computers or management or architecture. Read about the educational and personal skills required for success in these careers. Do they sound like you?

Are you aware that not all broadcasters, advertising copywriters, or newspaper correspondents were communications majors, advertising majors, or journalism majors? They came from every major offered in college. In other words, even if you want to be in advertising or to become a writer, you don't have to find the college with the greatest number of students majoring in advertising or writing. A safer bet would be to go to the best college you can get into and study whatever interests you most. It's important for you to know that a psychology or philosophy or history major has great career potential and offers opportunities for all students who learn how to read and write and think well. There are many career opportunities in every major; it's what you learn through the major that counts.

As you read about these careers, notice where people work. Are they all on the East Coast or in a major city? Is that where you want to be? Notice how many workers are women, how many are black, how many are Hispanic.

So you see, you were already making career choices when

you selected your high school curriculum. And these choices will be influenced by your college choices, which will lead to your choice of major. No matter where you are in the process, it's your school and college record today that counts for your career choices of tomorrow.

Careers Are Developmental

How can you decide what you are going to be when you don't even know all the things there are to be? How can you decide what you are going to be when you aren't sure how much you'd like to do the things you've heard about? It's difficult to commit yourself to a career decision now when you aren't at all sure how your values and priorities will change later.

For many students, it is easier to think about what you don't want to be. Perhaps one thing you're sure of is that you don't want to be a dentist like your dad or an architect like your mom. Or you don't want to live in western Kansas like your family does. Or you don't want to be tied down to a lifestyle that takes every cent you earn to send all the kids to college.

Your career decision will be easier if you realize that you *will* change jobs and directions many times in your life. You aren't choosing one career now to last you until your retirement. Just as your values and priorities have changed in the last five years, they will keep changing in the next five years and during the next twenty-five years. Look at the men and women of different ages whom you know—your uncles and aunts, cousins and neighbors, and friends. Think about them and their occupational careers. Ask them what their priorities have been at different stages in their lives. Ask about the moves they may have made from one part of the country to another, the changes in their jobs, in their families, in the amount of money they made and spent, and about their changing interests during different periods of their lives.

Just as you yourself change over time, as a result of your experiences and the people you meet, the world of work is ever-changing too. It used to be that a young man or woman could plan for one job or one career. But today the average young person can look forward to six or seven different jobs, six or seven minicareers, which will make up a lifetime of work. For example, you may start out as a salesperson, go into management in a real estate agency, leave all that for a political appointment in your state government, venture into commercial real estate in a resort area, expand that position into a job as a recreational developer—and even then you may be open for several more changes before your work life is completed. Many young people who were interviewed for this book are already in their second or third different job, and they are still in their twenties. Some are picking up business training anywhere they can to get the experience they need to go into business for themselves. Others are making a change to get higher-level jobs and more money. And still others are changing jobs to get a broader base of experience in business because they plan a management career in the future.

Something good happens to you when you realize that you aren't choosing the one and only right job, or the wrong job, for you. Something good happens to you when you can use everything you experience to build what you eventually become. There is no way that you can, or even should, know now what your future will be. If you take the attitude that everything counts and that choosing your career is a long process, it may be easier for you to see how your schoolwork fits into this process. The subjects you are studying now, the sports you are playing, the music you are making or listening to, the jobs and internships at which you are working, the friends you make, and the test scores you get are all part of your career development.

The decisions you make now—what to do this summer and next summer, what to do on weekends, what to do at home, what courses to take, what clubs to join, what extracurricular and recreational activities to participate in—*are* career decisions.

One way to help decide what you are going to do is to get your focus off the outside pressures and back on yourself. You don't have to concentrate solely on possible prejudices and sex-role stereotypes, or on the school's expectations for you, or on the world of work, the inflated economy, the rising or falling dollar, the international market, the national debt, or the changing labor market.

All these things will influence your eventual career decision, but what you first need to do is explore your personal career opportunities, no matter what the external conditions and projected changes may be.

PART 2

College Planning

College Career Planning

Every college in the country has a career planning office. Not every college student in the country knows about it. Or uses it. Get to know the resources in your career planning office. You can expect to find information on:

1. Examinations for graduate school
2. Medical, law, business, and Ph.D. advisers
3. Résumé writing
4. Interviewing skills
5. Job-hunting strategies
6. Your personal credential file that you can use for the rest of your life
7. Corporate recruitment on campus
8. Summer jobs
9. Internships (summer, term, and year)
10. Alumni contacts for summer and full-time jobs
11. How to search the job opportunities
12. General career information (booklets, books, and articles on specific careers)
13. Employers (brochures, annual reports, and articles about particular companies, agencies, and firms)
14. Handouts (information sheets on résumé development and interviewing, free magazines, and career guides)

Let's say you are a junior engineering major at Vanderbilt University. You want a summer job in Chicago to be near your

15

friends who have an apartment there. You are thinking about getting a job waiting tables because you have no idea how to get an engineering job. Go to your career planning office. Ask for a list of all Vanderbilt graduates who work in Chicago engineering firms. And ask the career planning officers about other engineering job possibilities. You can learn a lot in a summer job about engineering options following graduation. Besides the summer job, you will have started a network for an engineering job search a year from now.

Graduate Record Examinations

Let's say you are a French major and have no idea what you are going to do after college. Maybe go to Europe for a year. Maybe teach high school French. You really haven't thought that much about it. Go to the career planning office. Find out about taking the Graduate Record Examinations (GRE) so that when you do decide to go for a master's degree or to get into a doctoral program—even five years from now—you'll have a GRE score reflecting your ability when you were in college and still studying. Or you may take a GRE in a particular subject (other than foreign languages). But check into examination dates and deadlines in your *junior* year, while you still have time to plan and study. Many of the subject exams are given only in the fall. You can imagine how many seniors asked about the GRE at Thanksgiving time and lost out because they hadn't planned ahead. The undecided student and the preprofessional have more in common than you may think. Both need to take examinations to apply to graduate school. The career planning office has all the information you need.

There are two types of Graduate Record Examinations: the general test, given for three and one-half hours in the morning, tests verbal, quantitative, and analytic ability. Subject tests include biology, chemistry, computer science, economics, education, engineering, English literature, geology, history, mathematics, music, physics, political science, psychology, and sociology. Each test is three hours and measures mastery and comprehension basic to graduate study in major fields. All education majors and liberal arts majors who are considering eventually getting a master's degree should take the GRE while they are still in college. Pick up a copy of the *GRE Information Bulletin* in the career planning office; the *Bulletin* explains all the details. Don't wait expecting someone else to tell you that these exams are required.

Many colleges expect students to take the responsibility for getting such information, so check out the GRE now.

Miller Analogy Test

The Miller Analogy Test (MAT) is required by some university graduate programs, especially for psychology and education majors. This test focuses on conceptual reasoning and vocabulary.

Trusty Tips for Career Planning in College

1. Plan now!
2. Make a friend in the career planning office (and of every interviewer you ever meet in your life).
3. Remember the crucial words of Mark Twain: "You never get a second chance to make a first impression."

Consider the Ph.D.

Much is said and written about medical school, law school, and business school. But what do you know about getting a Ph.D. degree? Who goes for a Ph.D. anyway? Did you know, for instance, that there are typically three groups of students going for their Ph.D. degrees?

First come the scholars who find a six- to ten-year university program a challenge. They love the academic environment, they don't find poverty a burden, and they are at home on campus. These scholarly graduate students feel alive in the library and don't mind sharing an apartment and food. They seldom think about the job market or where a Ph.D. will lead them.

The second group are the career students. Going through a long graduate program is worth the process to get what they want. The academic environment does not thrill them; they have little tolerance for esoteric professors. They know that the Ph.D. will provide them with an upper-middle-class lifestyle. Career graduate students are ambitious and are interested in the applied aspects of their study. They often choose their program by the prestige of the university rather than by the reputation of the particular department.

Last, there are the undecideds who don't know what else to do, especially in today's bleak job market. Often very "good" students, they are most comfortable staying in college for a few more years. This undecided group is made up of students who have always been very conscientious and have often been straight-A students since elementary school. They may end up in a Ph.D. program because they are frequently advised to stay in college while their more adventurous colleagues are urged to jump into the job world or the family business. Members of the undecided group often leave the Ph.D. program after three or four years of graduate work.

This division is oversimplified, but still, you'll probably recognize yourself as belonging more to one group than to another. Regardless of your group, you need to know which Ph.D. program is best for you. To begin your search, ask professors in your major. Send letters to graduate admission offices and ask for an application, a catalog, and the name of the chairperson of the department in which you want to study. Compare your grade-point average (GPA) and GRE scores with those of the students who have been accepted in the past few years. Let's say you are interested in a Ph.D. program in French. Go to your career planning office and ask for the guides to Ph.D. programs; like undergraduate college guides, many of them rate the programs. For example, one guide rated the top Ph.D. programs in French in the following order: Yale, Princeton, Columbia, University of California at San Diego (UCSD), University of Pennsylvania, and University of Michigan. Harvard, University of Texas, UCLA, and UCSD are considered tops in Spanish. In the career planning office you will also be able to find the name of the chairperson for each department and the phone number, the percentage of students accepted for a Ph.D. program, and the number of students in the Ph.D. program. It's all there for the asking.

A Ph.D. admission counselor at UCLA, Hilda Peinado, says the most important considerations for acceptance are (1) the letters of recommendation from your undergraduate professors in your chosen field of graduate study and (2) your statement of purpose. Peinado says that your professors must attest to your potential for graduate work in the field in which you are applying, your curiosity, your potential for research, and your analytic skills. Just as important as your recommendations is your own statement of purpose. Be sure to include your ultimate academic and career goal and your perceived intellectual ability. Are you focused, even as you are open to new ideas? Do you have specific areas that interest you most?

How do you pay for a Ph.D. program? Most graduate students must support themselves in graduate school. Few parents provide the money for a Ph.D., although some may help out. The typical Ph.D. candidate has a job as a teaching assistant (TA) or as a research assistant (RA). At Berkeley, for example, 3,200 out of 9,000 graduate students have graduate student instructorships, which pay $10,953 a year, with a four-year limit. These positions are competitive and usually require about 20 hours of teaching or research a week. At the University of Arizona, the TAs make around $1,265 a month and the RAs make about $917 a month. The University of Texas pays about $7,000 a year and waives tuition fees. Each university is different, although graduate students can plan on paying their own way with a 20-hour weekly commitment. At the University of Texas, the first-year program requires less commitment, and the TA may teach only 7 hours a week. At UCSD, Ph.D. candidates entering in 1993–94 were offered full tuition plus $12,015 for a teaching assistantship plus medical insurance for as long as they maintained a reasonably good record. Check into the various job opportunities and financial perks before you decide which Ph.D. programs to apply to.

Whatever your graduate school plan, you will find that your campus career planning office is the very best resource for getting started. Work closely with your college major adviser as you learn more about your options. If you have graduated, go back to your career placement office and catch up on the necessary information, starting your personal credential file at once. It's *never too late* to get help from your career planning office.

Medical School

Most colleges have a premed adviser. Ask at your career planning office who that person is. You will have to take the Medical College Admission Test (MCAT), which is offered only twice a year. Read *Medical Admissions Requirements*, the examination information booklet, available in the career planning office. Check with your college major adviser as well as the premed adviser.

Law School

Colleges usually have a prelaw adviser. Find out who that person is at the career planning office; it's never too early to meet the adviser. You must take the Law School Admission Test (LSAT). Find out where the law school catalogs are and be sure to see the *Pre-Law Handbook* in the career planning office. Keep your college major adviser posted about your law school plans.

Business School

Liberal arts and business students who plan to earn a Master of Business Administration (M.B.A.) will need to take the Graduate Management Admission Test (GMAT). Remember, you don't have to be a business major to go to business school. The competitive "B-schools" accept liberal arts students from every major—even art history. Ask for a resource book such as *The Official Guide to MBA Programs, Admissions & Careers*. The numbers of women and minorities enrolling in business school have declined, which means these candidates have the edge in admission at most institutions.

What Becomes of All Those History Majors?

When a law student becomes a lawyer, a medical student becomes a doctor, an education major becomes a teacher, an anthropology major becomes an anthropologist, and an M.B.A. goes into corporate management—it's easy. They are following a clear line that we understand. It makes sense. But what happens to all those history majors? And English and psychology and math majors? And what happens to art history people?

Just think. Over half of all college graduates don't go into a career that is even related to their major! Do you ever wonder what they do? What becomes of them? How they know what to look for? What interviews to go after? And what about the 26 percent of last year's class who are unemployed? How do they know what jobs to look for now that they are out of college, off campus, and without easy access to campus recruiters and the placement office?

When you choose your college by what programs it offers or choose your major because you want to go into business, computers, pre-this or pre-that, you should first be aware that if your college does a good job of educating, you will change your major at least three times in your first year. In other words, major choices change as fast as students learn who they are, what they are interested in, and what their options are. Go ahead. Talk to college juniors and seniors and ask them about their college majors to see what I mean. It often goes like this: "My major? Well, first of all it took me six semesters to get out of computers." Or, "I spent the first year in business before I went into psychology and then realized it's English literature that I want to study." Or, "My family said I couldn't major in music, so I went into engineering for two years before I finally switched into a math major in liberal arts so I could minor in music theory."

See what I mean? It doesn't make sense to focus on ideas for your career and college major if you're bound to change. It *does* make sense to realize that you will change majors and career directions as you learn more about yourself. You are *not* choosing one major and one career now to last a lifetime. Just think of how you've changed in the past four years because of your high school experiences and the people you've met. You can expect those kinds of changes in the next four years. And the next and the next.

Students are often told that the particular college they go to—the one with the most prestige, the one with the highest "rating" and a major in the hottest career—is the only route to success. Big money, fame, the big time. Making decisions on the basis of what others think often gets people of all ages into trouble. Go by what is right for *you*. Listen to your own assessment of your abilities, interests, hopes, and dreams. Go for music and not engineering if that's you. Go for law if you can't stand blood, even if your whole family have been doctors before you. The truth is that research from the Center for Entrepreneurial Management on what employers like in job candidates shows that corporations prefer liberal arts graduates to business management majors, but what counts most of all is shined shoes (78 percent) or a strong handshake (67 percent) compared to a degree from an Ivy League college (1 percent)! In other words, trust yourself. Follow your heart and intuition as well as the advice of others. Pay attention to which high school subjects you love to study, which you hate and never study, how you like to spend your leisure time. How you spend your time when it's up to you is *you*. Respect your assessment of yourself in all education and career decisions.

The careers in *The College Board Guide to Jobs and Career Planning* are arranged by groups: arts, business, education, health, social service, and so on. You will find the career you want to read about by looking for the group you expect it to be in. You expect to find doctor, nurse, physical therapist under health careers. You expect to find real estate salesperson, stockbroker, automobile salesperson under sales. But where would you expect to find environmental accountant? What does a toxicologist do? How does an intellectual property lawyer get into that kind of work? Because jobs aren't always classified as expected, a dozen hot jobs for the late 1990s were added to stretch your imagination from logical career groups to jobs that recruit from a great variety of college majors—jobs that people often "end up in" rather than plan to go into, jobs that are the outgrowth and offshoot of working for a firm that sometimes gives employees ideas for creating their own niche.

Read what the people who hold these odd jobs have to say. Read, too, to get a small sampling of the broad range of jobs that are out there in the career world for you to consider. Try to separate the world of college majors from the world of work. When you meet someone who works at something that intrigues you, ask about it. Find out what it's like to be an outpatient consultant, a restaurant site selector, a wireless specialist. What are the day-in, day-out tasks, the responsibilities, the hours and weekends and nights like? Look into odd jobs. They can lead you to other work that may be just right for you. Just because you can't define it doesn't mean you won't like it. Who knows? You may be proud to end up in an odd job!

Toxicologist and Other Odd Hot Jobs for the Mid-1990s

Environmental accountant
Analyzes the cost factors underlying environmental projects. College background in accounting, biology, engineering, or geology. Best job possibilities in former chemical and defense plants.

Network administrator
Figures out how to link computers and workstations to save company costs. College background in computer science. Best job possibilities in urban areas with a concentration of personal computers.

Outplacement consultant
Advises workers being displaced from corporate jobs. College background in psychology or a business degree and experience. Best job possibilities in large cities and suburbs where corporate headquarters are found.

Toxicologist
Measures pollutants and toxic wastes. College background in science or public health. Best job opportunities in industrialized areas.

Restaurant site selector
Buys or leases real estate for fast-food and specialty restaurants. College background in communications or food industry. Best opportunities: everywhere.

Training manager
Conducts employee training programs advocated by public health and corporate officers. College background in education, business, or communications. Best job opportunities wherever large corporations are located.

Intellectual property lawyer
Protects innovations and inventions through patents and legal actions. College background includes a law degree plus specialized training in patents. Best opportunities in Boston and San Francisco, areas with many high-tech firms.

Chief information officer
A specialist who bridges the information needs of insiders and outsiders linked by computers. College background includes training in computers and business. Best job opportunities where large corporate and nonprofit organizations are located.

Member service director
Over 100,000 professional associations require specialists to direct programs serving their members. College background in human resources, business, or communications. Best job opportunities in Washington, D.C., New York, and Chicago.

Electronic publishing specialist
Desktop publishing is growing faster than the numbers of college graduates trained to do the work. College background in com-

puters, design, liberal arts, and strong interest in publishing. Best job opportunities in major cities.

Computational chemist
Modeling molecules is a key to innovation in biotechnology fields. College background in chemistry, chemical engineering, mathematics, and computer science. Best job opportunities on the East Coast and in California.

Wireless specialist
The cellular phone industry has taken off without warning. College background in electrical engineering, marketing, and/or design. Best job opportunities in major cities.

Special
Considerations

There are many ways to work. Flexibility in the times you choose to work is increasingly an option. You can work full time, or you may wish to share a job and use the rest of your time to write, make furniture, or rear a child. You may want to work part time or volunteer some of your time. And you may want to create your own job. Flextime means you can select the hours of the day you prefer to work. Two-career families often arrange flextime to cover the hours when their children are at home. There is home-based work, growing as fast as people install computers in their homes. A compressed work week is another option, often used in the summer to increase the hours in a four-day week so employees can leave early on Friday.

In the mid-1990s, young men and women will have more options for lifestyle and workstyle alternatives than at any time in history. With fewer job opportunities, some of you may end up in flextime arrangements and temporary jobs whether you chose them or not. Some of you will choose either to work on your own and make all the money you need or to agree that your partner will take the major responsibility for making money while you do something else—or any system in between. Whether you choose a nontraditional work schedule or it is all you can get, focus first on *you* and the kind of life you want, and then on the job, as you make your choices and work out your career.

Workstyle Options for Women

As wonderful as the career opportunities will be for women in the late nineties compared with the eighties, and although it is true that women no longer have any trouble becoming dentists, lawyers, business managers, or engineers, it's important for you to be aware that women are still making 70 cents to the men's $1. It's important for college women to realize that one year after a divorce, a husband improves his standard of living an average of 42 percent, while a wife's income drops by 73 percent according to a Stanford University study. Read those facts one more time. They concern every woman. Women over 30 know they need to make money. It's often young women who don't take the need to make money seriously enough—those who are still in school or college, where they can do more to improve their prospects for making money than at any other time in their lives.

No one talks about it—you don't either—but if somewhere in your mind you have the idea that someone else will be financially responsible for you, then you probably think you don't have to make quite as much money as your brother does. What is it that keeps some young women from aspiring to make money? No one should have to choose between love and making money!

It's not marriage and children that make women choose their careers differently; both women and men plan to marry and have children. It's the *kind* of marriage where men have control that limits women. But you can choose between one kind of marriage that permits meaningful work for both husband and wife and another kind that doesn't.

What will your life be like five years from now? Ten years from now? Fifteen years from now? Will you be married? Will you have children? Will you be working? If you are like most women, you will be doing all these things at some time in your life. Everyone, especially young women, should know that in the United States almost half (48 percent) of all mothers with infants under two are employed full time outside their homes. That's with children under two years old! The rate is even higher for mothers with school-age children under 18; in this age group more than one in every two mothers (61 percent) is employed.

The U.S. Department of Labor projects that women will account for 15 million of the expected 26 million net increase in the civilian labor force between 1990 and 2005. With such an increase in the number of women in the work force, they must realize that it isn't just the glass ceilings that we have to worry about, but also the sticky floors that keep women in low-paying jobs. In 1990, women held 76 percent of the lowest grade-level jobs in the federal government work force. At the senior-executive service level, women held only 11 percent of the jobs. And in nonprofit colleges and universities, women make up only 11.6 percent of full professors nationwide. Women have made their greatest inroads at community colleges, where the pay is lowest. Even when they become full professors with tenure, women still earn less than men. At Harvard, male professors earn $93,600 per year on average while women of equal rank earn $79,000 on average. Many medical school departments do not have a single female full professor. And, the John F. Kennedy School of Government at Harvard has 20 male professors and only one female.

And yet, women are working because, like men, they need money to support themselves and their children. Helping you aspire to and plan for a career that makes money is a goal of this book. How does a young woman go about choosing a career? After all, you probably don't know the answers now to where you want to live, what the work opportunities will be, what your income will be, whether or not you will marry and, if so, what your husband will be doing, and whether you want to have children or how many you will want to have.

A career starts with education in early childhood and extends through retirement. There isn't any work you do that does not count as part of your career. Caring for babies and children, managing a home, fund-raising, working as an engineer, and working part time in sales all contribute to your career development. It's all work, even though some is paid and some unpaid, some is part time and some full time or overtime.

Work requires skills to be learned and managed. Many skills are transferable from one job to the next. Some transferable skills you may learn at work are speaking, listening, letter writing, leadership, decision making, persuasion, and managing time. Transferable career skills are learned everywhere, including in the home. Family work—for example, raising children—counts toward your career development as definitely as does work in the military or in apprenticeship or in college or in the first years of a paid job.

With the knowledge that everything counts—even motherhood—and that choosing your career is a long process, it may be easier for you to see how your school and family activities and current job and interests fit into this process.

Women are often brought up differently and treated differently from men, both in school and at work. Research shows that to succeed at work, women have to accept these differences—and the anxiety and frustration that go with them—before they can seriously plan their career strategies. You may always be in conflict between achieving success in your career and achieving success as a mother. You may always worry about personal criticism of your work even though it doesn't bother your husband or your male competitors. You may always find it difficult to be assertive and to initiate your ideas compared to the ease with which your brother initiates his. In other words, women have to learn to manage by accepting the traditional conflicts of successful women. A woman must be able to say with confidence that she wants a career and that she is willing to confront the problems that she will encounter because she is a woman. This advice is not only for women aiming for policy-making positions but also for women intending to go into law, politics, theology, engineering, medicine, mathematics, science, health administration, educational administration, or *any field where the men are*. For wherever the men are is where the money and policy-making are!

Workstyle Options for Men

Traditionally, a young man's focus in choosing a career has been very different from that of a young woman. The young man is expected to financially support himself plus others when he grows up. The young woman is expected to be financially supported when she grows up. You have been programmed to measure your success by the amount of money you make. She has been programmed to judge her value by the amount of money her husband makes. Do you recognize your own expectations in this description? The more you understand how you are systematically set up for certain choices, the more you will see a chance to expand those choices.

It's easy to see how young men have been raised to fit the stereotype from the time they are children and are asked, "What are you going to be when you grow up?" Your earliest answer was probably "a cowboy," "a fireman," or "an astronaut." Adults don't stop pressing little boys about what they are going to be until the little boys actually become grown-up wage earners.

Many teachers, counselors, and parents are not always conscious that they are preparing you to be a "success object." They advise you to take a strong academic program with a lot of math and science, leading to a profession or business career that offers a lot of money or prestige. Of course, they will say that everyone is different and each person is an individual, but when it comes to the nitty-gritty, the male stereotype is usually in the back of their minds. Most educators assume that a man will put his career first; his friendships and marriage will then just fall naturally into place. If a man's work life goes really well, it's believed, he won't be bothered by poor personal relationships anyway. The unspoken assumption is that he must primarily be the achiever and provider rather than a person who can choose to integrate his work life with his personal life.

Remember that you don't have to fit the stereotype. You can begin to see yourself developing as a whole person with many choices rather than as a man who has to earn more than anyone else and constantly compete with his peers. In the nineties you don't have to be a success object. You can endeavor to be successful at many things, not just making money; but of course you can choose that too. You can be successful in your work and the other aspects of your life. You can be successful with your friends, with your family, in the community, in the arts and music, in sports, and in other hobbies. In the nineties you will have a chance to work through your own values to develop your own lifestyle. You don't have to define yourself only as a breadwinner and measure yourself as a real man by the amount of money you make. You can consider sharing the stress and responsibility of being a breadwinner.

In the late 1990s, you can look forward to an equal partnership with your wife. As equal partners, you can both decide what each will do. Shopping, cooking, making money, raising children, painting the house, cutting the grass, doing the laundry all have to be done and should be shared for the partnership to work. But equal partnership doesn't mean you both have to paint the house. It does mean you will both decide who will do what based on who is better at a job or who has more time for it or who has greater interest in it or who hates it the least, instead of deciding on the basis of being male or female. Equal partnership doesn't mean that you are the same; it means that you both have equal opportunity and equal responsibility for making decisions about all the choices living a full life demands.

When you understand the options open to you, you won't be tied to the values of the man who says he is best because he makes the most money. When you value yourself as an individual, you can consider all the career possibilities on the basis of your interests, your abilities, your hopes and dreams and ambitions. You won't have to specialize too soon, as though the only purpose of life is to get to the top first. You'll be able to change careers as your interests change. You'll be able to redirect yourself as you grow. You'll be able to tie in your career with your family life. You'll be able to say, "Hey, wait a minute! That's not for me. I don't have to make the most money to feel that I'm successful. I can succeed much better in other ways." You can discover what kind of a guy you really are. You can work out your career with a partner and enjoy having someone else help bring in the bread. You can be free to explore many job opportunities that are unique for you and the kind of life you want to live.

Student Jobs

Choosing a college major, choosing an internship, and choosing a summer or part-time winter job experience are educational pathways toward career development. Your actual work experiences provide opportunities for you to try out your career goals in a real work situation.

Once you get a career idea that makes sense to you, use your student job or internship for a trial run in that career, whether it's paid work or volunteer work, or for college credit. Work at a car agency if you are interested in sales, or in a hospital if you are interested in health care. Work with a children's group in a day camp or child-care center if your interest is in education, or in a bookstore or publishing house if the book business interests you. Try an internship in a bank or real estate office if you are considering a career in finance.

Even though the kind of work you are likely to get is at the lowest level in that field and, therefore, reserved for beginners, the menial tasks become meaningful if you apply what you learn to your own career development. If you are doing a repetitious job that takes no thinking, you can look around at the workplace as a whole and figure out what the next step up is for people who have permanent jobs and are eligible for promotions. Who is your boss? Who is the top boss? Do any of those jobs look interesting? For example, a job in a real estate office may consist of painting front doors on homes to be sold. But you can look around and see the hours kept by the other salespeople, listen to the kinds of questions clients ask and the answers salespeople give, and notice which salespeople are making the most money, which are putting in the most time, and which are living a life you would like to live.

Getting ahead in a job is like learning to work or to ski. You've got to put so many hours and so many miles into learning, no matter who you are or how fit you are or how well-qualified you are. Often a job is disappointing, especially when you start at the bottom. Setting goals is important at any job level. It gives you something to learn right now and makes you realize that you won't always be at the bottom. It's especially important when you just begin a job and it turns out that the job isn't everything you had hoped it would be.

Your work may not always seem related to where you want to end up. But when you see how everything you learn in a student job counts for something, then your present work activity takes on new meaning. When the beginning architect understands how she can use her training to get ahead, then the tedious job of drafting other people's ideas becomes more meaningful. When the intern in special education sees the variety of programs offered for teenagers, he can picture himself supervising some of those programs. Besides making money, your purpose in a student job is career exploration and development to help you determine all the possible directions for your future.

Stopouts: Working Ways to Learn

Another work alternative, besides student jobs, is an internship or a voluntary program for an academic year. An internship is a full-time supervised work experience in which a student can learn about a career or field of interest. Usually students are not paid, but often they can earn college credit. Some students "stop out" of formal education for a year after high school or after their first year of college to test a career idea. A Princeton junior stopped out and took a job as a hospital orderly for 10 months; she returned to college convinced that medicine was her vocation and that she wanted to be a doctor. Even though a medical orderly's career is very different from a doctor's, she learned about medicine as a *system*, about the different jobs within it, and became certain about the job she was after.

Doug Patt, from the University of California at Santa Cruz, has stopped out of college twice to see what the world of work is like. His second stopout included a job in a management agency for recording artists, where he learned about the music business on his own. He also toured with a blues singer. When he returned to college, he had a practical sense about the career he had chosen: film production. What does he say he learned? "I learned that if you want something in business, you've got to learn about and experience every aspect, not just about performance."

One stopout placement agency for member colleges and universities is Venture, located at Brown University in Providence, Rhode Island. Specializing in undergraduate internships, Venture provides jobs for hundreds of students in business as well as in nonprofit organizations.

Internships, apprenticeships, and voluntary jobs while you stop out from college are like college credentials and paid jobs. They are all valid educational pathways to career development.

Career Planning Checklist for College Students

Freshmen
- Find the career planning office as soon as you arrive on your campus and ask about special freshman programs.
- Think about your short-term education plans and goals: courses you are taking, summer jobs, campus jobs, job-hunting skills.
- Develop three long-term career goals, such as choosing a college major, getting jobs and internships, researching careers, developing your résumé, or improving your job-hunting skills.
- Research the career options associated with each of your current courses.
- Interview your professors about career options and students they have known who found interesting jobs related to their majors.

Sophomores
- Go to the career planning office and ask about special sophomore programs and about workshops on time and stress management.
- Discuss options for your major with faculty members.
- Talk to seniors who are already in the majors you are considering.
- Be open to changing your mind about your major as you gather fuller understanding of your interests, abilities, and achievements.

- Explore all possibilities before you choose a major, and make the choice as late as possible in your sophomore year.

Juniors

- Go to your career planning office to inquire about special junior programs and ask about internships and summer jobs related to your major.
- Ask for a list of college alumni in your field in a city where you'd like to work in the summer or for a college term.
- Attend a résumé and interview workshop at the career planning office.
- Find out who the medical, law, business school, and Ph.D. advisers are in the career planning office.
- Attend a graduate school testing workshop at the career planning office *early* in your junior year to learn when to register and how to prepare for the examinations.
- Ask for a list of on-campus recruiters and set up job interviews.
- Ask for a list of nonprofit recruiters who interview on campus.
- Ask for a list of graduates from the past three years who are employed in a field related to your college major.

Seniors

- Go to the career planning office early in your senior year and ask about special senior programs.
- Begin your college credential file:

  (a) Ask three of your professors for letters of recommendation for your file.
  (b) Ask your summer and internship employers to send letters of recommendation to the college for your credential file.
  (c) Have all professional credentials copied for your file.

- Register for all required GRE, LSAT, MAT, and GMAT exams.
- Keep in close touch with your graduate school adviser.
- Attend a résumé workshop at the career planning office.
- Attend an interview workshop at the career planning office.
- Attend a job-hunting strategies workshop at the career planning office.
- Most important!! Make friends with a career planning officer!

Keeping Career Options Open

Students at four-year colleges and graduate schools can put off specific or specialized career decisions longer than can students at two-year community colleges or technology institutes. If you are a four-year student, or if you are stopping out from college, take advantage of this extra time and explore your options. Keep in mind all the technological and economic changes that have occurred in the job market in the past five years. These changes are still going on, even though the market looks pretty dreary. All the changes in you that you've noticed are still going on, too. In other words, in the next few years it could be a whole new ball game. If you stick with assessing your own skills and getting in tune with your values and interests as they change in your personal and work lives, and if you keep your career options open to new directions, you can't go wrong.

PART 3

Career Planning

Your Skills Assessment

There are hundreds of jobs for you to investigate, and there are three basic career steps to organize your search. The first is to learn about yourself—to assess your own skills, values, and interests. The second is to learn about work—to research your job opportunities. And the third step is to find the educational and job pathways that will lead you to where you want to go.

One of the purposes of education is to learn what you like to do and how well you can do it. You are discovering your skills in the classroom as you learn how adept you are at mathematics and languages, at history and science. At the same time you are finding out what you don't like and what you don't do well. In addition to learning content skills, such as how well you can handle physics and Spanish, you are also learning your transferable skills—how well you read, study, speak, and write. These skills will carry over into all your subjects and also into many career situations.

You learn what your skills are by your own evaluation as well as by your grades and test scores. Although your school grades may indicate how well you will do in college, they won't necessarily measure all the skills you've learned. You can't possibly tell what you're going to accomplish in life merely by assessing your school grades and achievements. For example, if you rank fourth in your mathematics class right now, that doesn't mean that you'll be fourth in money-making ability in your age group 20 years from now. Grades in high school and college do not predict who will be the happiest, the most miserable, the richest, the poorest, or the most powerful, either in work or in family life.

To find out more about your skills, take a look at your everyday actions—not only what you say you like or don't like to do but what you actually do with your time. Think about the subjects you study, the tasks you perform at work, the things you do at home that really excite you, make you feel special, and make the time go fast. Notice what activities make you feel good and what activities make you feel lousy and as though you can't wait to get out of there. Think about how your activities are related to having fun. To making money. To study or work or community achievement. Then, notice what skills are needed for the activities you love. Is time management one of them? Is decision making important? Are being your own boss and taking the initiative part of your enjoyment? Do you get along with almost anyone, or with one group of people more than another? Do your activities involve getting others to go along with you? Do they involve staying with the project after you've already lost your initial enthusiasm?

Here are a few more pertinent questions:

- Do you prefer to work in a particular geographic location?
- Do you prefer to work with particular types or ages of people?
- Is money your main goal? Is power?
- Do you think you would like a job that is short on money but long on prestige?
- Would you like a job where you can be left to work on your own? Would you like to be your own boss?
- Do you like structure on a job, with specific expectations and clearly defined responsibilities?
- What kind of physical surroundings do you prefer in your work environment?
- Do you mind traveling or working nights and weekends?

As you learn more about yourself, you will notice how well you relate to others—your ability to get along with other students, your family, and your co-workers; your leadership abilities in class and on the job; and your ability to get along with authority figures, such as your boss, your teachers, your coach, and your parents. Of course your skills, interests, and values will change. In fact, work experiences while you are in school often bring about major changes in how you think, feel, and act. But even though you know you will change, there is still a lot to be learned right now about your skills in school and college, at home and at work.

Researching the Job through Interviews

To find out about a career, it makes sense to talk to others who are willing to discuss their work. One good place to find people to interview about their work is in your own family. Ask your parents, aunts, uncles, and their friends to help you find people who are already in the career that you are thinking about entering. Go and talk with them. If a securities salesperson is what you want to be, find a stockbroker and ask her what it's like to be in securities. Does it sound like your kind of job? Ask another salesperson. How much of the job does he really like? What parts of the job does he hate and wish were over as soon as he starts? Listen to everything you hear, because you are the one who will be selling and either enjoying the hustle and competition or getting an ulcer by the time you finally make the sale.

In addition to your family members, many of your teachers and professors will be good sources for finding people in careers that you are ready to research. Your clergy, youth-group leaders, and others in your community, including alumni from your school and college, will often want to be helpful to you. Go ahead and ask your network if they know a forester, a computer systems analyst, a nurse practitioner, or a foreign service officer you can meet and interview in your career research. Don't wait until you are choosing a graduate school or hunting for a job to talk with others about their work. The more experience you have talking with people in careers that interest you, the more background you'll have

41

for your future decisions. Not only will your interview experiences be good information right now, they will also be great practice for the crucial job interviews you will be having later.

Even though you don't know someone you have read about in the paper, go ahead and write to that person, saying that you are interested in learning about his or her job or in working for them during the summer or school holidays. Usually, you will find the person is flattered by your interest. In this way you can learn how to make your own opportunities for future interviews and jobs. As a student, you are in a good position to explore. You have a positive image and are not a threat—people aren't afraid that you will take over their jobs. So, make the most of your status as a learner to find out about careers from the people already doing well in them.

When you have the names of some people to interview, call them. Tell them you would like to talk with them for a specific amount of time, so they will know you won't keep them too long from their work. Say, for instance, that you are interested in becoming an environmental scientist and would like to talk about what the job is like with someone who knows. Make an appointment, then have questions like the following in mind to ask during the interview:

- How did you get into this career?
- How did you view the work before you got into it? Is your view different now? How is it different?
- What do you like most about your work?
- What do you like least about your work?
- What are the greatest pressures, strains, and anxieties in your work? The biggest challenges?
- Why did you choose this type of work?
- What special problems might someone new to the job have in adjusting to it?
- Would you make the same career choice again? Why?
- Besides the environment in which you work, where else could someone perform your work?
- What other careers are related to your work?
- How much time do you spend with your family? Is this amount what you expected to spend when you began working in your career?
- How much time do you spend with hobbies?
- How do your family and friends fit into the lifestyle of your career?

- What advice would you give a high school or college student who wants to get into your career?

End the interview on time, as promised. And when you get home, write a short thank-you note to the person for sharing his or her time and thoughts with you. Try another interview—there are a lot of careers to learn about—and talking is fun!

In your career research, remember that everything you learn counts. Even though you decide that a given career isn't what you had thought it was before your research, you are still ahead because you now have more accurate information. You may learn about new careers indirectly, and your follow-up from reading and interviews may lead you in directions you didn't plan on taking. The more information you finally have for your career decision, the more sure you can be of it—at least for this phase of your life.

Best Companies

How do you define the "best" company? Your answer will very much depend on who you are and what you're looking for. Don't just assume that pay is the only thing that's important. A high salary is often compensation for a stressful environment or poor working conditions, which may be exactly what you *don't* want. Besides, high pay is not always what it seems. You may be hired at a substantial annual salary but find yourself lagging your friends in a few years because raises aren't all that hot and the company offers little chance for advancement. So, one rule of thumb is to consider the long range as well as the short.

Another factor to consider is benefits. It's easy for people just starting out to overlook pension plans, day care, or family medical coverage. After all, if you're young and single, the need for these benefits may be decades away. (Or at least seem like it is.) Also bear in mind that certain kinds of benefits, like profit-sharing or stock options, may wind up being as important as base pay.

Values will help you determine what "best" is. Do you want a nice office and pleasant surroundings? Or is it all the same to you if you work in a metal cube painted Army green? In some companies, the way to advance is through transfers. If you've always wanted to see new places, that would be ideal. But what if you like where you're living right now? Your values will also determine whether you want a "job" or a "career." If you're in the second group, then a best company will offer training programs and a chance to move up.

Women and minorities, gays and lesbians, may have different criteria for best. Some companies have reputations for actively recruiting and offering advancement to members of such groups. Pay equity is also an issue here. And for women, so is a company's stand on sexual harassment as well as child care and family leave policies. Gays and lesbians look for companies that offer health benefits to same-sex partners of their employees.

As this chapter only begins to suggest, there are numerous factors to consider in deciding where you'd like to work. As you read the career descriptions later in the book, keep these factors in mind in evaluating the options that appeal to you.

Hit the "Temp" Road!

It used to be that housewives and musicians, actors and writers wanted temporary work long enough to pay the rent and then wanted to get back to their lives at home or as artists. It used to be that companies needed temporary office help for a few days, a week, maybe for a special project, or substitutes for people who were out sick. But it's "Kelly Girls" no more. We are talking about a temporary work force earning $14 billion a year because companies will no longer pay their regular employee benefits, which can include $4,000 a year just to purchase health insurance. Businesses are down to bare budgets, quarterly deficits are common, and international competition is fierce. These factors have helped to create the worst job market in decades. Out of the recession has come an entirely new employment concept—temporary positions for professionals. For example, Mactemps, a temp agency in Cambridge, Massachusetts, started supplying temps to operate Macintosh computers from a shop where it took in desktop publishing jobs. Since then, Mactemps has grown from one office to 20 offices with $21 million in sales, and it is still growing. Affiliates, a temp agency in Menlo Park, California, supplies attorneys and paralegals to businesses on a daily or weekly basis, while Office Team in Chicago supplies highly skilled office workers.

Today you can be a temp doctor, lawyer, or merchant chief (CEO). Whether you work in an office at $8 an hour or as a computer consultant at $120 an hour for a few weeks or a year, you will get your paycheck from a temporary-help agency, and usually you will get no benefits and not know how long the job will last.

Currently, there are 1.15 million temps, and 265,000 of them are college graduates in professional-level jobs. That number is growing daily by leaps and bounds. The professional temp work force is expected to reach half a million by the late 1990s. According to financial analysts, due to the recession, in order to be most cost-effective, businesses must give temps a permanent place in their work force. Companies such as Johnson & Johnson, Ford Motor Company, and Fidelity Investments now hire professional temps as well as office temps. The telephone company and Gillette hire temp engineers; Ford hires scientists; private hospitals hire temp doctors; temp financial planners and directors are hired by small businesses.

College graduates who head to Seattle, San Francisco, or Los Angeles know the temp market well. Three recent graduates who shared an apartment in San Francisco are typical of today's college graduates on the big job hunt. Ned Mitchell, a University of California at Santa Cruz graduate, looked all over the West Coast for a publishing job for as long as his money held out. Neil Taurus graduated from Grinnell College, in Iowa, and moved to San Francisco looking for an acting job. The third roommate, a Wellesley graduate named April Kim, wanted a career-directed job in the computer industry. Kim got a part-time job developing software through a temp agency. After four months, she was hired as a regular employee. Taurus wanted a temp job so that he could regulate his time and give priority to auditions and working nights at the Magic Theatre selling tickets, where he could at least be near actors and meet the playwrights. Mitchell soon learned that just having your name registered at the temp office wasn't enough. As difficult as it is for young graduates eager to start working, even the temp jobs are competitive! Mitchell got his name on the list for skilled office work at three temp agencies. Whenever his phone didn't ring by 8 a.m. for a day's work, he pounded the pavement, personally going by the agencies to remind them that he was available for work and wanted to be called as soon as possible. Soon after starting at Pacific Bell, a day's work turned into a week and a week into a month. After three months, Mitchell was hired as a "permanent" temp and he started to earn raises and promotions as if he were a regular employee.

It turns out that temping has some of the advantages of college internships—it gets your foot in the door in a very competitive market. College graduates can search the Yellow Pages for professional temp agencies and, like Mitchell, call on them every day until the work starts to come in. Office work starts at $8 an hour, sometimes going up to $12.50 an hour for computer work. Professionals, such as a temp financial officer in a steel company, can make $60,000 a year, a part-time doctor can make $50 an hour, and a software engineer can make $60 an hour—all through temp agencies. Some temp agencies offer free training in computers and some offer benefits for long-term temp work such as paid holidays and vacations and partial payment for medical insurance. So if you are still unemployed when the rent comes due, don't call home for money. Hit the temp road and open the doors into a work world where you can be developing your skills, learning, networking, and exploring career options you may never have heard about in college.

Mid-1990s:
Prepare for Change
and Creativity

Some of you will already have left college and may now be looking for that second or third job. You may have already had some work experience. You may want to consider a new career group or learn more about a related job in the group in which you are currently employed.

Formerly a college student would go into accounting and stay there. Or a person would become successful in sales, perhaps switch companies, but never dream of leaving the field. A young woman would choose to become a teacher and then would teach until retirement. Today, the accountant may change to a computer career, the salesperson may open his own business, and the teacher may move to an entrepreneurial career in real estate development. A new group of creative job seekers has entered the job market. It does not comprise just graduate students or the 8 million unemployed or the 2 million homemakers who are looking for jobs each year. In the mid-1990s many job hunters are fully employed adults in career transition. Changes at every phase of a career are a new phenomenon in the United States. The National Institute of Education reports that each year 40 million adults, or 36 percent of our working population, are in career transition. Those who change careers are in every age group. They cite financial need as the primary motivation. Other reasons are overcrowded career fields, early retirement, entrance of women into the work force from home, having attained their career goals, failure to be promoted, and no possibility for growth on the present job.

If you are in the market for a new job, the principles guiding going after what you want are the same whether you are a student, a full-time parent, a temp, or a full-time employed worker. You need to know (1) what you can offer by making a personal assessment; (2) what your career options are, by researching the job market; and (3) how you can get what you want by applying job-hunting strategies that include how to locate the person who can hire you, how to write a résumé, how to interview successfully, and how to negotiate salary and promotion. In your personal assessment you should:

- Identify transferable skills (problem solving, budgeting, analyzing),
- Identify content skills (engineering, home management, nursing, advertising, international business),
- Identify interest areas (paid and unpaid activities, hobbies, sports, clubs, leisure-time activities),
- Clarify lifestyle values (friendships, family, children),
- Define the ideal job in terms of skills, interests, values, and purpose in life,
- Relate skills, interests, and values to jobs.

To begin your research of the job market, read the job descriptions in this book. If a particular job interests you, look at related jobs in the same career group. Next, follow through on your search by writing to the professional associations cited for each career. Go to the library and look for a related trade journal. Translate what you learn about a career to your locality, or to the part of the country in which you want to live. Finally, remember that changes in life, even good changes, tend to rock the boat. Handling change is easier with the support of people close to you. Reaching out to your family and friends as you plan a career change will help smooth the transition.

Career change is one more way to look at your career development. As soon as you make a career choice, chances are that a change is going to follow. Plan for those changes. Be creative. Think about what you are learning now that will keep your change options open later. Career and job change is a fact of today's career development. You can count on it.

PART 4

Career Groups

Getting the Most from This Book

Part 4 of this book, "Career Groups," describes job opportunities as well as job characteristics and requirements. Read about several careers in Part 4 that sound appealing to you. When one job in a group interests you, read about the related jobs, too. Using the groups in this way may help you find new ideas. Also read "What Becomes of All Those History Majors?" in Part 2, describing odd hot jobs for the mid- and late 1990s that aren't necessarily related to specific college majors.

Sometimes young people in a business-oriented family tend to look only at business careers, or military or government work if their relatives are active in those fields. Or perhaps someone in your family has told you "you ought to be" a professor or a dentist or a new-car dealer, and you may not like the idea. You may reject it before you seriously consider whether or not the career is a good one for you. Explore career possibilities that *you* have in mind, not those your family or friends say you should or should not look at. After researching these possibilities, you'll either want to learn more, or you'll be able to safely eliminate them.

Defining the Job

Each job description in Part 4 begins with a definition, followed by a discussion of the tasks involved, usually with examples from

young people in their twenties or thirties who add their perceptions to the description. Following the description, each job lists
the requisite educational and personal skills.

Number of People in the Field

Information about the number of people in the career appears next
in the description, citing percentages for women, blacks, Hispanics, and those who are self-employed whenever those figures are
available. This entry also gives a specific number or percentage
for the type of firm or agency and the geographic location as well.

The Money Factor

As you research the careers in *The College Board Guide to Jobs and
Career Planning,* notice that the average salaries are cited for each
career. It is easy to think of the average as the exact salary at
which you can expect to start working. For example, in 1993 electrical engineers with a bachelor's degree started at an average of
$33,754 per year. What that average figure really means is that
some engineers started at $23,754 a year while others started at
$43,754. Beginning engineers *averaged* $33,754. For a better idea
of the money you can expect in a particular career, you will want
to translate the average salary into a range of starting salaries.
Within this range, the salary you start with will depend on the
college you attended, your college record, your work experience,
where the job is located, and the type of employer. If you are a
student now, salaries will be even higher by the time you are ready
for the job market because of inflation and cost-of-living salary
increases. To give you an idea of the future rate of increase, let's
look at past salaries for elementary school teachers. In 1985 they
averaged $23,092, in 1988 they averaged $29,629, and in 1993–94
they averaged $34,800. Remember, when you read "average," that
means many people make less and just as many may make more
than the figure cited.

As you choose a career, what does money mean to you? Will
your income be high enough to maintain the standard of living
you want and justify your education costs? How much will your
earnings increase as you gain experience? Like most people, you
probably think of "pay" only as money. But money is only one
kind of financial reward for work. Paid vacations, holidays, and
sick leave; life, health, and accident insurance; and retirement and

pension plans are also part of the total earnings package. The earning issue of the mid-1990s is health insurance because of the soaring costs of health care. Some employers also offer stock options and profit-sharing plans, day care, savings plans, and bonuses.

Which jobs pay the most? This is a difficult question to answer because specific information is available for only one form of remuneration—wages. Obviously, some kinds of work pay better than others. But many times the same kind of work does not pay the same amount of money. Some areas of the country offer better pay than others for the same type of work. For example, the average weekly earnings of a beginning desktop computer specialist vary from city to city. Generally, earnings are higher in the north central and northeastern regions of the country than in the western and southern areas. You should also remember that cities that offer the highest earnings are often those in which it is most expensive to live.

Earnings for the same kind of work also vary according to the type of organization you work for. For example, Ph.D. chemists in marketing and production earn more than Ph.D. chemists in industrial research and development; however, those in industrial research earn more than chemistry professors, who do research as well as teach.

Job Opportunities

You undoubtedly wonder what the economy will be like when you enter the labor market. Each career description anticipates your chances of getting a job through the year 2005. These chances are estimates developed by the United States Department of Labor. They are based on general assumptions about the future of the economy and the country—for example, the assumptions that there won't be a major war or an energy shortage, that allocations of federal money to state and local governments will continue to decline, and that current technological and scientific trends will continue.

Finally, you should remember that job prospects in your community or state may not correspond to the description of job opportunities given here. The opportunities in your area may be better or worse for the particular job you are interested in. The local office of your state employment service is the best place to ask about employment projections in your area.

Related Careers

The category of related careers gives you suggestions for other careers using similar skills and interests. Go ahead and read the listings of related work in order to broaden your choices.

More Information

When you write to the professional groups cited, you can expect to get lists of approved training institutions for that career. Most associations have career booklets and information written especially for college and high school students, and many will suggest books about their particular profession.

After you have looked at all the possibilities, choose one or two or three careers that sound interesting enough to read about and research further. Reading in detail about a career is a reliable way to acquire accurate information.

When you have read the career descriptions that interest you, look in your school or college and public libraries for trade magazines related to the career you are researching. If you want the inside story of what people in a career are reading, thinking about, and actually doing, read their trade magazines. The *Wall Street Journal, Variety,* and *Veterinary Economics* are where you will find out what the financial, theater, and vet people are really like. It isn't academic theory but the business of the job itself that you'll find in trade magazines. In addition to learning what people in a career are doing, you can't beat the trade magazine as raw material to prepare for a job interview. For example, nothing will impress a book publisher more than hearing you discuss facts about his or her business that you acquired from reading *Publishers Weekly*; or a physician if you can talk about the latest research published in the *New England Journal of Medicine*; or a banker if you have the latest economic reports from the *American Banker*; or an urban planner if you are aware of recent urban trends reported in *City*. If your school or college library doesn't have the trade magazines that interest you, check your local public library. Ask the reference librarian to help you out by selecting the trade magazines that relate to the job you are researching.

Arts: Performing and Visual

Performing Arts

- Actor, director, producer
- Dancer, choreographer
- Musician
- Singer

Design and Visual Arts

- Designer
- Interior designer
- Photographer, camera operator
- Visual artist

ABOUT PERFORMING AND VISUAL ARTS CAREERS

Talent, creativity, the ability to communicate, personal drive, and luck continue to be the necessary ingredients for success in the arts. There is no one best way to enter the arts. Determination is often as much the key to success as are creativity, skill, and formal education.

57

In the fine arts, formal training requirements do not exist, but it is very difficult to become skilled enough to make a living without some basic training. Bachelor's and graduate degree programs in fine arts are offered in many colleges and universities. In the graphic arts field, demonstrated ability and appropriate training or other qualifications are needed for success. Evidence of appropriate talent and skill shown in the "portfolio" is an important factor in getting into art programs and, later, in getting jobs. The portfolio is a collection of handmade, computer-generated, or printed examples of the artist's best work. Assembling a successful portfolio requires skills generally developed in a college art program. Even in good times, the number of performing artists always exceeds the number of job openings. Only the most talented actors, actresses, directors, and musicians find regular employment. Many in the arts field work intermittently or on a free-lance or contract basis. The difficulty of earning a living as a performer is one reason that many artists teach or take routine jobs, such as waiting on tables and word processing. They take on unrelated jobs that will support them while they continue to study and audition for performing arts work, as well as during the many, many between-job periods.

Evening work is a regular part of the performing artist's life. Rehearsals may be held late at night and on weekends and holidays. When performances are given on the road, weekend traveling is often necessary. Travel, irregular hours, and unemployment are all very hard on family and social life.

A college degree counts less in the performing arts than in many other careers. More important to artists are the professional schools of acting, dance, and music, which are usually located in the major cities where the work opportunities also exist. A professional school whose goal is to turn out the top musician or actor or dancer is the best place for your training. In order to find one, write to the professional association at the end of the career description that interests you and ask for a list of approved schools.

Camera operators, like news photographers, advance as their work gets around and they build a reputation. Camera operators can become directors of photography for movies and TV programs.

Commercial art, interior design, and photography require a two- or three-year professional or specialty school program. Write to the professional associations referred to under the career that interests you for a list of approved schools and colleges.

PERFORMING ARTS

Actor, Director, Producer

Entertains audiences through interpretations of dramatic roles on the stage and in film, television, and radio

What's It Like to Be an Actor, a Director, or a Producer?

Making a character come to life on stage or for film is a glamour job that attracts many talented young people each year. Directors and producers plan and supervise shows and performances. *Directors* interpret plays or scripts and usually choose cast members for stage, movie, television, and radio productions. *Producers* select plays or scripts and hire directors, principal members of the cast, and key production staff members. They coordinate writers, directors, and managers and arrange financing for the production. *Actors* usually struggle for a start in acting and pick up parts wherever they can, often as volunteers in community, church, and school theater groups whose productions, it is hoped, will be reviewed. The frustrations of being in a glamour career are the lack of money, the possibility of few big breaks, not knowing where the next job will come from or when, losing a good acting job because you are an inch too tall or too short, and constantly having to lay yourself on the line for auditions.

Al Ivy came to New York City from Little Rock, Arkansas, right after college. He joined the actor's union and has found a few small parts in the two years he has been in the Big Apple. "I spend every cent on seeing more theater," says Ivy. "I wait tables enough to pay for acting lessons, and my mom and dad still help out a little. I just need to give myself a chance at the theater, and I'll stay with it for five years before figuring out what to do next."

What Education and Skills Will I Need?

High School   College preparatory courses and as much acting experience as possible.

College   A theater arts or drama major is offered in over 700 colleges. However, many actors are trained in dramatic arts schools, particularly in Los Angeles and New York City. Most producers and directors have a strong interest in theater productions or film and are experienced in business and fund-raising.

Acting experience in local productions as well as in summer stock is more important than the number of years in college. Experience in your community theater can be the best way to become recognized as you build your acting record for future recommendations.

Personal Skills   Acting demands patience, physical stamina, and total commitment, since aspiring actors and actresses must wait for parts or filming schedules, work long hours, and travel often. Evening work is a regular part of a stage actor's life.

How Many Actors and Directors Are There and Where Do They Work?

There are 129,000 actors, directors, and producers working in stage plays, films (including TV films), industrial shows, and commercial. Thirty-six percent are women. Many others are between acting jobs, so the total number is actually much higher. In the winter, most job opportunities on the stage are in New York, Chicago, Los Angeles, and other large cities. In the summer, stock companies in suburban and resort areas provide employment, although most casts are selected in New York City. Film employment is centered in Hollywood and New York City, although there are studios in Florida and Seattle. Increasingly, small, competitive film companies are springing up in many interesting locations in the country. Even the Northeast Kingdom in Vermont has a new film company, and *Ethan Frome* was shot in that New England landscape.

How Much Money Will I Make?

Professional actors belong to unions. In 1993 the minimum salary for a Broadway actor was $950 a week. Off-Broadway paid from $340 to $579 a week. Motion pictures offered a minimum of $485 a day to actors and $99 a day to extras. Most actors get little if any unemployment insurance because they seldom have enough employment in any state to meet the eligibility requirements. The

Screen Actors Guild, which has over 40,000 members, reports that in 1991 20,000 members had *no* earnings, and 80 percent earned less than $5,000. Only 6 percent earned over $35,000. Therefore, your parents are right, most actors must supplement their acting incomes by working at nonacting jobs.

What Are the Job Opportunities?

Earning a living as an actor, a director, or a producer is often nearly impossible and almost always difficult. New York City is flooded with young, talented, well-trained people looking desperately for the few available jobs. The best places to look are commercial theaters, nonprofit acting companies, and television.

Related Careers

Dancer

Drama teacher

Radio and TV announcer

Playwright

Where Can I Get More Information?

Associated Actors and Artistes of America
165 West 46th Street
New York, NY 10036

National Association of Schools of Theater
11250 Roger Bacon Drive, Suite 21
Reston, VA 22090

Dancer, Choreographer

Expresses ideas and emotions through body movements

What's It Like to Be a Dancer or a Choreographer?

Most dancers work together as a chorus in dance productions for the stage, movies, and television. Some are selected for special dance numbers, and a very few top artists do solo work. The few dancers who become choreographers create new ballets or dance routines, teach them to performers, and sometimes direct and stage the presentations of their work. Others become dance directors who train dancers in new productions. Teachers usually teach in professional dancing schools or teach dance courses in colleges and universities.

Stephen Wynne, a 19-year-old scholarship dancer in the American Ballet Theater of New York City, says, "Seek out a reputable dance school, one associated with a company. Or ask a professional ballet dancer to recommend a good school. Get several opinions. Take as many classes as you can, as soon as you can, to get in shape. And most important, don't wait! If you aren't sure you want to be a dancer, you'll know after a week or so in ballet school.

"The only part of being a ballet dancer that I don't like," explains Wynne, "is the dieting. I don't like to diet. Some dancers don't have to, but diet or no diet, we must all stay away from junk foods. The best part of dancing is the noticeable improvement—being able to do things today you couldn't do the day before. I like the excitement of controlling movement and the viewer's appreciation. I also love the discipline that dancing demands. In other words, the best thing about dancing is dancing!"

The only thing that Janine Ceballos, a ballet dancer just chosen for a Belgian dance company, wants to add is, "I like working closely with a teacher, relating to him or her and listening to the music. I love dancers. They are nutty, but interesting."

What Education and Skills Will I Need?

Professional Training   Performers begin their training at age 7 for ballet and by age 12 or younger for other kinds of dance. Professional training includes 10 to 12 lessons a week for 11 or 12 months a year and many hours of practice. By 17 or 18 years of age, the dancer is prepared to audition.

Professional School or High School   A good professional school is very important for the training it offers and for the connections it provides for employment. In addition to dancing, students study music, literature, and history. An alternative to professional school is a high school program that leads to a dance major. Two hundred and forty colleges offer a dance major, usually modern dance, and it is often studied within the physical education or the theater arts department. This option can lead to a performing or a teaching career. Professional schools require their teachers to be experienced performers.

Personal Skills Dancers must have agility, coordination, grace, a sense of rhythm, and a feeling for music; they must also possess self-discipline, patience, a good body build, physical stamina, and the ability to work as part of a team.

How Many Dancers and Choreographers Are There and Where Do They Work?

There are about 18,000 performing dancers and choreographers, plus another 23,000 dance instructors in high schools, colleges, and dance schools. Seventy-eight percent of dancers are female, 22 percent are black, and 5 percent are Hispanic. Performers work mostly for theatrical producers, bands, and entertainers (36 percent). Some work in recreation (19 percent), restaurants and bars (16 percent), and motion picture production (15 percent). About half the dancers in major dance companies work in New York City. Other cities with dance companies are San Francisco, Seattle, Chicago, Dallas, Houston, Salt Lake City, Cincinnati, Cleveland, Milwaukee, Boston, Philadelphia, Pittsburgh, Atlanta, Washington, D.C., and Miami. About 12 percent of dancers are self-employed.

How Much Money Will I Make?

Performers belong to a union that sets their contracts and salaries. In 1993–94, dance salaries in ballet and stage production were $587 a week. Television dancers averaged $99 a performance. Choreographers earned from $970 to $30,000 for 8 to 10 weeks of rehearsals and performances. Films paid them $3,000 a week and television up to $10,000 for two weeks. College dance teachers with a master's degree received the same salary as other instructors, usually beginning at $19,200 a year.

What Are the Job Opportunities?

Jobs in the field of dance are very competitive. Excellent health and unusual physical vitality are always needed. Dancers rarely perform after 35 years of age, although there are many exceptions in modern dance. The best job opportunities are with regional ballet companies. Dance has become more popular, leading to more jobs. Tap dancing is now making a comeback.

Related Careers

Dance therapist   Dance critic
Dance teacher   Recreation worker

Where Can I Get More Information?

National Association of Schools of Dance
11250 Roger Bacon Drive, Suite 21
Reston, VA 22090

American Dance Guild
31 West 21st Street, Third Floor
New York, NY 10010

Musician

Expresses ideas and emotions through music

What's It Like to Be a Musician?

Professional popular musicians play in concerts, in dance bands at
nightclubs and restaurants, and at special parties. The best-known
bands, rock groups, jazz groups, and solo performers often give
concerts and perform on television. *Classical musicians* play in
symphony, opera, and theater orchestras and in chamber groups.
Instrumental musicians play string, brass, woodwind, or percus-
sion instruments in orchestras, rock groups, or jazz combos. *Composers* create original music. They transcribe ideas into musical
notation using harmony, rhythm, melody, and tonal structure.
Many composers now compose and edit music using computers.
Choral directors direct choirs and glee clubs. They audition and
select singers and direct them at rehearsals and performances to
achieve the sound they want.

Princeton student Lewis Flinn left for Hong Kong as soon
as he graduated. He tended bar to pay his rent and started calling
ad agencies about singing or writing music for advertising commercials. Since there are only a handful of music production companies in Hong Kong compared to the big time in New York City,
this experience provided the perfect opportunity for Flinn to get

his foot in the door and his ideas on tape. With a year's experience under his belt, Flinn couldn't wait to get to New York City. Like many other young musicians, he quickly got a part-time job to pay the rent. Then he got together his own band, the Acoustic Blue. Flinn plays keyboard and does the vocals. Unlike many other young musicians, Flinn has been successful in getting gigs in New York's downtown clubs. He also contacted commercial production companies for jobs as a "jingles singer." After several years in this very competitive field, Flinn has written an opera that was produced in New York, he was commissioned to write the music for a dance group, and he has gone from jingles singer to composer and producer of some major TV commercials. He now has several commissions to write advertising commercials and music scores for videos. Tough competition for creative work? Yes, but not impossible!

What Education and Skills Will I Need?

Professional Training   Professional musicians usually begin their training early in elementary school with intensive study in private lessons. They audition for symphony orchestras, chamber groups, and other professional groups whenever they are ready.

High School   Preparation for college, with as much music experience as possible. Many high school students choose their colleges by the quality of the instruction in their particular instrument. Most popular musicians do not have a college degree.

College   There are about 500 colleges, universities, and music conservatories that offer training in musical performance, history, and theory. There are an additional 100 institutions that offer music education.

Personal skills   Self-discipline, talent, versatility, creative ability, and stage presence are necessary for success.

How Many Musicians Are There and Where Do They Work?

There are 236,000 employed musicians; 31 percent are women, 10 percent are black, and 5 percent are Hispanic. Many of them work for theater producers, bands, and entertainers (36 percent); others are employed by churches (30 percent), and still others work in eating and drinking places (21 percent). The majority of musicians work in New York, Chicago, Los Angeles, Nashville, Miami Beach, and New Orleans. Classical musicians perform with one of the 30 major symphony groups, the 39 regional orchestras, the 96 metropolitan orchestras, or hundreds of smaller groups.

How Much Money Will I Make?

Musicians belong to the American Federation of Musicians (AFL-CIO), and concert soloists belong to the American Guild of Musical Artists. In 1993–94 major symphony orchestra musicians earned from $1,000 to $1,400 a week; regional orchestras paid from $400 to $700 a week. Television pays musicians $226 for a 3-hour session. Music teachers received the same salaries as did other teachers in their school systems or colleges.

What Are the Job Opportunities?

All music jobs are extremely competitive. There are many more talented musicians of all kinds—classical, pop, teaching, and performing—than jobs.

Related Careers

Arranger   Music therapist
Music salesperson   Librettist

Where Can I Get More Information?

American Federation of Musicians
1501 Broadway, Suite 600
New York, NY 10036

National Association of Schools of Music
11250 Roger Bacon Drive, Suite 21
Reston, VA 22090

Singer

Interprets music through voice production, melody, and harmony

What's It Like to Be a Singer?

Singers sing character parts or perform in their own individual styles. They are classified by the type of music they sing, such as opera, rock, folk, jazz, blues, or country and western, or according to their voice range—soprano, contralto, tenor, baritone, or bass. "It takes experience and exposure to make it in a singing career," says Linda Smyth, who at 38 is an understudy at the New York City Opera. "Holding out for star roles in opera means you understudy rather than sing in the chorus. I've had to take many jobs, preferably in music, to pay my way until I get that audition acceptance to star in the company. I love singing and the discipline required. Music is what I want to do." More common are the thousands of singers who take lessons and sing in small clubs or church choirs and weddings in addition to a teaching or related job. Allison Greene, mother of two young children and former private school teacher and administrator, studies voice in New York City and plans a singing career as soon as she can fit it into her family schedule. The pleasure of voice lessons energizes her enough to make the long hours of practice and discipline worthwhile. Music, like many talents in the arts, enriches the life of the artist in a way that no other career can.

What Education and Skills Will I Need?

Professional Training   Voice training does not begin until after a singer has matured physically. It continues for years after the singer's professional career has started.

High School   Dance and piano are often assets in getting a singing job; working on these skills and preparing for a music career by studying music theory are helpful.

College   About 500 colleges and conservatories offer degrees in music. Popular singers often get started in their careers by performing in local college and community shows or restaurants.

Personal Skills   Musical talent, stage presence, unique style, and self-discipline are crucial for success.

How Many Singers Are There and Where Do They Work?

There are 21,000 employed singers; 53 percent work for theatrical producers, bands, and entertainers, and 15 percent work in restaurants and bars. Many others are between jobs. Most of the singing jobs are in New York, Los Angeles, Las Vegas, San Francisco, Dallas, and Chicago. Nashville is the major center for country and western singers. In addition, there are singers all over the country working part time in church and synagogue choirs and in local restaurants and bars; they also often give private singing lessons.

How Much Money Will I Make?

The union minimum for concert singers in a chorus was $85 per performance in 1993. Opera company members earned slightly less per performance. Principal singers earn $485 a day in television and much more in solo concerts. Like other performing artists, most singers have a hard time earning enough to live on because their jobs are so irregular.

What Are the Job Opportunities?

As in all the performing arts, singing jobs are very competitive, regardless of the economy. There are always more talented, hard-working, ambitious singers than there are jobs.

Related Careers

Composer   Arranger
Songwriter   Choir director
Music teacher   Music salesperson
Music technician   Music librarian

Where Can I Get More Information?

American Federation of Musicians
1501 Broadway, Suite 600
New York, NY 10036

National Association of Schools of Music
11250 Roger Bacon Drive, Suite 21
Reston, VA 22090

DESIGN AND VISUAL ARTS

Designer

Designs or arranges objects and materials to best show off a product's appearance, function, and value

What's It Like to Be a Designer?

Designers study their company's product and competing products to consider possibilities for change. Designers create designs for products as diverse as dresses, cars, home appliances, computers, stethoscopes, filing cabinets, fishing rods, pens, and piggy banks. Designers usually specialize in one type of product or activity— for example, cars, fashion, furniture, home appliances, industrial equipment, movie and theater sets, packaging, or floral arrangements. Pleasant surroundings, beautiful clothes, and floral arrangements can be the product of specialized designers. They combine artistic talent with research on product use, marketing, materials, and production methods to create the most appealing design for competition in the marketplace. Fashion designers, for example, make fashion news by establishing the "line"—the colors and fabrics that will be worn each season. Other clothes designers cater to specialty stores or high-fashion department stores. They design original clothes as well as fashions in keeping with established trends. Most fashion designers, however, work for apparel manufacturers, adapting men's, women's, and children's fashions for the mass market. Josie Erickson wanted to have an art career, but because there are so few women in industrial design, she never thought of that specialty until her art professor suggested it as an alternative to the overcrowded art field. She tells what her job in a manufacturing company in Pittsburgh is like: "After our team selects the best design for a product, I make a model of it, often of clay so that it can be easily modified. After any necessary revisions, I make a working model, usually of the material to be used in the finished product. The approved model then is put into production. When I learned that all industrial designers experience the frustration of having many designs rejected, I began to find my job a real challenge. I like working with the team, and I like the business side of learning about how to market products."

What Education and Skills Will I Need?

High School Preparation for college, with courses in art, drafting, mathematics, and computer science.

College One of the 166 accredited college or art school programs. Computer-aided design (CAD) is an essential skill for all designers.

Personal Skills Creativity, a strong color sense, an eye for detail, artistic and drawing skills, ability to see familiar objects in new ways, ability to work with people who are not designers, and an interest in business and sales are needed for success.

How Many Designers Are There and Where Do They Work?

There are 302,000 designers; about 50 percent are women, 2 percent are black, and 4 percent are Hispanic. Designers work for large manufacturing companies, department stores, hotels, and design consulting and architectural firms—mostly in New York, Chicago, Los Angeles, and San Francisco. About 32 percent are self-employed.

How Much Money Will I Make?

Designers with experience working for manufacturers earned a median of $38,000 in 1993. The top 10 percent earned over $75,000. Industrial designers started at $27,900 a year in 1992; those with six years of experience averaged $38,000, while managers earned up to $75,000 a year. Floral designers are paid by the hour, from $5.40 to $9.40 in 1993.

What Are the Job Opportunities?

Jobs are competitive as they are in all artistic professions. The markets for new products are very dependent on the economy each year, except for floral design because of its low pay and limited opportunities for advancement.

Related Careers

Visual artist   Package designer

Photographer   Interior decorator

Where Can I Get More Information?

Industrial Designers Society of America
1142-E Walker Road
Great Falls, VA 22066

National Association of Schools of Art and Design
11250 Roger Bacon Drive, Suite 21
Reston, VA 22090

Interior Designer

Plans and supervises the design and arrangement of building interiors and furnishings

What's It Like to Be an Interior Designer?

Carol Durfee is an interior designer at a Denver, Colorado, architectural firm and has a Bachelor of Fine Arts in Architecture from the Rhode Island School of Design. She spends her day talking with field supervisors about space planning for current construction and with salespersons about new products and colors. She attends meetings with clients, visits construction sites to check the progress and quality, and spends afternoons in local shops looking at draperies, carpets, and furnishings. Durfee often meets with building committees to present her plans to clients. Interior designers work closely with architects to check their plans against the blueprints and building requirements. Boston designer Michael S. Abdou, a member of the American Society of Interior Designers, says, "Your work is never duplicated. Every day and every client are different. A designer is a guide who helps homeowners get the style and colors they want. Developing the color schemes after you work with a client takes most of the time." Abdou is well established in his own firm, and he always takes the summers off because clients usually are not in their city homes in the summer. He advises students who like to create things "to go to the best school of art or design you can get into."

What Education Do I Need?

High School   Preparation for art school or a degree in fine arts. Begin to develop your portfolio (collection of your best artwork) while in high school.

College   Go to a three-year art school or institute of interior design, or take a degree in architecture. A college degree or a three-year professional school degree is required to become a professional member of the American Society of Interior Designers, which is necessary for the top jobs.

Personal Skills   Artistic talent, color sense, good taste, imagination, good business judgment, and the ability to work with detail are needed to be a successful designer.

How Many Interior Designers Are There and Where Do They Work?

There are 69,000 full-time interior designers; about 50 percent are men. They work for design and architectural firms in major cities. Some have their own firms; others work in department and furniture stores, for restaurant chains, and for home magazines. There are thousands more who work part time; 40 percent are self-employed.

How Much Money Will I Make?

In 1993 the median salary for beginning designers was $25,000; experienced designers averaged $38,000, and project managers averaged $50,500.

What Are the Job Opportunities?

Jobs are competitive. The slower the economy and home construction market, the more difficult it is to find full-time employment. This field is expected to grow 35 percent, however, to 93,000 jobs by 2005. Needless to say, the numbers aspiring to those jobs will grow too!

Related Careers

Set designer   Floral designer
Fashion designer   Fabric designer

Where Can I Get More Information?

American Society for Interior Designers
608 Massachusetts Avenue, NE
Washington, DC 20002

National Association of Schools of Art and Design
11250 Roger Bacon Drive, Suite 21
Reston, VA 22090

Photographer, Camera Operator

Uses cameras and film to portray people, places, and events

What's It Like to Be a Photographer or a Camera Operator?

As a writer uses words, a photographer uses a camera for artistic or technical purposes—such as portrait photography, commercial photography, television entertainment and news, or photojournalism. Some specialize in scientific, medical, or engineering photography, and their pictures enable thousands of people to see the world normally hidden from view. Others specialize in portraits, commercial photography, industrial work, or photojournalism. *Photojournalists* combine photographic ability with news reporting. *Camera operators* film news events, television shows, movies, commercials, and cartoons. They use video cameras for live transmission by satellite to their television newscasting stations for instant viewing on TV.

John and Rosanna Nelson have been in partnership in a photographic portrait business in a small city for 30 years. They have two galleries in neighboring suburbs and are successful because they work long hours and have always been careful in their work. The Nelsons want students to know that "if you are going into the business, you will need to know about business management, how to relax people, and how to promote your business, as well as how to use a camera. Photography has come of age in the last 15 years; the latest technology and new materials enable more photographers to be more creative. With the tools available, there's no limitation on creativity." Photographer Lita Semerad learned that there is always opportunity to turn a hobby into a professional talent. Before a trip to Papua New Guinea, she took several classes in composition, perspective, and "how-to" with professional photographers. Semerad studied her subjects well, photographed several stories, and upon return sold many of her photographs to archives and publishers.

What Education and Skills Will I Need?

High School   Take art courses along with college preparatory courses.

College   Education required varies from on-the-job training to courses leading to a degree in photography from one of 160 colleges. The future belongs to photographers whose training and experience enable them to do more than other photographers can do. Preparation for a career in photography must include knowledge of the field in which photography is to be applied. Economics, geography, international affairs, and journalism are important fields of study for the photojournalist. A career in advertising photography requires knowledge of art and design and some background in advertising.

How Many Photographers and Camera Operators Are There and Where Do They Work?

There are 118,000 photographers and camera operators; 23 percent are women, 3 percent are black, and 6 percent are Hispanic. They work in portrait studios (26 percent), for the government (11 percent), for commercial art firms (11 percent), for printers and publishers (11 percent), and for educational services (9 percent). Forty percent of photographers are self-employed.

How Much Money Will I Make?

The median salary for photographers was $21,200 a year in 1992. Camera operators made slightly more. Portrait photographers in business for themselves and with national reputations earn much more. The top magazine photographers with national reputations earn over $75,000 a year. Most photographers, however, work very hard in offices in their homes for annual incomes between $16,500 and $35,600, with the top 10 percent averaging $49,200.

What Are the Job Opportunities?

Portrait photography is a very competitive business. Areas such as newspaper publishing, business and industry, law enforcement, and the sciences are expected to need more photographers in the coming years. Well-trained people with strong technical backgrounds will have the best opportunities. Because they are in an exciting and glamorous field, camera operators will continue to find the job market very competitive through the year 2005. The best opportunities will be in video training films and sales videos for corporate businesses.

Related Careers

Designer	Illustrator
Painter	Visual artist

Where Can I Get More Information?

Professional Photographers of America
1090 Executive Way
Des Plaines, IL 60018

American Society of Magazine Photographers
419 Park Avenue South, Suite 1407
New York, NY 10016

Visual Artist

Creates artwork to communicate ideas and feelings

What's It Like to Be a Visual Artist?

Most people in the field work in either illustration or design for publications, films, textiles, greeting cards, and industrial products. *Illustrators* paint, draw, or create pictures on a computer. The major specialties are fashion art, medical and scientific illustration, cartooning, and animation. *Designers* create or supervise the visual impressions of advertisements and industrial products. *Art directors* are designers who decide the art, design, photography, and type style that go into published materials and TV advertisements. *Animators* work in the motion picture and television industries. They draw the series of pictures that, when transferred to film or tape, form the animated cartoons seen in movies and on TV. *Computer graphics* is the newest method of creating artwork. In place of knives, glue, art boards, overlays, marking pens, and films, the computer graphics artist uses the computer screen to create uniform and irregular shapes, change colors, choose the number or size of an image, scale, rotate, duplicate, and move and erase objects—all of which are much faster to do by computer than by hand. Because the technology changes so fast, most visual artists learn computer skills on the job. Nelson Johnston, a visual artist who learned on the job, says that the common questions and concerns of artists who are training on computers are these: "Will I be able to operate this device? Does this mean that everything I do will be created by computer? Will I have to go back to school? Will I be so caught up in this computer and keyboard that I won't be able to think creatively anymore?" Johnston points out that for the artist, these are computer-anxiety questions, and after a very few hours with the computer, artists see it as another tool that does its job very well. Advertising visual artist Paula Randall says she still likes to use water color, pen and ink, and crayons, but computers are the best way to handle 90 percent of her work in multi-image graphics.

What Education and Skills Will I Need?

High School Preparation for an art school or a fine arts major in college. Art schools require an art aptitude test and an example of your work. Start assembling your portfolio (a collection of your best work) now.

College A two-year art school or four-year college art program will prepare you for the better commercial jobs. As in all the arts, demonstration of your ability and talent is more important than a degree.

Personal Skills Artistic ability, imagination, a distinctive style, and the capacity to translate ideas onto paper or film are necessary in the visual arts.

How Many Visual Artists Are There and Where Do They Work?

There are 302,000 visual and fine artists; 50 percent are women, 3 percent are black, and 5 percent are Hispanic. About 20 percent work in advertising, 13 percent for mailing, reproduction, and commercial art businesses, and another 13 percent in printing and publishing. They are employed in the major cities, although New York has by far the largest concentration because it is the center of the advertising and publishing industries. Boston, Chicago, Los Angeles, and San Francisco also have many artists. Sixty-two percent of visual artists are self-employed and work part time in order to devote the rest of their time to fine arts. In the arts, that is not always a good sign, because many (not all) visual artists would prefer an employer.

How Much Money Will I Make?

Artists in entry-level pasteup or layout jobs often make as little as the minimum wage. Income for a full-time artist ranged from $17,600 to $30,800 in 1992. Art directors, designers, and well-known free-lance illustrators make from $48,000 to $75,000 a year and more.

What Are the Job Opportunities?

Chances for work and promotions will continue to be very competitive through the year 2005. Those with outstanding talent and a mastery of visual art skills and computers will continue to be in demand despite the competition.

Related Careers

Account executive
Industrial designer
Interior designer
Art director

Set designer
Fashion designer
Photographer

Where Can I Get More Information?

American Institute of Graphic Arts
1059 Third Avenue
New York, NY 10021

Society of Illustrators
128 East 63rd Street
New York, NY 10021

Society of Publication Designers
60 East 42nd Street, Suite 1416
New York, NY 10165

Aviation

- **Air traffic controller**
- **Flight attendant**
- **Pilot**

ABOUT AVIATION CAREERS

Pilots make higher salaries with less education than any other workers in the country. There are 1.5 million workers in aviation; 240,000 of them are college graduates.

Even though airline pilots are usually college graduates, many of them get their flight training in the military. Air traffic controllers come from many college backgrounds; flight attendants usually have two years of college.

In aviation, jobs involve shift work around the clock. Air traffic controllers work a basic 40-hour week; however, they are assigned to night shifts on a rotating basis. Air traffic controllers work under great stress. They must keep track of several planes at the same time and make certain all pilots receive correct instructions.

Pilots work 100 hours a month, but because their schedules are irregular, some actually fly only 30 hours while others may fly 90 hours a month. Although flying does not involve much physical effort, the pilot often is subject to mental stress and must be constantly alert and prepared to make decisions quickly.

Flight attendants have the opportunity to meet interesting people and to see new places. The work, however, can be strenuous and trying. Attendants stand during much of the flight and must remain pleasant and efficient, regardless of how tired from jet lag they may be.

Advancement in aviation is usually very clearly determined. Seniority is established by union contracts. After 5 to 10 years, flight engineers advance on the basis of seniority to copilots, who are in charge of aircraft scheduling and flight procedures. Advancement for all new pilots is generally limited to other flying jobs. Advancement opportunities for flight attendants are very limited.

Aviation changed drastically in 1985, when government controls were relaxed, causing great demand for more pilots and other aviation personnel. The demand for pilots is so critical that many of the age and flight-hour requirements have been dropped in order to attract the numbers of pilots needed.

Air Traffic Controller

Keeps track of planes flying within an assigned area and gives pilots instructions that keep planes separated

What's It Like to Be an Air Traffic Controller?

Air traffic controllers are number one on the burnout list. They have a very stressful career because of the deep concentration required on the job. Air traffic controllers' immediate concern is safety, but they must also direct planes efficiently to minimize delays. Some regulate airport traffic; others regulate flights between airports. Relying on both radar and visual observation, they closely monitor each lane and maintain a safe distance between all aircraft, while guiding pilots between the hangar or ramp and the end of the airport's airspace. Air traffic controllers work in a tower near the runway to keep track of planes on the ground and in the air. They radio pilots to give them permission to taxi, take off, or land. They must keep track of many planes at once. Controllers notify en route controllers to watch the plane after take-off. Each en route controller is responsible for a certain airspace; for instance, one controller may be responsible for all planes that are 30 to 100 miles north of the airport and flying between 6,000 and 8,000 feet. All commercial planes are under the responsibility of an air traffic controller at all times.

Controller Maria Messier of Hardwick, Vermont, knew she wanted a career in aviation, so after high school she went straight to Embry-Riddle Aeronautical University in Florida. After completing a major in aviation management, she took the Federal Aviation Administration (FAA) air traffic controller test to qualify for the air traffic controller training program. Having met the competitive requirements, Messier went through training and was sent to Santa Rosa, California. She worked with seven other controllers on an 18-hour day schedule consisting of 2 hours on and 15 minutes off. Four years later she was transferred to Savannah, Georgia. "The most challenging situations," says Messier, "are when pilots have trouble with their landing gear. They call us after they have tried their backup plans, and our technical staff comes on to help them. Sometimes, we even have to call the manufacturer of the equipment to talk to the pilot." Messier says that working with student pilots can be difficult, "because they get scared and can't take in the directions you are giving them. All in all, I can't think of a more satisfying career—it feels good at the end of each day to have successfully met all the challenges and brought all the pilots safely back to land."

What Education and Skills Will I Need?

High School Preparation for technical, community, or four-year college.

College Most air traffic controllers complete four years of college before taking the federal civil service exam and training program at the FAA Academy in Oklahoma City. After they are selected, controllers are trained on the job. It takes two to three years to become fully qualified. Other controllers train during military service.

Personal Skills Speech skills must be perfect and vision correctable to 20/20. A physical exam every year is necessary for this crucial job in air safety. A stable temperament, ability to articulate well, decisiveness, and good judgment are also required.

How Many Air Traffic Controllers Are There and Where Do They Work?

There are 23,000 air traffic controllers; 33 percent are women, 4 percent are black, and 6 percent are Hispanic. They all work for the FAA. Most work at the major airports or at air-route traffic control centers near large cities.

How Much Money Will I Make?

In 1993 starting salaries for air traffic controller trainees were $22,800 a year. The average salary for experienced controllers was $53,800 a year.

What Are the Job Opportunities?

Competitive. High pay for a minimum of college education and a good retirement program attract more qualified applicants than available job openings. Even though burnout is high, jobs will be hard to get in the late 1990s.

Related Careers

Airline radio operator   Airplane dispatcher
Flight service specialist

Where Can I Get More Information?

Call (800) 555-1212 for U.S. Civil Service Commission Job Information and ask for the number of the nearest Civil Service Job Information Center, or check your local phone book. Also write:

Future Aviation Professionals of America
4959 Massachusetts Boulevard
Atlanta, GA 30337

Flight Attendant

Makes the airline passengers' flight safe, comfortable, and enjoyable

What's It Like to Be a Flight Attendant?

Before each flight, flight attendants check supplies, food, beverages, and emergency gear in the plane's cabin. They greet the passengers, check their tickets, and help with coats and luggage, small children, and babies. During the flight they give safety instructions, sell and serve cocktails, and serve precooked meals. Jimmy Williams, a flight attendant with American Airlines, flies 80 hours a month with 35 hours of groundwork duties. He points out to newcomers that all airline jobs with passenger contact have some required shift work. Because the airlines run flights 365 days a year, 24 hours a day, they require their personnel to take turns with this schedule. Planes generally carry 1 to 10 flight attendants, although 747 jetliners carry as many as 16 attendants. Williams says that what he likes best about his work is the amount of travel and time off compared to other jobs. Being young and single, he loves the one-third time on the job away from his home base when he can explore other cities, resorts, and every place American flies.

What Education and Skills Will I Need?

High School   Preparation for community, business, or four-year college.

College   At least two years of college are required by major airlines. The ability to speak a foreign language fluently is essential for an attendant on an international route.

Physical Qualifications   You must be in excellent health with good voice and vision. You must be at least 19 years old. Even though airlines specify physical attractiveness, you don't have to be tall, dark, and handsome or a beauty queen to be a flight attendant.

Personal Skills   Poised, tactful, and resourceful people are necessary to effectively serve the many customers, some of whom are afraid of flying.

How Many Flight Attendants Are There and Where Do They Work?

There are 93,000 flight attendants; 83 percent are women, 11 percent are black, and 6 percent are Hispanic. They work for scheduled airlines, usually headquartered near large cities where most airlines fly.

How Much Money Will I Make?

In 1993 union contracts set the minimum salaries of beginning flight attendants at an average of $13,000 a year. The major airlines pay $20,000 to $30,000 a year to attendants with more than six years of experience. A major strike by flight attendants in 1993 against American Airlines raised the pay and the consciousness of unions and management about poor employment practices in a female-dominated industry. The salaries are low, but extra compensation is paid for overtime and for night and international flights. Reduced airfare for attendants and their families is an additional benefit of the job.

What Are the Job Opportunities?

Competition is sharp for this glamour industry. The best opportunities will go to applicants who have at least two years of college and some experience dealing with the public. If you speak Spanish, French, or German, you will improve your chances for a job.

Related Careers

Tour guide   Reservations agent
Social director   Waitress

Where Can I Get More Information?

For specific information about qualifications and jobs, write to the particular airlines that interest you. Remember that local and regional airlines may have good opportunities and be less competitive than national airlines. Beware of "air attendant schools" because the airlines will give you their own training after you are hired. Also write:

Future Aviation Professionals of America
4959 Massachusetts Boulevard
Atlanta, GA 30337

Pilot

Flies planes to transport passengers and cargo, to dust crops, to inspect power lines and monitor other situations, and to take aerial photographs

What's It Like to Be a Pilot?

The pilot, referred to as the captain by the airlines, operates the controls and performs other necessary tasks involved in flying the plane, keeping it on course, and landing it safely. Third in line to the pilot, the flight engineer monitors the operation of the different mechanical and electrical devices aboard the plane, helps the pilot and copilot make preflight checks of instruments and equipment, and watches these instruments during the flight. Airlines are now hiring more women as flight engineers.

First Officer Charles T. Huggins, Jr., United Airlines, advises young people to get a college education, because airlines have not hired pilots without college degrees for years. "Then," says Huggins, "get plenty of experience. That means the military. Even though it's a five- or six-year obligation for pilots, the flying experience in the military is unparalleled by anything else. My daily activity includes jogging and exercising because the length of a pilot's career depends on his taking care of his health—that is, how long he can hold a Federal Aviation Administration medical certificate." Huggins has two children and is expecting a third. He says that "a person unable to adjust to a job in which he or she is not home every day would not like it." When his 15 workdays per month are over, the rest of his time is spent with his family.

What Education and Skills Will I Need?

High School   Preparation for college or technical school or military service.

College Most pilots are college graduates and have traditionally been trained through the United States military service. Because of the incentives for military pilots to stay in the service and the high demand for pilots in the deregulated aviation industry, a much larger percentage of pilots are trained through flying schools.

It takes 250 hours of flight time to get a commercial license. Most airlines hire flight engineers who are licensed as commercial pilots. Flight engineers work their way up to copilot and then to pilot. Pilots must be at least 23 years old and can fly as long as they can pass the required physical examination.

Personal Skills Decision making and accurate judgment under pressure are required of pilots.

Physical Requirements Excellent physical condition, 20/20 corrected vision, and good hearing are required.

How Many Pilots Are There and Where Do They Work?

There are 85,000 pilots; 5 percent are women, 3 percent are Hispanic, and less than 1 percent is black. Most (three-fifths) work for scheduled airlines; others work as instructors, for business firms, for agricultural services, or for the government. There are several thousand more flight engineers, first officers, and copilots.

How Much Money Will I Make?

Captains and copilots are among the highest-paid wage earners in the country. In 1993 the top pilot pay—$186,000 a year—went to a senior pilot flying a Boeing 747 for Flying Tigers, a cargo carrier. On the other hand, a senior captain piloting a small, twin-engine BAC 111 for Florida Express made $41,000 a year. A beginning flight engineer may start at $1,600 a month but will make $3,000 a month within a year. Average pay for a senior captain is $128,000. Flight engineers start at $21,000, and captains for non-union airlines and for corporations earn much less. The salary range for a corporate pilot is $46,000 to $66,000 and $38,000 to $48,000 for a copilot.

What Are the Job Opportunities?

There is a shortage of pilots. A 34 percent growth to 120,000 jobs is predicted by 2005. Opportunities in aviation have increased in every job category in the industry since deregulation. At the same time, the military has a shortage of pilots and is increasing the incentives for pilots to stay in the service, resulting in more demand than ever for commercial pilots.

Related Careers

Helicopter pilot	Air traffic controller
Flight engineer	Aviation dispatcher

Where Can I Get More Information?

Airline Pilots Association
1625 Massachusetts Avenue, NW
Washington, DC 20036

Business: Administration and Management

- Business Executive
- Hospitality Manager
- Management Consultant
- Operations Manager
- Personnel or Labor Relations Worker
- Property Manager
- Purchasing Manager
- Underwriter

ABOUT ADMINISTRATION AND MANAGEMENT CAREERS

Managers make a lot of money. There will be 15.9 million of them in the United States by the year 2005, up from 13.6 million in 1990. The number of service industry management jobs will be up in the 1990s, while the number of goods-producing industry jobs will be down. The president of Ford, mom and pop at the corner store, the local postmaster, the manager of the private tennis club, the local branch bank manager, and the chief executive officer of the city hospital are all managers. They plan, organize, direct, and control the major functions of their organizations.

The competition is stiff for getting into a management training program in a major corporation, even with a college degree. A Master of Business Administration (M.B.A.) is your best bet for the top management programs. People in business have varied college backgrounds. Many are from liberal arts programs with majors in economics, accounting, statistics, or prelaw. A law degree or a CPA certificate is a good way to beat the competition of the traditional M.B.A. Computer skills are now a basic requirement for managers in every field. Management is not an entry-level job. Teachers become principals, doctors and nurses become hospital administrators, salespeople become managers, and bank tellers become branch managers.

During the past 10 years there has been an upsurge in corporate education institutes where you can learn the specific business management skills you need for advancement. You can get a master's degree at Arthur D. Little's Graduate Management Education Institute in Cambridge, Massachusetts. Merrill Lynch has opened its own college for stockbrokers. McDonald's Hamburger University teaches management. Both IBM and AT&T spend millions of dollars to educate their full-time employees in skills needed on the job as well as in management skills for advancement. When you are planning advancement through education, first be sure to check the company you work for. You may be able to get further education at company expense instead of your own, and a company that invests in you is likely to take a strong interest in your advancement.

Working conditions vary according to the position, employer, and industry. In a large corporation a top-level manager might have a plush office and several private secretaries, whereas a production-line manager may have a simple office and use a secretarial pool. Most managers work long hours, some up to 80 or 90 hours a week. Some, like those in newspaper publishing, regularly work the night shift. Others, like hospital administrators, are on call 24 hours a day to deal with emergencies. And almost all managers are expected to work late when necessary.

The pace of work also varies. In the radio and television broadcasting industry, managers are subject to constant deadlines. For hotel managers, checkout time can be hectic. In retail trade businesses, seasonal changes in activity are pronounced. In the drug manufacturing industry, research projects may be long-term, with schedules for completion months or even years in the future.

Managers are decision makers. The difference between managers and other workers is that managers set goals and policies and work through other people to reach them.

Business Executive

Organizes, directs, controls, and coordinates the operations of an organization and its major departments and programs

What's It Like to Be a Business Executive?

Business executives, or managers, direct others in sales, research, production, accounting, and purchasing. They often work in company teams to decide about sales, personnel, public relations, and how the work should be done. Directors of training programs, who hire future managers for their corporations from among college graduates, look for self-starters—those people who can use initiative, who have an observing eye to see what needs to be done, who like responsibility, and who have high standards for fairness. To be good in their job, they must be thorough, though not necessarily brilliant, and persistent. There are as many different management titles as there are job categories. Loan officer and branch manager are banking managers; dean and superintendent are education managers; mayor and senator are government managers; program director and public affairs director are communications managers; publisher and editor in chief are publishing managers; and plant manager and quality control manager are production managers. In the corporate world the top job, the number one management position, is the chief executive officer (CEO). The CEO's fundamental objective is to maintain efficiency and profitability in the face of accelerating technological complexity, economic interdependence, and domestic and foreign competition. The educational pathway to CEO is usually through an M.B.A. program. Although the number of women in these programs is steadily increasing, the number of women in top management jobs is no-where near representative of the number of women in entry-level management. No women are on the fast track to the top management job at any Fortune 500 corporation. Even nonprofits are slow to promote women to management positions. For example, the University of Pennsylvania elected its first woman president in 1993 and is the first Ivy League college to select a woman for the top post.

What Education and Skills Will I Need?

High School   Prepare for college in whatever area interests you; take as broad a program as you can do well in. Participate in extracurricular activities that teach such management qualities as leadership, assertiveness, and sensitivity to others. Sports are especially important for learning teamwork and competitive skills, which are absolutely essential in management.

College   Most executive training programs recruit liberal arts majors. Ability to think and make decisions, computer skills, and an interest in a particular training program are special qualities corporations are looking for. An M.B.A. is one good route to management; a law degree is another, and a CPA still another. Also, sales experience has always paid off in management jobs.

Personal Skills   A highly analytical mind and sound intuitive judgment are crucial. Decision-making skills, assertiveness, fairness, and an interest in business are important. Self-starters and team players are what corporations are looking for. Familiarity with computers is increasingly important because firms rely on computerized management information systems.

How Many Business Executives Are There and Where Do They Work?

About 13.1 million top executives manage the nation's businesses, and about 2.9 million are college graduates. There are thousands more (13 percent) who are owners of their own businesses.

How Much Money Will I Make?

In 1993 college graduates entering management trainee programs averaged $20,200 a year. The median salary for middle managers with experience was $59,400. Size of company and field of management make a difference in salary. Top managers in health made $142,500; in human resources, $136,000; in computer companies, $83,900; and in retail, $56,000. When you think about middle-management and top-management salaries, be aware that salaries have become only a small part of what is known as the executive compensation package, or perks. For example, the manager with a salary of $70,000 a year gets an additional $90,000 in rewards. The CEO with a $200,000 salary may make as much as $580,000 more a year in bonuses, long-term incentives, fringe benefits, and perks. In 1993 CEOs at 200 major corporations made $3,200,000, including the value of their stock options.

What Are the Job Opportunities?

Between now and 2005, the number of managerial jobs in the service industries is expected to reach 15.9 million. The employment of health services administrators outside hospitals is expected to increase much faster than other managerial jobs. The numbers of business consultants are also expected to grow fast in management and public relations as well as data processing management positions. Managerial positions in goods-producing industries and production will decline.

Related Careers

College president   Department store manager
Governor   Hospital CEO

Where Can I Get More Information?

American Management Association
135 West 50th Street
New York, NY 10020

Hospitality Manager

Owns or manages food and lodging establishments as a profit-making business, providing maximum good food and maximum comfort for guests

What's It Like to Be a Hospitality Manager?

The Culinary Institute of America in Hyde Park, New York; the New England Culinary Institute in Montpelier, Vermont; the Lausanne Hotel School in Lausanne, Switzerland; the Cornell University School of Hotel Administration in Ithaca, New York; the hotel/motel restaurant management program at the University of Nevada at Las Vegas; and the Florida International University School of Hospitality Management in Miami have a new and high visibility in the mid-1990s. All indications are that hospitality is the fastest-growing opportunity through the end of this century. Students in these programs learn how to cook and manage kitchens and dining rooms, to decide about room rates and credit policy, and to manage the housekeeping, accounting, and maintenance departments of hotels and restaurants. Managers of eating and lodging businesses are responsible for any problems that guests or staff may have. The details of the job depend on the size of the establishment. Large hotels and chains offer more specialization. A manager of a small hotel or a self-employed hotel or motel owner often does all the jobs, including front-desk clerical work, advertising, and hiring staff.

Women have always been in the restaurant business, and 42 percent of the students at the Lausanne Hotel School are women, from 22 countries. An enterprising young woman in Philadelphia followed her dream and opened her own restaurant, after borrowing money from friends and the Small Business Administration for the initial investment. Now working 16 to 20 hours a day, Cindy Ayres is just where she wants to be—owner and chef of "the best new inexpensive restaurant in town." Of the top 50 women business owners in the United States, two are in the food business. Marian Illitch has been the financial brain behind the mom and pop business that started with one Little Caesar store and is now the third largest pizza chain in the country. At last count, the 4,500 stores brought in $2.26 billion under Illitch's financial leadership.

CEO Ruth Chris bought a 60-seat steak house in 1965 and has expanded it into a chain of 13 company-owned and 25 franchised restaurants with sales of $80 million a year.

What Education and Skills Will I Need?

High School Preparation for college or business college. Summer work in resorts, hotels, and restaurants will help you gain experience and find out what the job is like.

College Enroll in one of the 160 college programs offering a hotel management degree. Best known for hotel management, in addition to those colleges cited above, are the University of Denver, the University of Houston, the University of Massachusetts at Amherst, and Michigan State University. Or go to a community college or take a correspondence course for hotel and motel management.

Directors of training programs for the large hotels look for graduates of hotel and restaurant administration programs. Managing small hotels and owner-operated lodges and restaurants does not require a degree, but it does require interest, motivation, original ideas, and capital.

Personal Skills Initiative, self-discipline, and the ability to organize and concentrate on detail are needed in hospitality management careers.

How Many Hospitality Managers Are There and Where Do They Work?

In 1993 there were 2.7 million hotel and motel rooms in the United States, and the number is increasing. There were 99,000 hotel and motel managers, and more than 50,000 of them were owner-managers. In addition, 496,000 persons were employed as restaurant and bar managers. Forty-two percent of managers are self-employed.

How Much Money Will I Make?

A beginning graduate from a hotel school starts at $20,200 in a training program in large hotels. Raises can be expected to double the beginning salary within three to four years. In 1993, the salaries of experienced hotel managers ranged from $44,900 to $86,700 a year depending on the size of the hotel. Assistant managers averaged $32,500. Most managers are provided with board and room in addition to their salary. Managers of restaurants earned from $27,900 to $45,000 and more for large, outstanding restaurants. Cafeteria directors averaged $29,300 a year.

What Are the Job Opportunities?

Chances for jobs for the college graduates who have specialized in hotel management will be very good through 2005. Population growth, working families, and growth in the elderly population will increase the numbers of meals consumed outside the home. Small lodges and restaurants in cities and resort areas are often started by young people; even though the business is competitive, many original ideas have resulted in a comfortable living and a satisfying lifestyle for the owners.

Related Careers

Resident manager
Sales manager

Office manager
Convention services manager

Where Can I Get More Information?

American Hotel and Motel Association
1201 New York Avenue, NW
Washington, DC 20005

National Restaurant Association
250 South Wacker Drive, Suite 1400
Chicago, IL 60606

Council on Hotel, Restaurant, and Institutional Education
1200 17th Street, NW
Washington, DC 20036

Management Consultant

Collects, reviews, and analyzes data; makes recommendations and assists in the implementation of proposals

What's It Like to Be a Management Consultant?

"Fresh out of Yale's M.B.A. program, I went to work for a major consulting firm in Boston," says Chuck Irwin. "I was the junior employee on a team working on a computer contract for an international corporation that needed to change its basic computer system throughout the company. I was given an assignment to collect data on what computers they had, on the general profile of their business needs, and on the firm's internal computer organization. The computer project lasted a year; then I was assigned to three different team projects in my second year with the firm. Promoted to team leader, I now can choose which projects I want to take on and what part of the country I want to work in. I chose to specialize in computer consultations, although I debated an environmental specialization. I'm working long hours and asking for more work. An ambitious guy, I hope to be a consulting partner in my own firm in seven years."

What Education and Skills Will I Need?

High School   Prepare for a liberal arts college program with the strongest curriculum you can handle well.

College   Any major that interests you, along with economics courses and computer literacy, will prepare you for the best M.B.A. program you can get into. Many consultants come from majors in engineering, architecture, environmental design, communications, and marketing, as well as education.

Personal Skills   Ability to analyze and interpret data, draw conclusions, and make recommendations is essential for success. Oral and written communication skills are also required. Independence and self-motivation are important, because most consultants work with little or no supervision.

How Many Management Consultants Are There and Where Do They Work?

There are 208,000 management consultants. Forty-five percent of them are self-employed, primarily working for consulting, accounting, and law firms in the private sector. Most of the rest work for the federal government (Department of Defense), and state and local governments.

How Much Money Will I Make?

In 1992 consultants started at $31,300 to $39,100 a year, depending on their education and the location and size of the firm. Experienced and successful management consultants make big bucks, and many self-employed consultants go over the $150,000 mark early in their careers. Experienced consultants made $56,300; senior-level consultants made $76,700; junior partners averaged $105,600, and senior partners earned $166,100.

What Are the Job Opportunities?

Excellent for technically educated young people. Businesses are increasingly relying on consultants to help reduce costs and streamline operations. A Certified Management Consultant (CMC) designation gives a job edge to job seekers without technical training.

Related Careers

Marketing analyst
Operations manager

Business executive
Financial analyst

Where Can I Get More Information?

The Council of Consulting Organizations, Inc.
251 Fifth Avenue
New York, NY 10175

Operations Manager

Improves productivity and performance of an organization

What's It Like to Be an Operations Manager?

Also known as assistant principal, assistant superintendent, deputy commissioner, assistant director, and vice president in charge of operations, the operations manager oversees an organization's day-to-day business. Rather than focusing on competing organizations or visionary policies, operations managers are concerned with how efficiently and effectively everyday tasks can meet management goals. Operations managers are primarily problem solvers. The problems typically involve inventory control, personnel schedules, security, forecasting, resource allocation, product mix, and distribution systems. Operations managers work closely with the chief executive officer (CEO). The CEO of a manufacturing company may want to determine the best inventory level for each material in a process. Working with flowcharts, engineers, purchasing agents, and industrial buyers, and taking into account storage costs, operations managers use mathematical analysis to work out recommendations to solve problems. Once a decision has been made, operations managers work with their staff to ensure successful implementation. Service organizations such as hospitals, colleges, museums, and other nonprofits use the same process.

What Education and Skills Will I Need?

High School   Preparation for college, with emphasis on mathematics and computer science.

College   You can major in operations research at 120 colleges, or in business management, engineering, mathematics, statistics, or computer science.

Personal Skills   This job requires logical thinking, ability to work well with others, and oral and written communication skills.

How Many Operations Managers Are There and Where Do They Work?

There are 226,000 operations managers; 41 percent are women, 5 percent are black, and 4 percent are Hispanic. They work in industry, public utilities, banks, hospitals, and government agencies. Five percent are self-employed.

How Much Money Will I Make?

In 1993 the starting salary for experienced managers was $28,000 to $58,000. The average salary was $48,000; the top 10 percent made over $100,000.

What Are the Job Opportunities?

Chances for work will be very good through the year 2005 for young people who have a mathematical background, primarily due to the increased importance of quantitative analysis in decision making. College majors in operations research or operations management have 100 percent employment right out of college. Most opportunities are with financial businesses, health organizations, and nonprofit organizations such as universities and museums.

Related Careers

Computer scientist   Statistician
Applied mathematician   Economist

Where Can I Get More Information?

The Operations Research Society of America
428 East Preston Street
Baltimore, MD 21202

Academy of Administrative Management
550 West Jackson Boulevard, Suite 360
Chicago, IL 60661

Personnel or Labor Relations Worker

Personnel worker hires and keeps the best employees available for the success of a business or a government agency; labor relations worker handles union-management relations in unionized firms

What's It Like to Be a Personnel or Labor Relations Worker?

Personnel and labor relations workers represent management for a business or a government agency, providing the link between management and employees. Commonly known as human resources managers, they may oversee several departments, each headed by an experienced manager who most likely specializes in one personnel activity such as employment, compensation, benefits, training and development, or employee welfare. Human resources managers oversee the hiring and termination of employees and supervise equal employment opportunity and recruitment specialists. Personnel workers try to attract the best employees available and match them to the jobs they do best. Dealing with people is the essential activity of personnel workers. Some specialize in filling job vacancies by interviewing, selecting, and recommending applicants for job openings; some handle wage and salary administration; others specialize in training and career development on the job; and still others work in employee benefits. Lise Steg graduated from Northern Illinois University in August and found a job by mid-September. A business administration major in college, Steg worked part time getting personnel experience in banking, which gave her an edge in the job-hunting competition. Steg describes what it's like: "My title is personnel records manager for a security guard placement business that places guards in Illinois, Michigan, Wisconsin, and Indiana. They guard anything from nuclear plants to hotels. We have a high turnover—30 to 40 a week—out of 1,000 guards employed at any given time. I handle all the new hires, terminations, unemployment claims, and public aid, and will eventually handle insurance and workers' compensation. I'm also going to learn about the payroll and computer departments. I know there's not a lot of advancement opportunity here, but the experience is of infinite value. It's a perfect first job, and I love being out of college and starting my career!"

Labor relations is not an entry-level job. Workers in this field advise management in collective bargaining sessions and participate in contract negotiations with the union. They also handle day-to-day labor relations matters. Arvid Anderson, director of New York City's Office of Collective Bargaining, is the country's outstanding labor referee. He studied labor economics at the University of Wisconsin and says that his success "flows from an insistence on being low-key, methodical, and totally committed to the concept of collective bargaining."

What Education and Skills Will I Need?

High School   Preparation for college, with emphasis on English and social studies.

College   Personnel and labor relations workers come from a great variety of college majors. Some have majored in business administration, psychology, sociology, or industrial relations. Most companies look for a college graduate with the personal characteristics they think would be good for the company. A law degree is becoming highly desirable for participation in contract negotiations.

Personal Skills   Ability to speak and write effectively, work as a member of a team, see opposing viewpoints, and work with people of different educational levels are necessary skills in personnel and labor relations.

How Many Personnel and Labor Relations Workers Are There and Where Do They Work?

There are 474,000 personnel and labor relations workers: half of them are women (mostly in personnel), 7 percent are black. They are employed in every industry. About 10,000 are managers, and another 10,000 are self-employed. Over 85 percent of salaried jobs are in the private sector. Labor unions—the major employers—account for 11 percent of all salaried jobs. Other important employers include management, consulting, and public relations firms; educational institutions; hospitals; banks; personnel supply agencies; and department stores. There are many more women than men in personnel; the reverse is true in labor relations, where men dominate and also receive the highest salaries.

How Much Money Will I Make?

In 1993 the starting salary with a bachelor's degree was $22,900; $30,500 with a master's. The median annual salary for benefits planning analysts was $24,200. The median salary for personnel directors was $32,000. Labor relations workers averaged $63,900 to $70,000 in the private sector.

What Are the Job Opportunities?

Opportunities in personnel jobs for the new graduate are very limited and competitive. Labor relations jobs are even more difficult to get. The best chances will be for those with a master's degree in industrial relations or with a law degree.

Related Careers

Employment counselor   Psychologist
Lawyer   Sociologist

Where Can I Get More Information?

Society for Human Resources Management
606 North Washington Street
Alexandria, VA 22314

American Arbitration Association
140 West 51st Street
New York, NY 10020

Property Manager

Plans and directs the purchase, development, and disposal of real estate for businesses

What's It Like to Be a Property Manager?

Bill Cowell turned to property management from real estate salesperson three years ago when sales went down in Florida. Always interested in financial management and development, it was a natural time to change the direction of his career. His first client was the owner of several big condominiums who was looking for someone to assume the day-to-day management of the properties. Cowell has now taken on an industrial property for another client and an office building. He acts as the owner's adviser for these properties. He markets vacant space to prospective tenants, negotiates and prepares leases and rental agreements for tenants, and collects their rent payments and other fees. Cowell also handles the bookkeeping for the condos. He makes sure the rents are received and that the mortgages, taxes, insurance premiums, payroll, and upkeep and maintenance bills are paid on time. He prepares a financial statement for one of his clients and reports to the owners on the status of the property, occupancy rates, and lease expiration dates. After a few years of managing properties, Cowell hopes to get into acquiring land and planning the construction of industrial parks and other commercial buildings.

What Education and Skills Will I Need?

High School   Prepare for college by taking as much mathematics and computer science as you can.

College   Many property managers completed a business administration, finance, real estate, or public administration major, although liberal arts graduates sometimes turn toward business after they graduate from college.

Personal Skills   Good speaking and writing skills and an ability to deal tactfully with people are essential. Most people enter property and real estate management after previous employment in real estate sales.

How Many Property Managers Are There and Where Do They Work?

There are 243,000 property and real estate managers; 45 percent are women, 7 percent are black, and 5 percent are Hispanic. Forty percent are self-employed. Most work in urban areas or in the Sunbelt, where rentals and malls abound.

How Much Money Will I Make?

In 1992 the median salary for property and real estate managers was $21,800 a year. Shopping mall managers averaged $72,700, and office building managers averaged $75,000.

What Are the Job Opportunities?

Many job openings are expected to occur as experienced managers transfer to other jobs or leave the labor force. Most of the new jobs created will be in finance, insurance, real estate, and wholesale and retail trade.

Related Careers

City manager   Health service manager
Hospitality manager

Where Can I Get More Information?

Institute of Real Estate Management
430 North Michigan Avenue
Chicago, IL 60611

International Association of Corporate Real Estate Executives
440 Columbian Drive, Suite 100
West Palm Beach, FL 33409

Purchasing Manager

Negotiates and contracts to purchase equipment, supplies, and other merchandise for an organization

What's It Like to Be a Purchasing Manager?

Purchasing managers, sometimes called purchasing agents or industrial buyers, are responsible for getting the best dollar value for supplies for their firms. They buy raw materials, office supplies, furniture, and business machines. Purchasing managers check on deliveries to be sure the work flow of the firm isn't interrupted because of lack of materials. They work with other departments within the company, such as engineering and shipping, to coordinate the supplies with those who need them. Nonprofits such as schools, hospitals, libraries, and museums are increasingly hiring purchasing managers to figure out how to fund purchases as well as how to find the most cost-effective buys. Purchasing manager is a strong entry-level position that can lead to financial officer and vice-president in corporations and nonprofit institutions.

What Education and Skills Will I Need?

High School Preparation for college. Large firms hire college graduates for their training programs.

College Many purchasing managers come from backgrounds in engineering, accounting, and economics. The top jobs go to M.B.A.s.

Personal Skills Analyzing numbers and technical data, making buying decisions and spending within a budget, the ability to work and get along with others, memory for detail, and computer skills are all necessary qualifications for a purchasing manager.

How Many Purchasing Agents Are There and Where Do They Work?

In 1993 there were 208,000 purchasing agents and managers; 32 percent were women, 5 percent were black, and 4 percent were Hispanic. Half of them worked in manufacturing industries; the federal government employs another 20 percent of them. Construction companies, hospitals, and schools are also major employers of purchasing managers and agents.

How Much Money Will I Make?

In 1993 purchasing agents averaged $33,067 a year. Purchasing managers earned from $23,092 to $44,684, and the top 10 percent made more than $54,000.

What Are the Job Opportunities?

Graduates who have an M.B.A. and a bachelor's degree in purchasing, engineering, science, or business will have the best opportunities. Many opportunities will arise as service-producing organizations such as hospitals, health agencies, and schools begin to recognize the importance of professional purchasers in reducing costs.

Related Careers

Retail buyer

Service manager

Traffic manager

Manufacturing sales
representative

Where Can I Get More Information?

National Association of Purchasing Management
P.O. Box 2216
Tempe, AZ 85285

National Institute of Government Purchasing, Inc.
115 Hillwood Avenue
Falls Church, VA 22046

Underwriter

Appraises and selects the risks an insurance company will insure

What's It Like to Be an Underwriter?

An underwriter analyzes information in insurance applications, reports from loss control consultants, medical reports, and actuarial studies that describe the probability of insured loss, and then decides whether to issue a policy. If the underwriter is too conservative in estimating risks, customers will go to another company; if the underwriter is too liberal, the company will lose profits. Ian McGregor, an underwriter in Hartford, Connecticut, specializes in property and liability insurance. His career options included a specialty in life, property, health, or commercial insurance. Many of his cases involve drivers who have had several accidents and therefore present a high risk. McGregor corresponds with policyholders, agents, and managers about policy risks.

What Education and Skills Will I Need?

High School   Preparation for business or liberal arts college.

College Trainees are recruited from all kinds of college majors. Many major in mathematics or business administration, but this is not necessary. An underwriter must pass a series of examinations. Advanced courses are necessary to qualify as a fellow of the Academy of Life Insurance Underwriters.

Personal Skills Imagination, assertiveness, and the ability to make quick decisions and to communicate effectively are necessary for an underwriter, as well as the ability to work with detail and evaluate information.

How Many Underwriters Are There and Where Do They Work?

There are 100,000 underwriters, with very few women or blacks. Almost half work for fire, marine, and casualty insurance companies; 39 percent work for insurance agents and brokers, and 14 percent are in life insurance. The majority of underwriters work in the major insurance centers in New York, San Francisco, Chicago, Dallas, Philadelphia, and Hartford.

How Much Money Will I Make?

In 1992 the median starting salary was $28,000 a year. Experienced underwriters averaged $32,800 a year; supervisors $45,500 a year; and managers $61,000. Most insurance companies have liberal vacation policies and provide better-than-average benefits to their employees.

What Are the Job Opportunities?

Jobs are expected to be good through 2005, although the trend toward self-insurance is expected to lower the demand for underwriters. Computer technology will further reduce the need for underwriters.

Related Careers

Auditor
Financial officer

Budget analyst
Accountant

Where Can I Get More Information?

Insurance Information Institute
110 William Street
New York, NY 10038

Society of Chartered Property and Casualty Underwriters
P.O. Box 3009
Malven, PA 10355-0709

Business: Advertising, Marketing, and Public Relations

- **Advertising worker**
- **Marketing analyst**
- **Public relations manager**

ABOUT ADVERTISING, MARKETING, AND PUBLIC RELATIONS CAREERS

Outside of television and movies, advertising, marketing, and public relations are the most competitive, glamorous, and popular careers in New York City and in many other major cities in the country. Finding ways to sell products and services to the consumer is big business. So big, in fact, that businesses pay $500 per U.S. citizen per year for public exposure in the form of handbills, posters, newspaper ads, TV commercials, radio spots, billboards, and direct mail. Lobbying firms, a special type of public relations firm, attempt to secure favorable public opinion about their clients and to influence legislators on behalf of their clients' special interests. They work for large businesses, industry trade organizations, unions, and public interest groups.

There are half a million jobs in advertising, marketing, and public relations. Twenty percent of the workers in this field are self-employed. Many employers prefer college graduates who have a liberal arts education with a degree in journalism or business. There is no correlation, however, between a particular educational background and success in these fields. Hustle, enthusiasm, creativity, and aggressiveness, not a college degree, are the requisites for success.

People in advertising and public relations work under great pressure. They are expected to produce quality ads in as short a time as possible. Sometimes they must work long and irregular hours to make last-minute changes in ads and meet deadlines. Advertising and public relations can be satisfying careers for men and women who enjoy variety, excitement, creative challenges, and competition. Unlike people in many other careers, advertising workers experience the satisfaction of having their work in print, on television, or on radio, even though they themselves remain unknown to the public.

The marketing field is loaded with M.B.A. graduates who find fascinating careers in advertising and selling the country's products and services. They start as assistant brand managers and work up to product managers, looking for new avenues of potential sales. Advancement is very competitive in advertising, public relations, and marketing. Professionals are highly qualified in this industry, and by necessity it attracts the aggressive workers.

The most successful workers in major advertising, marketing, and public relations firms advance by becoming officers and partners of the firms, or by leaving to establish their own agencies.

Advertising Worker

Persuades people to buy a firm's products or use a firm's services

What's It Like to Be an Advertising Worker?

To many people, Madison Avenue in New York City represents the pinnacle of glamour and success in an advertising career. But wherever the company is located, the job is creative and challenging and the salary can be very high. The commodity is the person's talent, and the person must produce the idea, the copy, and the business that will make the client's product profitable. Careers in advertising include a number of different positions: *advertising managers* are responsible for planning budgets and for overall supervision; *creative workers* such as *writers, artists,* and *designers* develop and produce print, radio, and television commercials; *business* and *sales workers* handle the arrangements for broadcasting commercials on radio and TV, for publishing ads in newspapers and magazines, and for mailing ads directly to the public.

Most of us are familiar with the advertising world of products and services. Not so familiar is political advertising. Every presidential candidate has a staff of political advertising consultants. When you see the TV spots, newspaper ads, and fliers in the mail for your state legislators, you can be sure advertising firms or consultants were behind the ideas. When Bill Clinton started attracting attention, he called on Mandy Grunwald to help him with a TV ad, and later he asked her to try to turn around the negative press he was getting as a top runner in the field. Just out of college, Grunwald chose political advertising like most liberal arts graduates choose a career—she backed into it. She had learned how to read, write, and think at Harvard, and she had an interest in politics. One Saturday during her senior year, she woke up and decided to attend a workshop on a political view of the world, and all of a sudden she had a career! Under 30 and excited about life and career, Ms. Grunwald is in demand in many political hot spots around the country.

What Education and Skills Will I Need?

High School College preparatory program, with as much work in language as possible. Writing skills are particularly important. Working on school publications, learning to be a good observer, noticing how people respond, and selling are experiences that will be helpful in advertising.

College Most advertising agencies prefer a liberal arts graduate with a major in advertising, marketing, journalism, or business. Community college, business college, and art programs can get you started in advertising. The most common way to enter the field without a degree is to begin in a department store advertising program.

Personal Skills   Imagination, creativity, and a flair for language and selling are required for success in advertising.

How Many Advertising Workers Are There and Where Do They Work?

Almost half of the 432,000 people (one-third are women, 3 percent are black, and 3 percent are Hispanic) in advertising, marketing, and public relations work in New York and Chicago. About 100,000 work in advertising agencies. The rest work for manufacturers, retail stores, broadcasting stations, publishers, nonprofits, and political candidates.

How Much Money Will I Make?

The top beginning salaries are paid to outstanding liberal arts graduates, usually men. In 1993, they started at $20,300 to $24,000 a year. The median annual salary ranged from $41,000 for a top sales promotion manager to $79,000 for a regional sales manager. Salaries vary according to the size of the agency. An account executive in a large New York agency averages $67,000 a year, and a few make over $100,000.

Related Careers

Public relations manager   Lobbyist
Fund-raiser   Consultant

Where Can I Get More Information?

American Advertising Federation
1101 Vermont Avenue, NW
Suite 500
Washington, DC 20005

American Association of Advertising Agencies
666 Third Avenue, 13th Floor
New York, NY 10017

Read the trade journal *Advertising Age*.

Marketing Analyst

Evaluates the product, the consumer, and the marketplace and defines new avenues of potential business growth

What's It Like to Be a Marketing Analyst?

Pressured! Marketing analysts have a simple criterion to measure their success or failure: sales. Everything they do either produces more sales or it doesn't. They use market research to plan, implement, and analyze surveys to learn more about the consumers' wants, needs, and spending patterns. This information provides the direction for the sales component of the company as well as for its advertising and public relations programs. Marketing information is used to determine brand names, packaging, product design, and new outlets for the company, among other management decisions. Manufacturers rely on market research information to plan their product strategy, positioning, and promotional and pricing strategies. Although less familiar, marketing services and people is big business too. Colleges, publishers, and politicians all hire marketing analysts, as do some small firms. Marketing is a fascinating and challenging job that is attracting top M.B.A. students because of its influence on company business strategies. Marketing is one of the best fields in which to learn a business. Top management personnel often come out of marketing.

What Education and Skills Will I Need?

High School College preparatory program, with emphasis on English and mathematics.

College Attend business, community, or four-year college. Many marketing analysts come from the nation's top M.B.A. programs.

Personal Skills Decision-making skills, assertiveness, creativity, and an interest in business and profits are important.

How Many Marketing Workers Are There and Where Do They Work?

There are about 432,000 people in advertising, marketing, and public relations; one-third are women, 3 percent are black, and 3 percent are Hispanic. Most of them work in New York, Los Angeles, and Chicago. About 80 percent work for companies, and the remainder are self-employed or work for marketing consulting firms.

How Much Money Will I Make?

In 1993 marketing professionals earned from $22,000 to $67,000. The median salary was $41,000 for all marketing workers. The top 10 percent made more than $79,000.

What Are the Job Opportunities?

Marketing is a growing field, but the number of highly qualified students attracted to it is growing even faster. Very competitive for beginning jobs and for promotions. The growth in health-care facilities will result in good job opportunities in marketing at nonprofit institutions and organizations—a growing career area. For the best job opportunities anywhere in the country, apply through New York City headhunters (employment agencies) that specialize in marketing. If you don't know which employment agency is best, call the firm where you want to work and ask which agency it uses to hire most of its marketing people.

Related Careers

Business manager   Advertising worker
Public relations manager   Statistician

Where Can I Get More Information?

American Marketing Association
250 South Wacker Drive
Chicago, IL 60606

Public Relations Manager

Develops and distributes persuasive materials in order to create a favorable public image

What's It Like to Be a Public Relations Manager?

Public relations (PR) managers plan publicity they think will be most effective; communicate to consumers, stockholders, or the general public; write press releases for newspapers and magazines; and write brochures and pamphlets about a company or a product. They arrange special speaking engagements for company officials and often write speeches for them. They work in desktop publishing and with films, slides, videotapes, and all types of audiovisual equipment. They often work under tension and pressure caused by tight deadlines and last-minute changes in schedules. Public relations managers must be knowledgeable about all media and decide the most effective way to put across their ideas. Michael Wolf, a Cincinnati PR man just starting his own firm, has had four years of experience in Chicago. He says that he now works twice as hard and at much more risk, but he thinks he is where he wants to be—using every idea he ever had. "My long hours seem to be easier on the family now that the business is my own. Besides that, they wanted to be back in Cincinnati, the place they consider home." Public relations managers supervise staff specialists and assist in the preparation of copy for speeches and interviews.

Lissa Lareau, PR specialist for publications at the Nightingale-Bamford School in New York City, has shaped her own career after starting out fresh from college in the development office. She landed the job because while at the University of Maryland, she volunteered for phone-a-thons in the development office, giving her a foot in the door to do and learn more. Soon Lareau was putting in 15-hour weeks while completeing her junior and senior years at the university. She went to her first interview in New York City, where she wanted to live, with first-hand knowledge of what development is like gleaned from her college volunteer and work experiences. After two years in the development office at Nightingale, she found she was most interested in desktop publishing and creative layout. Lareau is a good example of how college graduates can develop their own specialties once they find an environment where they can experiment with what interests them most.

What Education and Skills Will I Need?

High School Preparation for two- or four-year college.

College Major in English, journalism, psychology, sociology, or any other field that interests you and in which you want to do public relations work. Public relations managers come from a wide variety of college majors, including liberal arts and applied arts. Writing skills are mandatory.

Personal Skills Self-confidence, assertiveness, an outgoing personality, understanding of human behavior, enthusiasm, and imagination are important for success in public relations.

How Many Public Relations Workers Are There and Where Do They Work?

There are about 98,000 jobs in public relations; one-third are held by women, 3 percent by blacks, and 3 percent by Hispanics. Most public relations managers work in New York, Los Angeles, Chicago, and Washington, D.C.

How Much Money Will I Make?

In 1993 the median income for college graduates starting in PR was $21,000 a year; the range, with experience, was from $28,000 to $44,700; the top 10 percent made over $75,000 a year. Salaries vary with the level of managerial responsibility and with the size and location of the firm. For the top 10 percent in New York City, making over $100,000 is not uncommon.

What Are the Job Opportunities?

Public relations jobs are very competitive because thousands of college graduates who want to work in large cities look for jobs with glamour, like public relations. Chances will be best for enthusiastic people with sound academic and computer credentials and some media experience.

Related Careers

Advertising worker   Fund-raiser
Lobbyist   Marketing analyst

Where Can I Get More Information?

Public Relations Society of America
33 Irving Place, 3rd Floor
New York, NY 10003

Business: Computer and Mathematical Operations

- **Mathematician**
- **Statistician**
- **Systems analyst**

ABOUT COMPUTER AND MATHEMATICAL OPERATIONS CAREERS

One of the oldest and most basic sciences, mathematics is the foundation for engineering, physical sciences, technology, and computer science. If you are making a curriculum choice between more mathematics or science or computer science as a high school student, always choose mathematics. You can select science later, when you specialize. You can go a lot further in computer science with a solid calculus background than with the latest computer science course, which will be out of date next week.

The computer industry has been projected to grow 90 percent between 1990 and 2005, making it the third fastest growing industry in the economy. Most college graduates will be in the following computer jobs: systems analyst, sales, software development, consulting, operations, and management.

Growth in the computer industry will result from advances in computer capabilities, especially networking and E-mail. Among the fastest growing segments of the computer industry will be consulting and integration services, prepackaged software, and information retrieval services. The demand for networking will drive the demand for consulting and integration. Employment is clustered around major cities. San Jose, California, is the West Coast center and Boston's Route 128 is the East Coast center for developing computer software. Many young graduates head for these two centers to work for established firms, and as many more start their own software companies. The education and training of computer personnel will continue to be inadequate for the demand.

Mathematician

Creates new mathematical theories, and solves scientific, managerial, engineering, and social problems in mathematical terms

What's It Like to Be a Mathematician?

Jennifer Hoyt, a mathematician for Merrill Lynch, has been on the job for two years and loves her work solving financial forecast problems through mathematics. Hoyt emphasizes doing the best you can in your college subjects because you never know how you will use them. "In high school I had no intention of doing anything with math! I took the usual math courses for college, but not until my junior year in college did I plan to major in it." Major corporations such as Merrill Lynch, IBM, and GE offer graduate courses at nearby universities in quantitative analysis, so employees can keep upgrading themselves in their careers.

Many young women think that math is a natural for men. "Not so," says GE mathematician Delbert O. Martin. He urges high school students to be persistent. Martin says, "Don't take the first failure seriously. I had to take elementary calculus three times before I passed it. I like being a mathematician because my work is exciting, challenging, and creative."

What Education and Skills Will I Need?

High School Preparation for college, with emphasis on mathematics and computer science. Be sure to select calculus if it's offered in your school.

College Major in mathematics, or in a related field with a minor in mathematics, to prepare for an advanced degree in mathematics, which is necessary for research and university teaching jobs.

Personal Skills Good reasoning ability, persistence, and the ability to apply basic principles to new types of problems are required.

How Many Mathematicians Are There and Where Do They Work?

There are 16,000 mathematicians plus several thousand math teachers and professors; 33 percent are women, 7 percent are black, and 3 percent are Hispanic. They work for the federal government (30 percent), private industry in manufacturing (20 percent), state governments (13 percent), business services (11 percent), and the insurance industry (7 percent).

How Much Money Will I Make?

In 1992, college graduates with a bachelor's degree started at $28,400 a year in private industry, at $33,600 with a master's, and at $41,000 with a Ph.D. The average salary for college professors in 1993–94 was $46,300 a year.

What Are the Job Opportunities?

Job prospects in applied mathematics in engineering and technology will be competitive through 2005. There is a shortage of Ph.D. mathematicians, which is providing more job opportunities for professors and theoreticians. Mathematicians are expanding into new areas such as law and management problems, creating more jobs for graduates. A critical shortage of math teachers is predicted for the late 1900s.

Related Careers

Engineer	Statistician
Actuary	Operations manager
Systems analyst	

Where Can I Get More Information?

Mathematical Association of America
1529 18th Street, NW
Washington, DC 20036

Statistician

Deals with the collection, analysis, and presentation of numerical data

What's It Like to Be a Statistician?

In the marketing field, statistician Bill Strand, who works for a TV rating service, determines the size of a television audience by asking a few thousand families, rather than all viewers, what programs they watch. Statisticians decide where and how to get the data, determine the type and size of the sample groups, and develop the survey questionnaire or reporting form. Statisticians are able to obtain accurate information about a group of people or things by surveying a small portion, called a sample, of the group. They use computers extensively to process large amounts of data for statistical modeling and graphic analysis. Statisticians often specialize in a particular subject area such as biology, economics, engineering, medicine, or psychology.

Mount Holyoke graduate Laura Marshall majored in mathematics, looked around at her best opportunities, including actuary science, which offered the highest starting pay, and then decided to go to the University of Massachusetts to get a master's degree in statistics. With the degree, her career opportunities will be broader and her mathematics foundation highly marketable in a sluggish job market.

What Education and Skills Will I Need?

High School   Preparation for college, with as much mathematics as possible and a few courses in computer science.

College   Over 80 colleges offer a bachelor's degree in statistics, and 110 offer a master's degree. Statisticians also major in mathematics, operations research, or psychology with a minor in mathematics. Business administration and economics courses are helpful to expand job possibilities.

Personal Skills   Ability to reason well, to work under supervision, and to enjoy routine work.

How Many Statisticians Are There and Where Do They Work?

There are 16,000 statisticians; one half are women, 4 percent are black, and 2 percent are Hispanic. Most of the jobs are in industry, finance, and with insurance companies; one-fourth work for the federal government. Statisticians also work in the entertainment world, in the political arena, and of course in sports, the most "stats" crazy of all fields. Statisticians work in all parts of the country, although most are in metropolitan areas such as New York, Washington, and Los Angeles.

How Much Money Will I Make?

In 1992 college graduates started at $28,400 a year in corporate jobs, and a Ph.D. started at $41,000. The average salary for statisticians working for the federal government in 1993 was $54,109.

What Are the Job Opportunities?

Students who study statistics and computer science and combine them with specialties such as biology, economics, or engineering will have very good opportunities for jobs. Private industry will hire the largest number of statisticians. Opportunities will be particularly good in the pharmaceutical, chemical, and food products industries. Large numbers of college faculty are expected to retire within the next 10 years, creating many opportunities for Ph.D. statisticians.

Related Careers

Mathematician

Actuary

Systems analyst

Marketing analyst

Where Can I Get More Information?

American Statistical Association
1429 Duke Street
Alexandria, VA 22314

Systems Analyst

Decides how data are collected, prepared for the computers, processed, stored, and made available to users

What's It Like to Be a Systems Analyst?

Sally Aarons, a mathematics major at Stanford, was accepted in a major computer training program. After some work experience in programming, she is back in training as a systems analyst. Systems analysts are the problem solvers for the computer user. They begin work by discussing with managers the jobs to be performed. They learn exactly what kind of information is needed, what has to be done with it, how quickly it has to be processed, and how it is currently being collected and recorded. In most companies, analysts evaluate the computer equipment already owned by the company in order to determine if it can carry the additional data or if new equipment is needed. Next, analysts develop the computer system—that is, they decide how the data should be prepared for the machines, processed, stored, and made available to users. If the company decides to adopt the proposed system, the analyst prepares specifications for computer programmers to follow. Analysts usually specialize in business, scientific, or engineering applications. The problems that systems analysts deal with range from monitoring nuclear fission in a power plant to forecasting sales for a publisher.

Robert D. McCaffrey, married and the father of a six-year-old, is a systems analyst supervisor at Marriott Hotels. His day starts with a review of the previous night's computer processing to make sure that all regularly scheduled programs have run normally. Next, he reviews the progress being made on new development programs and systems to ensure that schedules are being met or that remedial action is being taken. Daily meetings with people who are using the data are necessary to discuss new development and maintenance projects. Usually, a weekly meeting is held with all programmers to review the preceding week's activity and modify short-term plans if necessary. Also, meetings with management are held to review long-term plans to ensure that the system is satisfactory and financially feasible.

What Education and Skills Will I Need?

High School   Preparation for college, with as much mathematics as possible.

College   Systems analysts come from majors in engineering, computer science, accounting, mathematics, and economics. It takes five years of experience and the successful completion of a five-step examination for certification. Regardless of your major, you must know programming languages. Most systems analysts come from other careers and learn the necessary skills on the job and in corporation-sponsored courses.

Personal Skills   The ability to concentrate and pay close attention to detail is important. You must be able to communicate well with technical personnel such as programmers and managers as well as with people who have no computer background.

How Many Systems Analysts Are There and Where Do They Work?

There are 666,000 systems analysts and computer scientists; 30 percent are women, 7 percent are black, and 3 percent are Hispanic. Most systems analysts have previous experience as engineers, managers, or computer programmers. More than half the jobs are in urban areas with manufacturing firms, computer and data processing services, and finance, insurance, and real estate firms. Nine percent of systems analysts are self-employed.

How Much Money Will I Make?

In 1992 the average starting salary for analysts was $25,200. With experience, the median was $42,100. The top 10 percent made over $65,000 a year.

What Are the Job Opportunities?

The more education, the better the opportunities. A systems analyst with training in health or business has an excellent chance for a good job. Computer technology is going into the fourth generation and a lot of help will be needed to keep the country's offices up to speed.

Related Careers

Computer programmer   Mathematician
Engineer   Operations manager

Where Can I Get More Information?

Association for Systems Management
1433 West Bagley Road
Berea, OH 44017

Association for Computing Machinery
1515 Broadway
New York, NY 10036

Business: Money Management

- **Accountant**
- **Actuary**
- **Bank manager**
- **Financial manager**

ABOUT MONEY MANAGEMENT CAREERS

Banking and finance are still trying to recover from the bad name they earned in the late 1980s. There are nearly two million jobs in these four money-management careers—accountant, actuary, bank manager, and financial manager—most of them held by men. Slower than average growth is projected because many banks are still closing or merging in the mid-1990s.

Money management requires a college education. For banking, a well-organized office-training program ranging from six months to one year is the best preparation.

Advancement in money management depends largely on job performance and qualifying examinations in accounting and actuary work, which require specialized study. Courses in every phase of banking are offered by the American Institute of Banking, an industry-sponsored school.

Money managers work in well-lighted, attractive, comfortable offices. Because a great deal of bank business and credit business depends on customers' impressions, money managers are encouraged to wear conservative, somewhat formal business clothes. Most jobs do not require travel, although accountants employed by national accounting firms may travel extensively to conduct audits and perform other services for their clients. Most money managers work overtime at home, and some are constantly studying for the qualifying examinations required for advancement. The demands of the first 10 years in a money-management career limit the time available for social and family life.

Accountant

Designs and controls financial records and verifies financial data

What's It Like to Be an Accountant?

Accountants prepare financial reports, profit and loss studies, cost studies, and tax reports. The three major accounting fields are public, management, and government accounting. Public accountants are independent and work on a fee basis for businesses, individuals, or accounting firms. Management accountants, also called industrial or private accountants, handle the financial resources of their company and work on a salary basis. Government accountants examine the financial resources of government agencies and audit private businesses to verify that they are complying with government regulations. Any of these accountants may specialize in auditing, taxes, cost accounting, budgeting and control, or investments.

Sue Jourdon, certified public accountant (CPA) for a small city, likes her work because she has the challenge of converting the city's present accounting system to a new computer program. She has a liberal arts college background with summer work in computer science, which she says adds to the excitement of accounting. "The hours are too long during the tax season—10 to 12 hours a day. But the good pay makes up for it." Marcel Renaud, CPA, says an accountant must love figures, and the study never stops. "It's a science and you must keep up-to-date, reading three to five hours a week." Marcel has specialized in health care, and at 32 he is making well over $75,000 figuring out innovative ways to bill rocketing health-care costs to government and insurance plans that will pay.

What Education and Skills Will I Need?

High School   A college preparatory program with strong interest and ability in mathematics is necessary for a certified public accountant (CPA) program. Alternatives include a commercial course leading to a business college program or a community college program in accounting, correspondence study in accounting, or a college course leading to a business administration major.

College   Accounting is offered in one-year business college programs, two-year community college programs, and four-year college programs. Nine out of 10 CPAs are college graduates, have passed the CPA examination in the state in which they work, and had two years of accounting experience before they took the exam. Currently, 17 states require CPA candidates to have 150 college credits, which usually means a fifth year of college.

Personal Skills   Aptitude for mathematics, ability to work independently, ability to work with systems and computers, accuracy, ability to analyze and interpret facts and figures quickly, and a high standard of integrity are necessary.

How Many Accountants Are There and Where Do They Work?

There are 939,000 accountants and auditors; 50 percent are women, 7 percent are black, and 4 percent are Hispanic. There are 475,000 CPAs; 10 percent are self-employed and 10 percent are part time. Accountants work in urban centers for accounting and bookkeeping firms (30 percent), manufacturing firms (17 percent), and government (13 percent). Ten percent are self-employed.

How Much Money Will I Make?

In 1993 starting salaries for accountants with a bachelors's degree averaged $28,000 a year. Beginners with a master's degree started at $30,000 a year. Accountants with experience averaged from

$70,000 to $80,000 a year. Chief accountants earned $85,000 and more.

What Are the Job Opportunities?

Accountants play a key role in management and seldom lose their jobs in a recession. Opportunities are expected to be good through 2005, since the numbers of graduates in accounting haven't increased since 1980.

Related Careers

Actuary

Financial manager

Bank manager

FBI special agent

Where Can I Get More Information?

Institute of Management Accountants
10 Paragon Drive
Montvale, NJ 07645

National Society of Public Accountants
1010 North Fairfax Street
Alexandria, VA 22314

Actuary

Assembles and analyzes statistics in order to design insurance and pension plans on a profit-making basis

What's It Like to Be an Actuary?

Why do teenage boys pay more for car insurance? How much is a life insurance policy for a 21-year-old female? Answers to these and similar questions are provided by actuaries. They calculate probabilities of death, sickness, injury, disability, unemployment, retirement, and property loss for accidents, theft, and fire. They use statistics to construct probability tables in order to develop insurance rates. They usually work for a life insurance or liability insurance company.

Actuary Mark Magnus, of New England Life Insurance Company in Boston, specializes in pension plans. This involves making sure that employers invest enough money wisely for retired workers to get a monthly pension for life. Magnus cautions college graduates to plan on a limited social life for the first few years as an actuary because the required actuarial examinations take 15 to 25 hours a week of home study. Or, he recommends, date another actuary and study together!

What Education and Skills Will I Need?

High School   College preparatory course, with as much mathematics as possible.

College   A degree is required, with a good background in calculus, probability and statistics, and computer science. Actuary science is offered in over 60 colleges; other good majors are mathematics or statistics. While still in college, you should begin to take the examinations required to become a professional actuary; it takes from 5 to 10 years to complete the exams after college while you are on the job. Thirty-eight colleges offer a degree in actuarial science. Employers generally prefer applicants who have a degree in actuarial science and those who have passed several examinations offered by professional actuarial societies.

Personal Skills   Mathematical skills, interest in studying and working independently to pass examinations on your own, and ability to do routine, detailed work are needed.

How Many Actuaries Are There and Where Do They Work?

There are 15,000 professional actuaries in the United States; one-third are women, 6 percent are black, and less than 1 percent are Hispanic. Almost half are employed in the five cities with major life insurance companies: New York, Hartford, Chicago, Philadelphia, and Boston. Others work for engineering and architectural firms (23 percent), for insurance agents and brokers (14 percent), and for fire, marine, and casualty insurance companies (13 percent). Virtually none are self-employed.

How Much Money Will I Make?

In 1993 the starting salary for college graduates who had not yet passed any actuarial exams was $31,800 a year. The pay increases rapidly as the exams are passed. Associates made from $36,000 to $41,000; fellows averaged $65,000.

What Are the Job Opportunities?

Opportunities are expected to be competitive through 2005. It is a small field and insurance companies recruit heavily on campus. The best jobs and the most money will go to the graduates who passed two or more actuarial examinations while they were still in college.

Related Careers

Mathematician   Statistician
Financial analyst   Engineering analyst

Where Can I Get More Information?

American Society of Pension Actuaries
4350 N. Fairfax Drive, Suite 820
Arlington, VA 22203

Society of Actuaries
475 North Martingale Road, Suite 800
Schaumburg, IL 60173

American Academy of Actuaries
1720 I Street, NW, 7th Floor
Washington, DC 20006

Bank Manager

Banks are in the "money" business; the bank manager is responsible for the management of the bank's business

What's It Like to Be a Bank Manager?

"If you're interested in money management," says Ian Burnham, "a bank training program is a good place to learn." Bank managers include the loan officer, who makes decisions on loan applications within the policy of the bank; the trust officer, who manages property, funds, or real estate for clients and whose duties include financial planning, investment, and taxes; the operations officer, who manages the bank's procedures efficiently; the customer manager, who is responsible for relations with customers and other banks; the branch bank manager, who has full responsibility for a branch office; the personnel administrator; and the public relations and operational research officers.

Overexpansion and competition have resulted in closings, mergers, and consolidations in banking. Public trust in the rapidly changing investment markets is at an all-time low. There is currently a need for bright, flexible, innovative young bankers who can bring a high level of integrity to the job.

What Education and Skills Will I Need?

High School   Preparation for college, with emphasis on mathematics and economics.

College   Bank management trainees usually must have a bachelor's degree in business administration with a major in finance, or a liberal arts degree with a major in accounting, economics, commercial law, or statistics. Some banks prefer trainees who have a master's degree in business administration (M.B.A.). Small-city and rural banks promote outstanding clerks and tellers to management positions.

Personal Skills   Ability to analyze detailed information, interest in working independently, good judgment in advising others, and tact are necessary in banking. Investment banking requires high motivation and a willingness to take risks.

How Many Bankers Are There and Where Do They Work?

There are 547,000 bank officers and managers; 37 percent are women, 3 percent are black, and 2 percent are Hispanic. They work in every bank in the country—from rural banks to big-city banks with well-developed training programs for managers.

How Much Money Will I Make?

In 1993 beginning college graduates in management training programs at large banks started at $21,200 to $31,000 a year. Those with a master's degree started with slightly more, and those with an M.B.A. made from $28,600 to $49,000 their first year. Bank managers averaged $42,600, and the top 10 percent made over $80,000. The officers of small-town banks work up from tellers and are paid much less than are city bankers.

Master of business administration graduates with little or no experience are starting at $50,000 a year in investment banking. With an undergraduate degree, they start at $33,000 if their other qualifications are outstanding. Liberal arts graduates show high growth potential, often ending up in top management jobs.

What Are the Job Opportunities?

Opportunities for work as a bank officer will be competitive through 2005. The failing of thousands of savings and loan banks in the past 10 years will result in continued hard times for banks. More services and a greater use of computers will require sound management and fewer jobs.

Related Careers

Stockbroker   Business executive
Accountant   Financial manager

Where Can I Get More Information?

American Bankers Association
1120 Connecticut Avenue, NW
Washington, DC 20036

Board of Governors
The Federal Reserve System
Constitution Avenue, NW
Washington, DC 20551

Financial Manager

Prepares financial reports required for company operations and to satisfy tax requirements

What's It Like to Be a Financial Manager?

A financial manager, also known as treasurer, business manager, and controller, oversees the cash flow and develops information to assess the future financial status of a business. Gail Chase, a Wharton School of Business M.B.A., is the financial manager of the University of California at San Diego (UCSD). She is responsible for the preparation of income statements, balance sheets, and depreciation schedules. She oversees the accounting, audit, and budget departments. Chase is responsible for managing the cash flow to meet the everyday cash needs as well as the investment needs of UCSD. "For example," she explains, "loans may be necessary to meet a cash shortage for the payroll, or surplus cash from federal grants and loans may need to be invested in interest-bearing instruments. I have to figure out the best way to borrow or invest these moneys."

What Education and Skills Will I Need?

High School Prepare for college with a strong curriculum in mathematics, computer science, and communications skills.

College Major in accounting or finance, or take a liberal arts program and prepare for an M.B.A., or go to a special training school after college in accounting management, budget management, corporate cash management, financial analysis, international banking, or data processing systems procedures.

Personal Skills Financial managers must be able to work independently and to analyze detailed information. People employed in this field must also have strong writing and speaking skills, tact, and good judgment. Knowledge of computer applications is vital for advancement.

How Many Financial Managers Are There and Where Do They Work?

There are 701,000 financial managers; 44 percent are women, 4 percent are black, and 2 percent are Hispanic. One-third are employed by banks, insurance companies, real estate firms, and securities dealers. Others work for service industries such as health, social, and management services.

How Much Money Will I Make?

The salary level depends on the size and location of the employer. The median salary was $39,700 in 1993, and the top 10 percent of managers earned over $77,800. Top financial managers earn much more than that, and they receive additional compensation in the form of bonuses and perks. The chief finance officer (CFO) earned $56,000 in small firms to $290,000 in the largest firms; controllers earned from $44,000 to $129,000.

What Are the Job Opportunities?

Opportunities for well-educated financial managers will be good through the 1990s; the best opportunities will be in health services.

Related Careers

Accountant   Bank manager
Insurance consultant   Securities consultant

Where Can I Get More Information?

American Financial Services Association
919 Eighteenth Street, NW
Washington, DC 20006

Treasury Management Association
7315 Wisconsin Avenue, Suite 1250 W
Bethesda, MD 20814

Business: Sales

- **Automobile salesperson**
- **Insurance salesperson**
- **Manufacturer's salesperson**
- **Real estate salesperson**
- **Retail and wholesale buyer**
- **Services sales representative**
- **Stockbroker**
- **Travel agent**

ABOUT SALES CAREERS

Sales is where the money is. You can make the most money with the least education in this career group. Sales is also where the experience is, and the road to top management is often through sales. Sales jobs have boomed in the past few years—from 12 million jobs to 16.3 million, a growth rate of more than 30 percent, mostly in real estate, travel agency, and stockbrokerage firms. About 26 percent of all salespeople have a college degree. They reflect a great variety of college majors, although manufacturers' salespeople often come from technical or scientific backgrounds.

Beginning salespeople work evenings, weekends, and holidays—whenever the customers and clients are free to buy. Some manufacturers' salespeople have large territories and travel a lot.

Others usually work close to their headquarters. The amount of time beginning salespeople put into building up their accounts is hard on family life and friends. But once they establish accounts, which takes about 10 years for stockbrokers and car salespeople, they can meet their clients at their mutual convenience—on the golf course, on the racquetball court, or at lunch. If you are interested in sales and have decided not to go for the big money, then you can put in fewer hours. In many fields, salespeople are free to set up their own time schedules. Real estate is the best example of a field that allows flexible hours. More than 25 percent of the 7 million people in sales work part time. A flexible schedule provides many opportunities for coordinating a career with parenting. Salespeople who have managerial ability may advance to assistant sales manager, sales manager, or general manager. Some managers open their own businesses or become partners in dealerships, agencies, or firms. Most sales advancement comes in the form of making more money and having more free time as customer accounts become well established. Advice from the million-dollar salespeople:

1. Believe in yourself.
2. Believe in your product.
3. Work on your timing.
4. Develop a sense of humor.
5. Realize your customer isn't necessarily telling you what he or she really wants.

Automobile Salesperson

Sells new and used cars for car dealers

What's It Like to Be an Automobile Salesperson?

An automobile salesperson must know about *selling*, not about the complicated details of the product. The main thing is to know how to close a deal—that is, how to overcome the customer's hesitancy to buy. Often, a new salesperson begins a sale and an experienced one helps close the sale. A new salesperson may quote prices and must learn how to give a trade-in allowance for the customer's present car.

Salespeople often arrange financing and insurance for the cars they sell. They learn to develop and follow leads on prospective customers. Car selling is an exciting job because there is a $300 to $500 profit on each car sold and much more on top-of-the-line models.

Commission selling, or getting paid a percentage of the product sold, is not a traditional position for women. The higher the price of the product, the fewer women are selling it. For instance, very few women sell cars, commercial real estate, or securities—the top-paying sales jobs. An exception is Elaine Atkins, daughter of a Ford dealer, who does sell strictly on commission. She says she would never have thought of getting into car sales if it hadn't been a family business. Now that she has gone through the steps from working on salary with commissions from walk-ins to building her own prospects list and working strictly on commission, she loves it. She loves being her own boss, taking off a month when she has filled her quota, and making more money than she ever thought possible. Another exception is Pat Moran, who took over JM Family Enterprises, the largest Toyota dealer in the country, with sales of $2.4 billion. Even though U.S. auto sales dropped 1 percent in 1992, Moran's sales rose 15 percent.

What Education and Skills Will I Need?

High School Most salespeople, but not all, prepare for a great variety of college majors. They are usually trained on the job by sales managers and experienced salespeople.

College Many new-car dealers have some college, but business and selling experience counts more than a degree.

Personal Skills Sales skills, initiative, assertiveness, enthusiasm for the product, and ambition make a successful salesperson. Innovation is a key to success in hard times. The Morans pioneered the use of TV advertising to get their market share.

How Many Automobile Salespeople Are There and Where Do They Work?

There are 294,000 automobile and boat salespeople; 8 percent are women, 5 percent are black, and 5 percent are Hispanic. They work in every city, town, and village in the country. New-car dealers employ from 1 to 50 salespeople.

How Much Money Will I Make?

In 1993 salespeople in the automobile business averaged $25,000 a year. The top 10 percent made over $90,000. Earnings vary widely, depending on geography, experience, and type and size of the dealership.

What Are the Job Opportunities?

If you prove yourself a seller, you can convince a dealer to hire you for a commission job that doesn't involve a financial risk to the dealer. If selling cars is what you want to do, you can suggest a plan to a dealer (after-hours, weekends, or after another job). Ask for a few months' trial, and if the dealer makes money, you will have a job. Car sales have been down. The spring of 1993 saw the first increase in sales in three years. The higher cost of used cars, better-made American cars, and the many people who have not bought in the past few years point to optimism in car sales.

Related Careers

Real estate salesperson　　　　　Insurance salesperson
Manufacturer's representative　　Stockbroker

Where Can I Get More Information?

National Automobile Dealers Association
8400 Westpark Drive
McLean, VA 22102

Insurance Salesperson

Sells policies that protect individuals and businesses against future losses and financial pressures

What's It Like to Be an Insurance Salesperson?

Insurance is one of the largest industries in the economy with over 2.1 million workers, and half a million people are in insurance sales. Other insurance jobs for college graduates include manager, security analyst, underwriter, and actuary. As insurance companies develop their financial planning services, they are expanding the kinds of careers they offer. The frontline workers are the salespeople and brokers. An insurance agent sells for one company, usually on a commission basis; a broker sells insurance for several companies. Managers are responsible for the administration of policy, accounting, investments, and loans. Underwriters review insurance applications to evaluate the risk involved in order to determine profit for the company. Accountants, bookkeepers, and lawyers are also employed by insurance companies.

John E. Wilson, Jr., business executive for the John Hancock Mutual Life Insurance Company, likes best the interaction with people. He likes motivating, guiding, and producing an end result. Wilson thinks it is important for students to realize that during a career, interests or circumstances may bring changes they might not have planned or intended. He would like to see young people plan their education with more flexibility than most think is needed. "Our top insurance sales and management people, for example, come from a great variety of college majors and work experiences. Their skills would lead them to excel in sales in any number of other fields, as well."

Monica Ladd, insurance broker in a family business, spends her day changing and rating policies, answering clients' questions about coverage, talking to special agents representing their companies, and contacting people about accident reports. She finds the work very stimulating, because of the constant change in policies and people's needs and because she makes very good money.

What Education and Skills Will I Need?

High School   Prepare for business, two-year, or four-year college.

College   Major in business administration, personnel, insurance, or liberal arts. Insurance salespeople come from all kinds of educational backgrounds, and a degree is not necessary to get good sales jobs. Most insurance salespeople come from other jobs. They tend to be older than entrants to other careers. All agents and most brokers must be licensed in the state where they plan to sell insurance. The College of Insurance in New York City trains college graduates for top-level positions in the industry.

Personal Skills   Enthusiasm, self-confidence, discipline, and ability to communicate well are necessary to be successful in selling. You must be able to inspire confidence.

How Many Insurance Salespeople Are There and Where Do They Work?

There are over 439,000 full-time insurance agents and brokers; 33 percent are women, 5 percent are black, and 4 percent are Hispanic. Thirty-two percent of them are self-employed. There is a high turnover of agents; at the end of four years only about 15 percent are still full-time agents. High turnover and part-time work provide entry-level opportunities. There are insurance agencies and brokers in every city, town, and village in the country. The headquarters of most insurance companies are in California, Connecticut, Illinois, Massachusetts, New Jersey, New York, and Texas.

How Much Money Will I Make?

Beginners start at a salary of about $1,200 a month for six months before they go on commission. After five years of building a clientele, insurance salespeople make from $20,900 to $42,200, the top 10 percent averaging $62,000. Top agents make $80,000, and some earn over $200,000 a year.

What Are the Job Opportunities?

This is certainly a time of transition, and there are many opportunities for ambitious and talented graduates interested in insurance sales. Selling jobs have a big turnover, giving many beginners an opportunity. The overall insurance industry is changing rapidly, with a growing demand for long-term health care and pension benefits. The biggest change is using insurance to provide educational funds for college and for retirement. Rising incomes and concerns about financial security will stimulate sales of insurance, annuities, and financial services.

Related Careers

Real estate salesperson   Manufacturer's salesperson
Financial manager   Stockbroker

Where Can I Get More Information?

Independent Insurance Agents of America
127 South Peyton Street
Alexandria, VA 22314

National Association of Professional Insurance Agents
400 North Washington Street
Alexandria, VA 22314

Manufacturer's Salesperson
Sells manufactured products to businesses and institutions

What's It Like to Be a Manufacturer's Salesperson?

A manufacturer's salesperson, sometimes called a sales engineer, industrial salesperson, or sales rep, spends most of his or her time visiting prospective buyers to inform them about available products, analyze their needs, and take orders. Salesworkers visit firms in their territory. They prepare reports on sales prospects or customers' credit ratings, handle correspondence, and study literature about their products. Sales reps usually promote their product by displays at conferences or by giving demonstrations to companies on how to use their products. Stacey O'Sullivan, salesperson for Dell, sells highly technical computer equipment. She says that in addition to learning all about her product, she also must be able to help prospective buyers with technical problems, show them how to use the software more effectively, and inform them about other equipment that is available for expanding their computer systems. It often takes months to negotiate a sale. O'Sullivan loves the challenge of selling and the money she makes in computer systems, the fastest-growing product in the world.

What Education and Skills Will I Need?

High School Preparation for college; college graduates are preferred.

College Many technical or specialized salespeople are engineers, pharmacists, or chemists. Others majored in business or liberal arts. Over half of all entrants transfer from other occupations, and more than half do not have a degree.

Personal Skills Selling skills, assertiveness, pleasant appearance, interest in the product, and the ability to get along well with people are necessary for all work in sales.

How Many Manufacturers' Salespeople Are There and Where Do They Work?

There are 1,613,000 manufacturers' and wholesale sales representatives; 20 percent are women, 3 percent are black, and 4 percent are Hispanic. They are employed by the printing and publishing, chemical, fabricated metal products, electrical, and other machinery industries, as well as by the transportation and food products industries. Most work out of branch offices, usually in big cities near prospective customers.

How Much Money Will I Make?

In 1993 the mid 50 percent earned from $22,300 to $46,500 a year. The highest salaries were in electrical and electronics equipment, construction materials, and pharmaceuticals. The majority of salesworkers get paid on a combination of salary, commission, and bonus. The top 10 percent make more than $62,200 a year.

What Are the Job Opportunities?

Jobs will be competitive in the tough manufacturing market through 2005. The best opportunities will be in computers, chemicals, and electronics.

Related Careers

Real estate salesperson   Automobile salesperson
Retail and wholesale buyer   Stockbroker

Where Can I Get More Information?

Manufacturers' Agents National Association
23016 Mill Creek Road
P.O. Box 3467
Laguna Hills, CA 92654

Real Estate Salesperson

Represents property owners who want to sell or rent residential and commercial properties

What's It Like to Be a Real Estate Salesperson?

Anne DeMarzo, number one agent for the biggest rental agency in New York City, started as a trainee stationed in one building to show apartments. The month she got her real estate license, she rented 18 apartments. She makes a lot of money—$100,000 last year. Starting the day at her desk with telephone calls to clients, she spends a lot of time going over apartment listings and deciding which would be just right for them. She credits her success primarily to a knack for remembering hundreds of apartment listings.

Experienced Neil Gallagher, number one salesperson for another agency in New York City, says the key to top sales is to show precisely the right apartments to customers. "The best job a salesperson can do," he said, "is in the selection of *what* to show, because anyone can show an apartment or a house or a building." He always visits the property he is going to rent or sell before he shows it—checking the size of bedrooms, dramatic views, and any unique features he can use to make it special for particular clients.

What Education and Skills Will I Need?

College   A degree is not necessary to become a real estate salesperson or broker, although a state real estate license is required. More than 200 colleges and many correspondence schools offer one or more courses in real estate to enable applicants to qualify for the licensing examination.

Personal Skills   Outgoing personality, neat appearance, assertiveness, enthusiasm, tact, and a good memory for faces, names, and listings make a successful real estate salesperson. The ability to sell is the key to success in this career.

How Many Real Estate Salespeople Are There and Where Do They Work?

There are 397,000 full-time agents and brokers, and as many part-time sales agents; half of them are women, 3 percent are black, and 4 percent are Hispanic. This career is known for its part-time workers. There are over 4 million licensed realtors; 62 percent are in small firms and are self-employed.

How Much Money Will I Make?

Commissions on sales are the source of income in the real estate business. Commissions vary from 5 percent to 10 percent, depending on the type of property and the part of the country; Vermonters make much less than do agents in San Francisco or New York City. The median income is $28,000 for salespeople and $46,600 for brokers. Top salesman Neil Gallagher makes $300,000 in New York City.

What Are the Job Opportunities?

Good jobs in real estate are very competitive and will continue to be so. The best chances for work will go to the well-trained, ambitious people who enjoy selling. The housing market and the economy, which always influence the job market, have been down in spite of low mortgage rates. There is great turnover in the field; beginners are often discouraged because they can't close enough sales to get started.

Related Careers

Automobile salesperson   Travel agent
Insurance salesperson   Manufacturer's salesperson

Where Can I Get More Information?

National Association of Realtors
430 N. Michigan Avenue
Chicago, IL 60611

Retail and Wholesale Buyer

Purchases merchandise to resell at a profit

What's It Like to Be a Retail and Wholesale Buyer?

Retailer Emily Woods designed the preppy clothes that made J. Crew the successful catalog company that it is, and later became president of this rapidly expanding retail business. She opened three retail stores in 1989 and in 1993 opened 36 stores in Japan. Buyers working for J. Crew or any retail business purchase for resale the best available merchandise at the lowest possible prices to profit from the flow of goods from manufacturer to consumer. Wholesale buyers purchase goods directly from manufacturers or from other wholesale firms for release to retail firms. Retail buyers purchase goods from wholesale firms or, occasionally, directly from manufacturers. Buyers work on a very busy schedule with a lot of hustle and with all kinds of people. Retail buyer Irv Lief, a former trainee at Macy's in New York City, has just taken a new job in merchandising at Innes of Wichita, Kansas. He loves the fast pace of the work and doesn't think it matters whether you work for a large or a small store. "Getting the goods to the customers at the right time for the best profit is exactly the daily challenge I like to live with. My wife is also in business," says Lief, "and we both like a fast-track lifestyle."

What Education and Skills Will I Need?

High School Preparation for business school, art school, a merchandising program, or a liberal arts degree.

College Take a two- or four-year course that includes business, marketing, fashion, merchandising, and art. Prepare for a department store training program for buyers, such as the prestigious Bloomingdale's program.

Personal Skills Buyers must be able to work fast, be good planners, and be able to communicate with salesworkers, buyers, and sellers all at the same time.

How Many Buyers Are There and Where Do They Work?

There are 182,000 buyers and merchandising managers; 50 percent are women, 4 percent are black, and 4 percent are Hispanic. Two-thirds of them are retail buyers, working for clothing and general department stores in major cities. Thirteen percent are self-employed.

How Much Money Will I Make?

In 1993 most buyers started at $21,100 to $29,500 a year. The median income for buyers was $32,500. The top 10 percent of all buyers made over $64,000.

What Are the Job Opportunities?

Jobs will be competitive through 2005 because buying is a glamour job and many college graduates go for it. Also, the economy has been down long enough to negatively affect retail sales. Assertive, fast-working people who like to hustle will get these jobs.

Related Careers

Automobile salesperson
Merchandise manager

Manufacturer's salesperson
Sales manager

Where Can I Get More Information?

National Retail Federation
100 West 31st Street
New York, NY 10001

Services Sales Representative

Sells a wide variety of services from advertising to communications systems

What's It Like to Be a Services Sales Representative?

It can be complex—selling data-processing services such as inventory control, payroll processing, sales analysis, and financial reporting systems. Or educational—selling states a particular licensing examination or insurance laws and regulations. Or nationwide—a hotel sales representative contacts government, business, and social organizations to solicit convention and conference business for the hotel. Or creative—Patricia Gallup pioneered fast, inexpensive mail-order sales of computer software with an emphasis on service by phone. Her philosophy is "Why go to a store, when you can buy from us without leaving home." Even though services sales representatives sell a great diversity of services, they have a lot in common. All sales representatives must fully understand and be able to discuss the services their company offers. They must develop lists of prospective clients. They must meet with clients and explain how the services being offered can meet their needs. And after making a sale, representatives call on their customers to make sure the services have met their needs and to try to sell them additional services. Technical services representatives often work as part of a team and receive technical assistance from support personnel.

What Education and Skills Will I Need?

High School   Preparation for business or technical school or an engineering, marketing, or liberal arts major in college.

College   If computers, or hotel management, or another area is your interest, major in that area. Both liberal arts and business graduates work in services sales. Most companies have extensive training programs for recent college graduates.

Personal Skills   Outgoing personality, assertiveness, high motivation, and ability to organize make effective services sales representatives. The abilities to communicate well and to work under pressure are also important.

How Many Services Sales Representatives Are There and Where Do They Work?

There are 488,000 services sales representatives. Most of them work in business services (53 percent), including computer and data processing, advertising, personnel, equipment rental and leasing, and mailing, reproduction, and stenographic services; 11 percent work in engineering firms.

How Much Money Will I Make?

In 1993 the median annual salary in advertising sales was $29,000. Representatives selling other business services earned $27,000. Representatives working for Fortune 500 companies started at $39,000; those with five years of experience averaged $60,000, and the top 10 percent made over $100,000.

What Are the Job Opportunities?

Because of high turnover in sales jobs, there are usually positions to be found. The number of jobs depends on the particular service—health services and computer services are expected to grow through 2005.

Related Careers

Real estate salesperson

Insurance salesperson

Travel agent

Manufacturer's salesperson

Where Can I Get More Information?

Contact businesses that sell services in your area of interest.

Stockbroker

Sells stocks, bonds, or mutual funds to individuals and institutions

What's It Like to Be a Stockbroker?

A stockbroker, sometimes called a securities salesperson, gets an order for stock and relays the order through the firm's order room to the floor of a securities exchange or the firm's trading department. After this transaction is completed, the stockbroker notifies the customer of the sale. Other duties of the broker include explaining the stock market and trading practices to customers, suggesting when to buy and when to sell, and often managing the money of institutions with millions of dollars to invest. Vermont stockbroker Argie Economou reports that after 15 years in the business, and despite the valleys and the peaks, he wouldn't be anywhere else. "I'm my own boss," explains Economou. "I can come and go as I please. I can make 126 phone calls in one day, as I have done, or I can take off and make none. It's an exciting business of endless variety. Everything you see in this world—everything you see or smell or touch—relates to business. It's all-consuming and I love it."

Ann Williams, a young lawyer from Little Rock, Arkansas, President Clinton's home base, was looking for an opportunity to make the big time. She decided to change careers when a former professor needed a sales assistant in the securities business. Williams had been working for the Arkansas legislature but was looking for an opportunity to move to New York City. Although fulfilling the six months required before she could take the necessary securities examination, Williams stayed in her first job in New York for a little less than a year. She went on to another short-term job before going to work at a firm where she has been for more than two years. She says that Wall Street has been slow to computerize, and she hates the paperwork that goes along with each sales transaction. It's also tough, she thinks, to be responsible for other people's money when you have no control over the market. Her attraction to a career in selling stocks is the unlimited money she can make. "There's no ceiling on how much you can make," says Williams. "If you work hard and are smart, the sky's the limit. I like the entrepreneurial spirit of sales. To a large extent you're your own boss in this job, unlike a corporate job at the same level." She loves researching companies, reading annual reports, and looking into every facet of a business. For example, the annual report of the Gap retail chain interested her, so she went to a store to see for herself how many people were buying what. Williams loves the excitement of U.S. business and wants to learn more about how each firm manages its profits.

What Education and Skills Will I Need?

High School   Preparation for college. Read the financial pages of newspapers—especially the Sunday business sections of *The New York Times*, and *The Wall Street Journal*—in order to learn about the financial market.

College   Almost all trainees for stockbrokerage firms are college graduates. Most come from other careers, primarily professional or sales jobs.

Personal Skills   Selling skills, interest in making big money, love of finance and business, and ambition are needed for success in the stock market.

How Many Stockbrokers Are There and Where Do They Work?

There are 200,000 stockbrokers; 23 percent are women, 4 percent are black, and 3 percent are Hispanic. They work for brokerage firms, investment banks, and mutual funds firms. Most work for a few large firms that have offices in large and small cities all over the country. Twenty-five percent are self-employed.

How Much Money Will I Make?

Trainees start at $1,200 to $1,500 a month, depending on the size of the firm, until they are licensed and working on commission. In 1992 full-time stockbrokers who sold to individuals earned from $20,800 to $47,000. The top 10 percent made $70,000 a year, while brokers selling to institutions averaged $156,000 a year.

What Are the Job Opportunities?

In the current economic downturn, job seekers outnumber job openings. Jobs are always very competitive, however, regardless of the economy. Merrill Lynch advises college graduates to get two or three years of successful business experience before they apply for a training program with a major investment firm. If you don't get into a major firm's training program, small firms are the best bet for getting a foot in the door.

Related Careers

Insurance salesperson

Financial manager

Real estate salesperson

Bank manager

Where Can I Get More Information?

New York Stock Exchange
11 Wall Street
New York, NY 10005

Securities Industry Association
120 Broadway
New York NY 10271

Travel Agent

Organizes, schedules, and sells travel services to the public

What's It Like to Be a Travel Agent?

Travel agents are dealers in dreams—other people's dreams—and in the course of a day they plan many round-the-world trips, vacations, and special event trips, as well as routine business trips for regular customers. An agent must possess a great deal of specialized knowledge about climate, accommodations, fares, places of interest, tariffs and customs laws, currency exchange, and reference sources for new information. When an anthropologist schedules a trip to Taute, New Guinea, the agent must supply exact information about connections between airlines and time changes from time zone to time zone. The agent must know that when the anthropologist ends up on a missionary plane in Lumi, walking through the bush is the only means of transportation left to get to his or her destination. Travel agencies are service agencies. Goodwill and good client relations are vitally important to making a profit in these services. That's not always easy, especially when a customer changes travel plans for the sixth time. Knowing details, excursion rates, charters, and frequent-flying deals, and the ability to figure out how to make trips more convenient and comfortable are necessary skills for a successful agent.

What Education and Skills Will I Need?

High School Most travel agents have some college background, although it is not a requirement. Courses in geography, history, and a foreign language are helpful.

College Some travel agents have taken travel agency courses that are offered in adult education programs, correspondence schools, community colleges, and private programs. Others are college graduates who have learned on the job, usually after coming from other careers.

Personal Skills Sales skills, business ability, interest in details and accuracy, together with a pleasant personality are necessary to be successful as a travel agent.

How Many Travel Agents Are There and Where Do They Work?

There are 115,000 full-time travel agents and many more who work part time and moonlight from other jobs in order to get reduced travel fare benefits as well as commissions. Urban and resort areas have the greatest number of agents. Twenty percent are self-employed. The travel industry is expected to grow to 214,000 agents by 2005, a 62 percent increase.

How Much Money Will I Make?

Entry-level salaries are low. The job situation is competitive because so many people want to work in the travel industry. In 1993 agents started at $12,428. They averaged $15,610 after three years and $20,775 after 10 years; senior agents made $25,000 a year. Owners of their own businesses make 5 percent on domestic travel, 10 percent on international travel, and 10 percent on cruises and hotels. Young people often go into this career for the fringe benefits, which include vacations at reduced rates and transportation and hotels at a discount when they travel. Often, agents are invited for free holidays to see and recommend the facilities of an airline or resort hotel.

What Are the Job Opportunities?

The travel industry is one of the fastest-growing fields, and spending on travel is expected to increase through 2005. Travel is sensitive to economic downturns, however, and jobs will remain very competitive since travel is one of the glamour careers that attract many qualified people. The surest way to get a start in travel is to take any job a small agency offers you and work toward a promotion after learning the job. Another strategy for getting into the field is to bring in customers while you work another job, until you have impressed the boss enough to get a full-time position.

Related Careers

Airline reservations agent   Salesperson
Tour guide

Where Can I Get More Information?

American Society of Travel Agents
1101 King Street
Alexandria, VA 22314

The Institute of Certified Travel Agents
148 Linden Street
P.O. Box 812059
Wellesley, MA 02181

Communications

- **Cable television broadcasting**
- **Radio and television broadcasting**
- **Reporter**
- **Writer, editor**

ABOUT COMMUNICATIONS CAREERS

Responses such as "I'm a writer," or "I'm in TV," to the question "What work do you do?" almost always evoke envy. Communications careers are glamorous, and because they are, competition for most jobs is tough, with many more job seekers than there are job openings. Except for news broadcasting, relatively few workers in this industry are involved in the production of television programs because most are prerecorded by motion picture companies. Some people are attracted by the image of media jobs—the opportunities to meet public figures, to appear before nationwide audiences, and to attend special events. It is often difficult to see the hard work required when you are looking at the exciting aspects of communications careers.

The broadcasting business is undergoing a tremendous change, from three major networks to soaring numbers of independent stations operating on cable and by satellite. The independents have increased to 250 stations, and the number of households with cable increased from 41 million in 1985 to 54 million in 1990. Even more dramatic is the growth of the video cassette

155

recorder (VCR) market; VCR's are selling at the rate of almost 1 million a month and are already in a third of U.S. homes. With all the television choices, the average time a household spends watching the tube each week rose to 49 hours and 58 minutes— more than seven hours a day, seven days a week! Radio listening and advertising rates are up as well. Even though there are many more broadcasting jobs today, the field is as competitive as ever. For example, a major Boston radio station reports that it receives 5,000 résumés a year but has only 20 openings.

The intellectual skills acquired at college are important for a communications career. Acute powers of observation and the ability to think clearly and logically are necessary qualities, because people in communications need to understand the significance of the events they observe. A feeling for language enables newspaper reporters and broadcast journalists to breathe life and meaning into the overwhelming number of events that occur every day. A knack for creating drama through the spoken word makes radio and television announcers attractive to audiences of all kinds. Even though the competition is tough, there will be jobs through the 1990s for talented persons who have acquired the appropriate education and experience. Entering on the business side is usually the easiest way to get into communications. Advertising sales, a very demanding job, is a common entry-level professional position. Another strategy is to find a small station hundreds of miles from a major city, maybe in the town or small city where you grew up, and be prepared to take any job that's offered. You need a combination of talent, education, motivation, imagination, and luck.

Cable Television Broadcasting

Prepares, produces, and sells cable TV programs

What's It Like to Be in Cable TV?

"You have to be hungry, ambitious, and energetic to compete in this industry," says Vivian Horner, vice-president of program development for Warner Amex Cable in New York. At this time cable television is the fastest-growing communications career in the country. When we think of television, often the first jobs that come to mind are announcer and actor. But there are lots of other careers involved in setting up and running a cable system. Here are some of them: *winning the franchise*—jobs include engineer, market analyst, financial analyst; *building the system*—jobs include engineer, electronics and satellite technician; *running the system*—jobs include electrical engineer, sales specialist, marketing and advertising director; *programming and production*—jobs include director of public access, director of local origin programs, studio manager, sound and lighting technician, and newswriter.

After graduation from Oberlin, Mark Irish headed for New York City's cable TV world and landed a programming and production job at Showtime. His whole life is wrapped up in his work, which often lasts until 7 or 8 p.m. in the office, followed later in the evening by a screening of a film where "everyone" in the industry has to be seen. "A social life is almost impossible unless you take your date to the screenings," says Irish. "This life is just as crazy and glamorous and tough as they say it is. I love it. I wouldn't be anywhere else—except maybe Los Angeles, doing the same thing."

What Education and Skills Will I Need?

High School Preparation for college, with as much writing, speaking, and reading as you can get.

College Major in communications, electronic engineering, radio and television, journalism, theater arts, business, or liberal arts.

Personal Skills Programming careers require an interest in business, a lot of hustle, and attention to detail. The entertainment side of cable requires a well-modulated speaking voice and a reasonable command of the English language, plus knowledge of dramatics, sports, music, and current events.

How Many Cable TV Workers Are There and Where Do They Work?

There are 86,000 jobs in the system level of the cable TV industry, and the jobs are clustered around major cities. About 16 percent of the jobs are held by women, 9 percent by blacks, and 6 percent by Hispanics. Cable employment projections are that the current number will more than double by the mid-1990s.

How Much Money Will I Make?

Members of a franchise team for a major cable TV company make from $27,000 to $44,000 a year. Selling is an important job in cable, as subscriber fees are the major source of income. Entry-level salaries range from $16,000 to $26,000 in sales, depending on geographic location. Experienced account executives can earn over $36,000. Operations is the business-management side of the TV industry. An operations manager oversees capital expenditures, customer service, accounts payable, installation and maintenance, and other administrative functions. Entry-level salaries for operations range from $16,000 to $21,000 in small systems and are over $24,000 in major cities.

What Are the Job Opportunities?

Along with computers, cable television and VCRs are the fastest growing industries of the 1990s. As in other communications fields, it is a glamorous career with many talented and ambitious young people applying for jobs. Starting work at ground level can provide a wonderful opportunity to learn and grow with the industry. Program and production jobs are very limited as cable stations tend to buy packaged programs. See "Radio and Television Broadcasting" for information on television production jobs.

Related Careers

Commercial or public radio worker
Commercial or public television worker

Business manager
Salesperson

Where Can I Get More Information?

National Cable Television Association
1724 Massachusetts Avenue, NW
Washington, DC 20036

Radio and Television Broadcasting

Plans, prepares, produces, and presents radio and television programs

What's It Like to Be in Radio and Television Broadcasting?

The glamour and excitement of radio and television make broadcasting attractive to approximately 200,000 people who are employed in this career. Whether in commercial or public broadcasting, radio and television producers and directors plan and supervise individual programs or series of programs. They coordinate the shows, select the artists and studio personnel, schedule and conduct rehearsals, and direct on-the-air shows. They are often assisted by entry-level *associate producers* who arrange details, distribute scripts and script changes to the cast, and help direct shows. They may also arrange for props, makeup service, artwork, and film slides and help with timing. *Announcers* are probably the best-known workers in the industry. They introduce programs, guests, and musical selections and deliver most of the live commercials. At small stations, they may also operate the control board, sell time, and write commercial and news copy. *Musical directors* select, arrange, and direct music for programs, following general instructions from the program producers and directors. News gathering and reporting are another key aspect of radio and television programming. *News directors* plan and supervise all news and special events coverage. *News reporters* gather and analyze information about newsworthy events for broadcast on radio or TV. They may specialize in a particular field, such as economics, health, or foreign affairs, and often report special news events from the scene. *Newswriters* select and write copy for newscasters to read on the air. In many stations, the jobs of newswriter and newscaster are combined. In addition, broadcasting stations have video and film editors, engineering technicians, a sales department that sells time to advertisers who sponsor the programs, and a general administration department.

Two disc jockeys, one on the East Coast and the other on the West Coast, have a lot in common. Both Peter Standish and

Tammy Heide started volunteering for their college radio stations in their freshman year at college. By the time they graduated, they had four years of experience and a lot of contacts. Standish had worked at the campus radio station, as an intern for a music trade publication, and for KQAK, a leading radio station in San Francisco, all at the same time. Even with contacts, Standish and Heide are quick to point out that you need a lot of luck to get the breaks in this competitive job market. They've worked hard and have been lucky. They wouldn't change anything except, perhaps, in their college curriculum; they might have taken a little more music history and liberal arts while they were in college.

What Education and Skills Will I Need?

High School   Preparation for college and a liberal arts or communications major, with as much writing, speaking, and reading experience as you can get.

College   Major in any of the liberal arts, communications, radio and television, journalism, theater arts, or a related area. Most broadcasters worked part time in related jobs while in college.

Personal Skills   Announcers must have pleasant and well-controlled voices, good timing, excellent pronunciation, and good grammar.

The videotaped audition that presents samples of an applicant's delivery, style, and appearance is often the most important factor in hiring. Programming careers also require an interest in business and in details.

How Many Radio and Television Workers Are There and Where Do They Work?

There are 56,000 announcers and newscasters and 120,000 full-time and 30,000 part-time staff employed in commercial broadcasting; half are in radio. Eighteen percent of the announcers are women, 7 percent are black, and 3 percent are Hispanic. Thirty-three percent work part time. They are employed in 7,000 commercial radio stations and 700 commercial television stations in the United States.

In addition, there are 700 educational radio stations and 220 educational television stations. There are also 3,150 cable TV systems, which hire about 9,500 workers.

How Much Money Will I Make?

In 1992, radio announcers started from $13,000 to $45,000 a year. Television broadcasters made from $28,000 in the smallest stations to $163,000 in the largest markets. Sportscasters made from $22,000 to $142,500 and weathercasters up to $103,321. News announcers averaged $41,000, with top salaries of over a million dollars going to some network anchors.

What Are the Job Opportunities?

Radio and television broadcasting are two very popular careers. The professional-level jobs are very competitive, and thousands of liberal arts graduates apply for the few jobs available every spring. For example, one Boston radio station had 5,000 applicants for 20 jobs. The small local stations are the least competitive and offer the beginner the most valuable diverse experience in communications. The chances are better with radio because there are many more jobs and more beginners are hired.

Related Careers

Actor

Public relations
  worker

Salesperson

Teacher

Where Can I Get More Information?

National Association of Broadcasters
1771 N Street, NW
Washington, DC 20036

Radio-Television News Directors Association
1000 Connecticut Avenue, NW
Suite 615
Washington, DC 20036

Reporter

Gathers news and prepares stories that inform the public about local, state, national, and international events

What's It Like to Be a Reporter or a Correspondent?

Reporters, also known as news correspondents and video journalists (VJ's), present different points of view on current issues. Ross Connelly and Susan M. Jarzyna, publishers of the weekly *Hardwick Gazette* in Vermont, say they expect their reporters to cover a story by researching the history of the event, reviewing public records, and interviewing a variety of people. As a rule, reporters take notes or use a tape recorder while collecting facts. However, more and more reporters are using small, portable computers to enter the story, which is then sent by telephone modem to rewriters. Most reporters use personal computers in the newsroom, and they are now expected to do much more editorial and layout work on their stories. Big-city news reporters, VJ's, and TV broadcasters often have "beats," such as police stations, courts, or political headquarters. Many magazine and wire service reporters specialize in medicine, foreign affairs, education, science, art, or movie or restaurant reviews. A daily newspaper has a fast pace and a deadline atmosphere not found in other writing jobs. Radio and TV correspondents who work for the major networks send their stories to rewriters who write the news in relatively short sentences for ease of understanding by listeners.

Video journalist Hannah Buchdahl got her start at CNN after graduating from Northwestern University's School of Journalism. While in high school, she was editor-in-chief of her high school newspaper. In her junior year of college, she worked as an intern for a semester at an Oregon daily newspaper. As she said, "I did some writing, copy-editing, junk jobs—everything. I had a police beat, an obits beat, and a school board meetings beat. I learned two very important things: how to build contacts to get the news, and that I didn't want to do newspaper work. When CNN came to campus in April of my senior year, I went to a large group information session and was given a writing test, mostly on my knowledge of current events. A phone call interview came next with Headline News. They offered me a starting job for $13,000 a year as an editorial assistant." She found a roommate, borrowed money, and ate at home in order to live on the meager salary. Ms. Buchdahl eventually got a raise, and then was promoted to writer and, most recently, to writer/associate producer for CNN.

What Education and Skills Will I Need?

High School Preparation for college, with as much training in language skills and reporting experience as you can get. Any part-time or summer work on a local newspaper will help you find out what a reporter's job is like. Work on as many school publications as you can while in high school.

College Reporters and correspondents come from a great variety of college majors. You don't have to be a journalism or an English major to be a reporter. Most reporters, however, have a liberal arts degree. Writing and communication skills, together with a special style, are what count.

Personal Skills Writing skills, imagination, curiosity, resourcefulness, an accurate memory, and the ability to work alone or in a bustling environment are all necessary qualities for reporters and correspondents.

How Many Reporters Are There and Where Do They Work?

There are 58,000 full-time correspondents and reporters; 51 percent are women, 3 percent are black, and 2 percent are Hispanic. Over half work for newspapers. Others work for radio, television, magazines, and wire services.

How Much Money Will I Make?

Newspaper reporters are unionized and salaries average from $20,000 to $47,000 a year, depending on the circulation and location of the paper. Experienced reporters get over $50,000, and the best reporters count on bonuses for top stories. Reporters for small-town newspapers start at about $18,000 a year. Radio and TV reporters begin at a meager $12,000 a year and may earn up to $33,500 with experience.

What Are the Job Opportunities?

Jobs for reporters and correspondents in urban centers are competitive. Thousands of English and journalism majors look for reporting jobs each year in New York and other major cities. Every bit of experience counts. If you can publish while you are in college, or work in a reporting job during the summer, you will have a head start on the competition. The best chances for newspaper jobs are in small towns and with special-interest papers. Connelly and Jarzyna, for example, hire a recent college graduate every two years. If you can take small-town life, you will find that the best opportunities for a reporting career begin there. Iowan John McCright started at the *Hardwick Gazette* right out of Dartmouth, and after two years as a full-time reporter, he beat out the competition for a reporter's job at the *Boston Business Journal.*

Related Careers

Copywriter   Translator
Screenwriter   Fiction writer

Where Can I Get More Information?

National Newspaper Association
1627 K Street NW, Suite 400
Washington, DC 20006

Newspaper Association of America Foundation
11600 Sunrise Valley Drive
Reston, VA 20041

Writer, Editor

Communicates ideas and information through the written word for the education and entertainment of readers

What's It Like to Be a Writer or an Editor?

Writers develop original fiction and nonfiction prose and poetry for books, magazines, journals, newspapers, radio and television programs, and advertisements. *Editors* supervise writers and select and prepare material for publication or broadcasting. They almost always do rewriting and editing, but their primary responsibilities are to plan the contents of the publication or program and to supervise the preparation by the writer. They decide what readers or viewers will like, assign topics to writers, and oversee the production of the book, magazine, or program. In broadcasting, editors are also known as *program directors*. *Technical writers* put scientific and technical information into understandable language. They prepare manuals, catalogs, and instructions for installing, maintaining, and servicing equipment. *Copy writers* write advertising copy for use by print or broadcast media to promote the sale of goods and services. *Magazine writers* write features or are magazine researchers, interviewers, or co-writers. Magazine production is similar to newspaper production in that both depend on advertising for profits. Magazine personnel work closely with their advertising agencies. The pace in magazine publishing is faster than in book publishing because magazine personnel have weekly or monthly deadlines. *Fashion writers* write about fashion for department stores, trade publications, advertising agencies, and newspaper columns. *Radio* and *TV newswriters* put the news into fairly short sentences for listening purposes rather than reading. The major networks have a staff of writers for their newscasters.

Andrew Potok, author of the poignant book *Ordinary Daylight*, says, "What I like best about writing is what I liked best about painting. The opportunity to sit and think and spin tales. It's an incredible privilege to lock yourself up in a room and plumb the depths to spin those tales. That's not to say it's easy and always goes well. Like psychoanalysis, it's terribly difficult, as self-discipline and interior work always are. But still, I am always awed by the privilege I have of spending my life writing."

What Education and Skills Will I Need?

High School   Preparation for college, with as much training in language skills and experience in writing as you can get. Part-time or summer work on a local newspaper will help you find out what some writing jobs are like. Work on as many school publications as you can while in high school.

College   Writers come from journalism, English, and other liberal arts majors, and from a great variety of programs. Most commercial writers have a college degree; however, college is not a necessity for success. Writing and communication skills, together with a special style and interesting experiences, are what count. Familiarity with electronic publishing, graphics, and video production equipment is increasingly important.

Personal Skills   Writing skills, imagination, curiosity, resourcefulness, an accurate memory, and the ability to work alone or in a bustling environment are all necessary for most writing jobs.

How Many Writers and Editors Are There and Where Do They Work?

There are 283,000 writing and editing jobs; about 53 percent go to women, 3 percent to blacks, and 2 percent to Hispanics. This number includes 58,000 technical writers in the electronics and aerospace industries. Most of the book publishing jobs are in New York City, while newspaper jobs are everywhere. Smaller and special-interest newspapers are flourishing throughout the United States. Thirty-four percent of writers and editors are self-employed.

How Much Money Will I Make?

In 1993 college graduates started at $16,000 to $18,000 with major book publishers, while experienced book editors made from $30,000 to $60,000 a year. Technical writers started at $26,700, and made up to $45,400 with experience. Editorial supervisors averaged $55,000 a year. A few well-known book editors made over $70,000 a year. Like all of the "performing artists," very few book writers can make a living with their craft. Writers often teach, work in publishing, or have other jobs to supplement their writing income.

What Are the Job Opportunities?

The jobs in urban centers are competitive. Each year, thousands of English and journalism majors look for writing and editing jobs in New York and other major cities. Every bit of experience counts. If you can publish while in college or work in a writing or editing job during the summer, you will have a head start on the competition. Technical writers are in less demand. Most technical writers enter the field after several years of experience in engineering or other technical areas. Advertising and public relations firms are another source of jobs.

Related Careers

Translator   Copywriter
Biographer   Screenwriter

Where Can I Get More Information?

American Society of Magazine Editors
575 Lexington Avenue
New York, NY 10022

Society for Technical Communications
901 North Stuart Street, Suite 304
Arlington, VA 22203

Education

- Adult education teacher
- College professor
- College student personnel officer
- Early childhood educator
- Elementary school teacher
- High school teacher
- Librarian
- Museum careers: curator, archivist
- Physical education teacher
- Private school educator
- School administrator
- School counselor
- Special education teacher

ABOUT EDUCATION CAREERS

Education careers require more education for less pay than any other career group. The oversupply of teachers graduating each year from college, the decrease in funding for education, the decreased enrollment in schools, and the closing down of many federally sponsored programs have made this field very competitive.

Almost 5 million teachers, professors, counselors, and librarians are represented by the descriptions in this section, and all these positions them require a college education. Most of the jobs also require a master's degree or a doctorate for professional certification or promotion.

Every state offers an education major in its state college or university. Write to the Department of Education in your state's capital to find which colleges offer this major. If you choose to go to a liberal arts college, there are several options for certification in elementary and secondary education, including summer school, a master's degree program, and correspondence courses.

If education is the field for you, your best bet is to specialize in elementary or inner-city teaching, vocational or technical education, bilingual education, math or science, or education for the disabled or disadvantaged. The computer industry has been draining education's supply of math teachers, thereby creating the biggest demand in public schools and colleges in the field of mathematics.

Times are changing, though, and by 1997, high school enrollments are predicted to increase, providing a new ball game for young educators.

Adult Education Teacher

Provides instruction unrelated to a degree or a diploma

What's It Like to Be an Adult Education Teacher?

Adult education teachers offer courses that can be trend-setting, career-building, or just plain fun. Typical courses are basic education for school dropouts, cooking, dancing, exercise and physical fitness, photography, the stock market, and foreign languages from Arabic to Croatian. Andrew Burnstein, who graduated in the 1970s from the Barnum & Bailey clown college, teaches a course called "Clowning Around" to those who have always wanted to join the circus. John Sirabella from the New School for Social Research in New York City is offering a film class called "The New Queer Cinema," a lecture course that considers the history of gay cinema and the emerging themes associated with avowedly "queer," post-AIDS culture. And boxing teacher Ron Rosenblum, who has been teaching boxing for twenty years, says that boxing has never been hotter than in the past two years. He teaches men and women, chemists, teachers, and all kinds of other professionals.

Like other teachers, adult education teachers prepare lessons, make assignments, grade papers, do related paperwork, attend faculty and professional meetings, and stay up-to-date in the developments in their fields. Many programs in adult education, sometimes called continuing education, are taught at night in local public schools, colleges, and Y's.

What Education and Skills Will I Need?

High School   Preparation for college.

College   Four years of college are necessary for most adult education jobs, although training requirements vary widely by state and by subject. In general, teachers need experience in their fields and a license or certificate if such is required for full professional status in a particular field. Most states require teachers of adult basic education to have a bachelor's degree from an approved teacher-training program. Teachers of sports, foreign languages, and the arts need only experience and an interest in teaching.

Personal Skills   Communication skills, patience, understanding, and interest in their students are necessary for success.

How Many Adult Education Teachers Are There and Where Do They Work?

There are about 540,000 adult education teachers, 40 percent of whom teach part time. About 40 percent are women, 10 percent are black, and 3 percent are Hispanic. They are employed by schools, hospitals, colleges, businesses, labor unions, and religious organizations.

How Much Money Will I Make?

In 1992 salaried adult education teachers who worked full time averaged $26,900 a year. The top 10 percent made $49,200. Earnings varied widely by subject, academic credentials, experience, and region of the country.

What Are the Job Opportunities?

Through the late 1990s the best job opportunities will be in the computer technology and medical technology fields. Most of the demand will be for teachers of English as a Second Language and for part-time teachers of basic academic programs. The change in U.S. immigration policy requiring basic competency in English and civics will increase opportunities in adult education.

Related Careers

Teacher

Counselor

Education administrator

Public relations worker

Where Can I Get More Information?

American Association for Adult and Continuing Education
1112 Sixteenth Street, NW, Suite 420
Washington, DC 20036

College Professor

Provides instruction for students in college-level learning

What's It Like to Be a College Professor?

"College teaching is not an occupation but a way of life. The involvement with the subject you are teaching, the reading of professional literature in your own field, and the discussions with students and colleagues become your point of view for living," writes Gail Bucknell, associate professor of economics at Northwestern University. College professors who teach full time average eight to twelve hours a week in the classroom. Higher-ranked professors who advise graduate students and are actively engaged in research may spend only four to six hours a week in actual classroom teaching. Outside the classroom, professors prepare lectures, grade student work, and keep up with their field of study. Most professors conduct research projects and write for their professional journals. Summers may be spent teaching summer school, doing research projects, or on vacation. Roberto Chavey, a Texas professor married to a professor, says that the lifestyle of two college professors can make a most interesting family life: "We take turns tending our children and sharing the domestic work as most of our career time is flexible and some professional work can be done at home."

What Education and Skills Will I Need?

High School Preparation for college, with as strong an academic program as you can handle well.

College Preparation for graduate school in the field in which you show the most ability and interest. Your graduate work doesn't have to be in the same field as your undergraduate work, although it is usually related. As you learn more about your academic abilities and interests, your major field may change. Plan to get your Ph.D. if you want to be a college professor. Keep in mind that teaching and research assistantships are offered to Ph.D. candidates but rarely to candidates seeking only the M.A. So apply directly to a Ph.D. program when you decide to start graduate school.

Personal Skills Professors need to be curious about learning and able to share their enthusiasm and interest in their field with their students. They must like detail and be persistent in order to follow through on academic research and writing.

How Many Professors Are There and Where Do They Work?

There are 812,000 college professors; 39 percent are women, 4 percent are black, and 4 percent are Hispanic. Almost a third work part time.

Half of all college professors are employed in eight states, each with a college enrollment exceeding 2 million: California, Illinois, Massachusetts, Michigan, New York, Ohio, Pennsylvania, and Texas.

How Much Money Will I Make?

In 1993–94 the average salary for a nine-month contract for a college instructor was $27,200; for an assistant professor, $36,800; for an associate professor, $44,100; and for a full professor, $59,500. Beginning salaries are much less than the average. Experienced professors averaged $46,300 a year. Academic deans averaged $74,000, medical school deans $182,600, and business school deans $73,700.

What Are the Job Opportunities?

College teaching will remain competitive through 2005 because of decreasing college enrollments and increasing numbers of Ph.D.'s looking for jobs. The largest number of jobs will be in business, science, math, health science, computer science, and engineering. Increasing numbers of retirements in the late 1990s will provide job opportunities in business and science. Community colleges are the other best bet for jobs.

Related Careers

College administrator
Government and corporate
 researcher

Writer
Librarian

Where Can I Get More Information?

American Association of University Professors
1012 Fourteenth Street, NW
Washington, DC 20005

College Student Personnel Officer

Helps students meet their personal, social, housing, and recreational needs

What's It Like to Be a College Student Personnel Officer?

Student personnel staff members are responsible for individualizing education for college students. This includes counseling students, advising student government officers, overseeing residence hall programs, directing orientation programs for new students; supervising fraternities and student honoraries, and guiding communications between faculty and students. All these activities become very meaningful because they enable students to take advantage of their educational opportunities. Marc Freidman, director of student personnel at a liberal arts college in the Northwest, encourages people to go into college personnel work if they like the academic lifestyle and if they have a commitment to education and students. Adult students have concerns different from those of younger students; adults often combine family life or single parenthood with student life and a job. College personnel also work with the special needs of off-campus students.

Morality, hate crimes, date rape, and ethnic diversity have all become major problems on campus that have to be confronted by student personnel officers.

What Education and Skills Will I Need?

High School   Preparation for college, with a broad range of academic subjects.

College   Many students prepare for graduate school with a major in social sciences or education. A master's degree is required for student personnel work in higher education, and a doctorate is required for the bigger universities and for top career jobs.

Personal Skills   The ability to work with people of all backgrounds and ages; emotional stability while under pressure from students, parents, and faculty; and patience when working with conflicting viewpoints are necessary skills in college personnel work.

How Many College Student Personnel Workers Are There and Where Do They Work?

There are 50,000 college student personnel workers; about half of them are women, 13 percent are black, and 5 percent are Hispanic. The jobs they hold include dean of men, dean of women, dean of students, director of admissions, residence hall dean, registrar, counselor, financial aid officer, foreign student adviser, student union worker, student government specialist, and activities director. Every two- and four-year college in the country hires student personnel workers.

How Much Money Will I Make?

In 1993 the median salary of student personnel workers was $36,800 a year. Beginners started at about $24,000.

What Are the Job Opportunities?

Competition is expected through 2005 because of decreasing college enrollments, especially among residential students.

Related Careers

High school counselor   Admission officer
School psychologist   Industrial personnel manager

Where Can I Get More Information?

American College Personnel Association
5999 Stevenson Avenue
Alexandria, VA 22304

National Association of Student Personnel Administrators
1875 Connecticut Avenue, NW, Suite 418
Washington, DC 20009

Early Childhood Educator

Instructs children from two through five years old; day-care workers take responsibility for infants as well

What's It Like to Be an Early Childhood Educator?

An early childhood educator works with small groups of children in an unstructured situation for a few hours a day. The program usually consists of reading to the children, painting, working with clay and crafts, free play, music, dance, teaching colors and numbers, and talking about community services and transportation and families. Day-care and child-care centers often run from 7 a.m. until 7 p.m.; children come and go according to the hours their parents work. As more two-career families send their preschool children to these centers, job opportunities will increase for professionals in this crucial field. Day-care director Mary Marshall says, "You learn how delightful human beings can be when you work with young children as they learn, become curious, and show their many interests. Early childhood education is just beginning to get the recognition it deserves for its importance in child development." Early childhood educator Kathleen Sampson graduated from Southern Illinois University and wasn't eager to have parents participate in the education of their children. After she had her own children and was told "no," she couldn't visit her child's classroom, she realized what an integral part of education parents can be. Sampson now believes that it is vital and absolutely crucial for parents and teachers to work together for the good of the child.

Kevin Seifert, teacher at the demonstration preschool at San Jose State University, writes that male teachers in a child-care center face special problems in that children often mistrust a man in this role. According to Seifert, most male childcare workers work part-time and don't remain long in the field—often just long enough to get experience for an administrative job.

What Education and Skills Will I Need?

High School   Preparation for college.

College   You can prepare for early childhood education with a two-year program in a community college, or a degree program in a four-year college, or an advanced degree. Most nursery schools are private, and a degree is not required for teaching. Many nursery schools are informal cooperatives where the children's parents are involved in teaching and planning school programs. Day-care centers and government programs for early childhood education will increasingly require degrees; master's degrees will be necessary for the administration of these programs.

Personal Skills   The ability to be firmly low-key to allow children to express themselves in a learning environment, an avid interest in the growth and development of small children, and the ability to be relaxed in an active setting.

How Many Early Childhood Educators Are There and Where Do They Work?

Of the 425,000 nursery and kindergarten teachers, 98 percent are women, 9 percent are black, and 6 percent are Hispanic. Most communities have several nursery schools and day-care centers in addition to the public preschools.

How Much Money Will I Make?

Like all "women's work," the pay is exceedingly low, even for college graduates. Salaries vary more than those for any other teaching jobs because the school may be in a parent's home, in a private business, or in an organized chain of schools. If the job is in the public school system, the teachers are paid a little less than elementary school teachers, beginning around $18,000. The median salary is $26,000. The highest paid teachers in child care centers averaged $15,488; those who worked for lower paying centers averaged $8,890 in 1992.

What Are the Job Opportunities?

The job opportunities are excellent—as enrollment of early childhood programs increases with the baby "boomlet" and as women continue to work full time, a shortage of teachers for this age level is expected.

Related Careers

Elementary school teacher	Salesperson
Librarian	Personnel worker

Where Can I Get More Information?

National Association for the Education of Young Children
1834 Connecticut Avenue, NW
Washington, DC 20009

National Education Association
1201 Sixteenth Street NW
Washington, DC 20036

Elementary School Teacher

Teaches science, mathematics, language, and social studies to children in kindergarten through sixth grade

What's It Like to Be an Elementary School Teacher?

Robert Braun, with 20 years of experience in business and technology, shares a fifth-grade teaching job with Elise Braun, his wife. He doesn't know of one male who has spent a lifetime in elementary school teaching. "Most try it for a few years, go back to college to study school administration, or switch to business as the financial pressure mounts." Elementary teachers play a vital role in the development of children. They teach the basics of mathematics, language, science, and social studies. They try to instill good study habits and an appreciation for learning. Teachers observe and evaluate each child's performance and potential. In addition, teachers work outside the classroom preparing lessons and grading papers, and they attend faculty and parent meetings after school. What is learned or not learned in these early years shapes children's views of themselves in the world, affecting later success or failure in school and work. Other than family, there is no more influential person for the growing child than the elementary school teacher.

First-grade teacher Cheryl Crytzer remembers her first year of teaching in Riverdale, Maryland, where she learned that a first-grade teacher has to be "on" every minute, because first graders are totally dependent on their teacher for everything. "However, absolutely nothing compares to the satisfaction of teaching reading," explains Crytzer. "You work all fall on reading and then—right after Christmas—light bulbs go off and 'Wow! I can read!' From then on they take off on their own."

What Education and Skills Will I Need?

High School   Preparation for college, with as broad a program as possible. Most elementary school teachers teach all subjects, including music, art, and physical education. So be prepared.

College   Four years of college, with a major in elementary education, are required. A teaching certificate is awarded by every state, and many states require a fifth year of preparation for a permanent certificate. Plan your fifth year or master's degree in a special area of education, such as administration.

Personal Skills   Dependability, good judgment, patience, creativity, and enthusiasm for the development of young children are needed.

How Many Elementary School Teachers Are There and Where Do They Work?

There are 1,634,000 teachers; only 18 percent are men, 10 percent are black, and 3 percent are Hispanic. In addition, there are 60,000 principals and supervisors, who are mostly men. School is taught in every city, town, and village in the United States.

How Much Money Will I Make?

Salary is determined by level of education, work experience, and the particular town in which the teacher is employed. Most states offer a minimum of $20,000 to $22,000 for beginning teachers, and the average salary for all elementary school teachers in 1993 was $34,800 for a 10-month contract. Teachers salaries are on the way up. Teachers are unionized in most parts of the country. Some average starting salaries for public schools for 1992 were:

Alaska	$39,000
California	$26,000
Idaho	$20,000
Mississippi	$17,800
New Hampshire	$20,522
Ohio	$24,337
Pennsylvania	$25,400
Wyoming	$26,709

What Are the Job Opportunities?

There is good opportunity in some parts of the United States; suburban schools continue to be competitive. Retirement will also produce job openings in the mid-1990s.

Related Careers

School administrator	Salesperson
Librarian	Public relations manager

Where Can I Get More Information?

American Federation of Teachers
555 New Jersey Avenue, NW
Washington, DC 20001

National Education Association
1201 Sixteenth Street, NW
Washington, DC 20036

National Association of Elementary School Principals
1615 Duke Street
Alexandria, VA 22314

High School Teacher

Teaches a specific subject in junior or senior high school, grades 7 through 12

What's It Like to Be a High School Teacher?

High school teachers instruct four or five classes a day and supervise study halls, lunchrooms, and extracurricular activities. If you're a current or recent high school student, you have a better idea of what a high school teacher does than any other career because you see teachers at work all the time! You certainly notice which ones enjoy their work, or which ones make the most sense to you. If you want a career like that of the teachers who are reaching you, you have a good example of what the life is like.

John Slayton, a high school teacher who is working abroad for the U.S. Department of Defense, has taught military dependents in Japan, Turkey, and the Netherlands. He loves the lifestyle, living in an apartment in the nearby village rather than on the military base where he teaches. Slayton socializes with other American, Canadian, and British teachers, enjoying the advantages of living in a foreign country. He says the frustrating part of his work is not having a solution for the small group of students who are trapped in our education system and who disrupt the learning process of their classmates. What he likes best is the satisfaction of helping young people prepare for an independent, successful career in our increasingly complex world as they respond to what they learn about themselves. "Teaching," says Slayton, "presents a daily challenge, and the students continually offer a wonderful variety of experiences."

What Education and Skills Will I Need?

High School Preparation for college, with as broad a program as possible.

College   Major in the subject you wish to teach, or a related subject if you are planning to attend graduate school. Each state has its own certification system, and many require a master's degree for permanent certification. There are many ways to do graduate work, including summer school, evening school, and correspondence courses.

Personal Skills   Good teachers have a desire to work with young people, an interest in a special subject, and the ability to motivate others and to relate information to them.

How Many High School Teachers Are There and Where Do They Work?

There are 1,263,000 high school teachers; about half are women, 7 percent are black, and 3 percent are Hispanic. They teach in every community in the United States; 90 percent teach in public schools.

How Much Money Will I Make?

Salaries vary with each community and with educational background and experience. In 1993 the average salary for a high school teacher was $36,000 a year. Most states now have a minimum salary of $20,000 to $22,000 for a beginning teacher with a bachelor's degree. Coaching, supervising publications, and working with clubs can add $1,000 to $5,000 a year to the salary. States with the highest average salaries for public school teachers include Connecticut ($47,811), Alaska ($44,725), New York ($44,200), and California ($41,811). Lowest are South Dakota ($23,000), North Dakota ($24,145), Mississippi ($24,428), and Oklahoma ($25,721).

What Are the Job Opportunities?

The number of high school teaching jobs is expected to increase 34 percent by 2005; 1,717,000 jobs will be created by increased enrollments, reductions in class size, and a large number of retirements in the mid-1990s.

Related Careers

School administrator   Public relations manager
Private school educator   Salesperson

Where Can I Get More Information?

American Federation of Teachers
555 New Jersey Avenue, NW
Washington, DC 20001

National Education Association
1201 Sixteenth Street, NW
Washington, DC 20036

National Association of Secondary School Principals
1904 Association Drive
Reston, VA 22091

Librarian

Selects and organizes collections of books and other media and provides access to information

What's It Like to Be a Librarian?

A librarian offers the services of getting books and other information to individuals and special groups, of educating the public about what is available, and of helping people of all ages to explore the wonderful world of books that so often gives new and first interest to readers. Library work is divided into three basic function: user services, technical services, and administrative services. Only librarians offering user services work with the public. In large libraries many librarians specialize and have a single function, such as cataloging, publicity, reference work, or working in a special subject area such as art, medicine, or science. *Public librarians* serve all kinds of readers; *school librarians* work only with the students and staff of their school; and *university librarians* provide services to students, staff, and researchers. "Students planning a career as a school librarian should know what the job is like," says Elizabeth Dow, elementary school librarian. "It helps if one has a capacity for remembering trivia, a capacity for keeping a lot of loose ends in mind, and a sense of humor. Nobody else really understands the joy of discovering the perfect Dewey number for an item that has been nagging you. The part of the job that makes it all worthwhile is connecting the perfect library item with a student at the exact moment the student needs it. This could be the right story, item of information, or curiosity stimulator. Seeing the click in children's eyes and knowing I've expanded their world or met their need is a great high."

What Education and Skills Will I Need?

High School Preparation for college, with as broad a program as possible. The development of verbal skills is important.

College Strong liberal arts program to prepare for a graduate degree in library science. A master's degree in library science (M.L.S.) is necessary for most jobs. A reading knowledge of at least one foreign language and advanced computer skills are essential to the job.

Personal Skills Good librarians have a strong intellectual curiosity and an interest in helping others to use library materials.

How Many Librarians Are There and Where Do They Work?

There are 141,000 librarians; 83 percent are women, 6 percent are black, and 3 percent are Hispanic. Most of the librarians work in schools and colleges. Others work for local governments, usually in public libraries. In addition, 7,800 audiovisual specialists are employed by libraries. Thirty percent of librarians work part time.

How Much Money Will I Make?

In 1992 a graduate school librarian started at $25,791 and a specialist started at $27,400 a year. Experienced school librarians averaged $27,400 a year, public librarians averaged $23,800, and college librarian managers averaged $45,200.

What Are the Job Opportunities?

The best chances are for specialized librarians in medicine, law, business, engineering, and science. Information management outside the traditional library setting is expected to offer excellent employment in industry and in government agencies needing qualified librarians with computer skills. Although school budgets are down, few students graduated in library science in the 1980s, so the job prospects are not too bad.

Related Careers

Museum curator	Research analyst
Archivist	Teacher

Where Can I Get More Information?

American Library Association
50 East Huron Street
Chicago, IL 60611

Special Libraries Association
1700 Eighteenth Street, NW
Washington, DC 20009-2508

Museum Careers:
Curator, Archivist

Creates museum exhibits and manages the work of an art museum, a natural history museum, a historical museum, or an industrial museum

What's It Like to Be a Museum Curator or Archivist?

Directors and curators of museums design and install new exhibits, organize gallery talks and educational programs, acquire new art objects for the collections, and revise existing exhibits. *"Operations workers* are the landlords and superintendents of the building. They are in charge of temperature control, security, admission, restaurants, installing and moving exhibits, and preparing budgets for their programs," explains Lita Semerad, executive assistant to the vice-president for operations at the Metropolitan Museum of Art in New York City. An art history major, she has been with the Metropolitan for 18 years. Semerad advises young people interested in a museum career to be ready to start at the bottom and to take any job offered to get a start. She has helped many aspiring museum workers get part-time jobs with a particular exhibit or project that have often expanded into full-time work.

Curators search for, acquire, catalog, restore, exhibit, maintain, and store items of interest. In the Greek and Roman department of New York's Metropolitan Museum is their youngest curator, Max Anderson. At 28 he became assistant curator, but his first job at the Metropolitan was a summer job between college and graduate school. When he started full time, Anderson got an edge on the competition because of his language ability. He speaks fluent Italian, exactly what was needed during the Vatican exhibit. Because of that, he traveled with the exhibit to Chicago and San Francisco. He also speaks French, German, and Spanish and reads Greek and Latin as well. Anderson, like other curators, knows that a job well done results in good attendance, good public relations, and increased revenue for the museum.

What Education and Skills Will I Need?

High School   Preparation for college, with emphasis on art and social sciences.

College   Most people in museum careers majored in art history and the classics; some majored in anthropology. A few universities offer graduate degrees in museum management; some colleges and universities offer courses on archival science. Most top management jobs go to M.B.A.'s.

Personal Skills   Creativity, an interest in history and art, and the ability to teach others are needed for success in museum careers.

How Many Curators and Archivists Are There and Where Do They Work?

There are 19,000 curators and archivists and many more professional museum workers such as lawyers and public relations and museum managers. About 40 percent work for the government and 30 percent in museums. Most curators in the federal government are employed by the Smithsonian Institution and the military museums of the Department of Defense. Most curators work in major cities where the large museums are located—New York, Washington, Chicago, Los Angeles, and Boston.

How Much Money Will I Make?

In 1993 beginning curators with a master's degree averaged $26,400 a year, and Ph.D.'s started at around $31,600. The average salary for a curator was $45,000, while assistant curators started at $22,000. Archivists earned less than curators. Conservators averaged $50,600. Chief curators earned a median of $49,800, and directors made $91,300.

What Are the Job Opportunities?

Very competitive. Despite low pay (except in the National Gallery of Art, the Metropolitan in New York City, and the Getty Museum in Los Angeles), every art history major wants to work in the country's great museums, and many of them apply for the few museum positions open each year. An advanced degree with some part-time or summer experience is the best chance for the new graduate to enter the field. Also, "getting hired part time by a project director, rather than going through personnel, often gets your foot in the door," advises Semerad of the Metropolitan.

Related Careers

Librarian	Art Designer
Anthropologist	Historian

Where Can I Get More Information?

American Association of Museums
1225 Eye Street, NW, Suite 200
Washington, DC 20005

Society of American Archivists
600 South Federal Street, Suite 504
Chicago, IL 60605

Physical Education Teacher

Teaches physical education and health to students from preschool through adult education

What's It Like to Be a Physical Education Teacher?

Physical education teachers get to know students well because sports and afterschool activities offer an informal learning situation. They are often called on to help other staff members, the guidance department, and the administration learn more about the behavior of a particular student. PE teachers often plan their own physical education programs, with an emphasis on the sports and activities in which they are interested, the special interests of the community in which they teach, and the available facilities. There is a trend in programs to emphasize wellness and physical fitness, and to include individual sports outside school, such as weekend skiing, biking, high-ropes courses, and backpacking. Grace Butterweck, director of athletics at Marymount College in New York, reminds students that "this career is not for you if you just live to play sports. It is an educational career, and sports are the medium for teaching students. Sports are one place where students can learn about leadership, aggression, and competition with everyone's approval."

What Education and Skills Will I Need?

High School   Preparation for college, with an emphasis on life sciences. Participate in as many sports as possible.

College   Major or minor in physical education. A master's degree is needed for certification in many states and is always required for college teaching. Anatomy, physiology, and health courses are required for a physical education major. It helps to get experience through summer work in recreation programs.

Personal Skills   Physical education teachers must be athletic, and they should have the ability to encourage those who are not athletic, an interest in the total development of students, a sense of fairness, and the ability to instill in young people the importance of good health habits.

How Many Physical Education Teachers Are There and Where Do They Work?

There are 221,000 physical education teachers and coaches. This number is expected to increase 24 percent to 274,000 by 2005. Every high school and most elementary schools have a physical education teacher. Summer recreational and administrative work is always available at camps and playgrounds.

How Much Money Will I Make?

Salaries are the same as those of all teachers within a particular school system. In 1993 high school teachers averaged $36,000 a year. Coaches are usually paid $500 to $2,000 extra for coaching each sport.

What Are the Job Opportunities?

Secondary schools are in critical need of coaches, and physical education teachers will increasingly be in demand through 2005. Opportunities are also excellent in special education, inner-city schools, and rural areas.

Related Careers

Teacher

Athletic director

Coach

Physical therapist

Where Can I Get More Information?

American Alliance for Health, Physical Education,
    Recreation and Dance
1900 Association Drive
Reston, VA 22091

National Education Association
1201 Sixteenth Street, NW
Washington, DC 20036

Private School Educator

Teaches a specific grade or subject in a private (independent) school or, as administrator, directs the school

What's It Like to Be a Private School Educator?

"I went stir-crazy being a carpenter in isolated Vermont, and I was so bored in a New Jersey insurance company," reports Frederick Von Rollenhagen, speaking about his first jobs out of college. "I love to read and talk about what I read and to be directly involved in athletics. Trusting my instincts finally led me to teaching English and coaching lacrosse and ice hockey at Newark Academy, in Livingston, New Jersey. As soon as I started teaching, I began work on my master's degree in English literature at

Middlebury College during my summers off. Teaching in an independent school is everything I hoped it would be, even though it took me three years to hit my stride. The first year I was very nervous in the classroom." Von Rollenhagen says that his business friends on Wall Street envy his summer opportunities. He spent two summers studying at Oxford University in England and is free to go anywhere in the world for two whole months each summer. Von Rollenhagen's advice to college students looking for a teaching job is to be sure to know the school well. For example, he wouldn't want a boarding school because he likes a private life when his day is over, even though coaching takes him late into the day. "One way to know a school," says Von Rollenhagen, "is to find out what the academic program is like in your discipline when you interview for a job. For instance, our tenth graders read two or three major books plus short stories and poetry, and they write three or four major papers a term. Newark Academy is a serious school, a warm and friendly place, and a wonderful place to work—unlike some schools where I interviewed and noticed that very little was expected of the students."

Duke University graduate Dorothy Hutcheson, from Atlanta, started teaching English at Shady Side Academy in Pittsburgh. As a first-year teacher she was teaching two sections of ninth-grade English, plus counseling students for college half time, plus coaching tennis, and besides all that she lived in a dorm with residence hall responsibilities. She stayed at Shady Side for seven years but changed from the girls' to the boys' residence hall when, after three years, she married the director of music. Hutcheson decided to switch to administration when she moved to Packer Collegiate Institute in Brooklyn, New York, as the director of college counseling and dean of students. After two successful years, she was elected to be interim head of the school. She went on to be director of development for two more years before being selected the youngest head of school at Nightingale-Bamford in New York City in 1993. An advocate of independent education, Hutcheson advises young people to start working on their master's degree as soon as they get a job. As she points out, most private schools will pay for it; she took two courses per semester for two years and spent two summers in summer school.

The advantages for private school teachers and administrators are the small classes, the liberal arts background of the faculty with whom you work (you do not need to be state-certified), the involvement of parents in their children's education, the prestige of the school, the high academic standards and expectations of students, and the freedom to choose a school with social rules that are important to you. For example, drugs, alcohol, and violence do not have to be tolerated; there is freedom for religious programs; and a dress code is often required in private schools.

What Education and Skills Will I Need?

High School Preparation for college, with as broad a program as possible.

College Major in the subject you wish to teach, or a related subject if you are planning to attend graduate school. You do not have to take education courses or be certified to teach. Private school educators usually come from a liberal arts college. Plan to start work on your master's degree as soon as you begin your teaching career. As in any education career, the higher the degree (go for the Ph.D.), the more opportunities for top-level teaching and administrative jobs and the better the pay.

Personal Skills Good teachers love to be with students. They have a passion for their special subject and the ability to communicate well with young people. Flexibility is a help, as many private school educators take on extracurricular activities.

How Many Private School Educators Are There and Where Do They Work?

There are 37,600 teachers and 6,623 administrators in the approximately 995 independent schools that belong to the National Association of Independent Schools (NAIS). They enroll 457,403 students. Among the teachers, 64 percent are women, 1.6 percent are black, and 1.2 percent are Hispanic. One-third of the schools are located on the East Coast, one-fifth are on the West Coast, and the rest are in major cities across the country. Even though these numbers represent fewer than one-third of all private schools, most of the competitive independent schools are in this group.

How Much Money Will I Make?

In 1993–94 secondary school teachers in independent schools averaged $29,145, beginning around $21,000; elementary teachers averaged $29,000 and began around $20,000. Top salaries (earned by 10 percent of teachers) in schools with over 500 students were between $55,940 and $81,875. In administration, the range for head of school was from $67,309 to $135,000; the top 10 percent earned more than $200,000.

What Are the Job Opportunities?

If you're willing to go anywhere, if you're an interesting person with the personal skills listed above, you will have many opportunities for a job. There are several well-known private school employment agencies that place teachers throughout the country. Contact Carney, Sandoe & Associates in Boston (1-800-225-7986) and Independent Educational Services (IES) in Princeton, New Jersey (1-800-257-5102), to get started on your job hunt.

Related Careers

Public school teacher   Public school administrator
College professor   Librarian

Where Can I Get More Information?

National Association of Independent Schools
1620 L Street, NW
Washington, DC 20036

School Administrator

Manages, directs, and coordinates the activities of elementary, middle, or high schools

What's It Like to Be a School Administrator?

Administrators manage schools and school systems and provide classroom teachers with the best possible environment in which to teach. They set education standards and goals and establish policies and procedures to carry them out. Principals visit classrooms, review instructional objectives, evaluate teachers, and examine learning materials. They confer with teachers and other staff members, talk with parents, and meet with students. Principals also oversee guidance and record keeping functions and prepare budgets. Their primary responsibility is to ensure high-quality classroom instruction. Milt Israel, an assistant superintendent of schools, says, "This job has grown more complex in recent years. The trend toward consolidation and answering the needs of many different vocal and often angry groups is hard work! Issues that confront most school administrators today include quality education, desegregation, developing curriculum to address family diversity, contract negotiations with teachers, spiraling costs, and taxpayer resistance to higher taxes. Not to mention afterschool care of young children whose parents work, health needs of children such as meals at school, and the AIDS epidemic."

What Education and Skills Will I Need?

High School   Preparation for any college major that relates to teaching or education.

College   Major in any subject you wish to teach in school or college. If you want to be a college dean, college president, or superintendent of a large-city high school, prepare for a master's degree and work toward your doctorate in administration.

Personal Skills   Interest in the development of students, business sense, and ability to communicate many diverse ideas to a wide variety of people are necessary.

How Many School Administrators Are There and Where Do They Work?

There are 351,000 administrators in education, 78,000 principals, and 16,000 superintendents; 54 percent are women, 10 percent are black, and 4 percent are Hispanic. Education administrators work in every community in the country.

How Much Money Will I Make?

Administrators usually get paid some percentage more than teachers earn. A superintendent of a small school system, with a master's degree, earns about $40,000 a year, and a superintendent of a large school system, with a doctorate, earns $75,000 a year and more. In 1993 an elementary school principal averaged $45,452, a junior high school principal averaged $48,650, a high school principal averaged $63,000, and an assistant principal $52,300 a year.

What Are the Job Opportunities?

The employment outlook will remain competitive as school enrollments decrease and ambitious teachers look for administrative promotions. Most administrators are recruited from the teaching faculty, assistant principals, academic department heads, or central office administrators.

Related Careers

Teacher   ,   Operations manager

School counselor   Private school educator

Where Can I Get More Information?

American Association of School Administrators
1801 North Moore Street
Arlington, VA 22209

National Association of Secondary School Principals
1904 Association Drive
Reston, VA 22091

School Counselor

Helps students understand their interests, abilities, and personality characteristics in the context of their educational decision making

What's It Like to Be a School Counselor?

According to David Phau, a school counselor in a suburban high school outside of Chicago, "I spend half my day with students, individually or in small groups; about a fourth of the day talking with parents and teachers, on the phone and in conferences; and the other fourth in administrative work, with records, college and work applications, and correspondence. Afterschool hours are also important because students and teachers like to drop by the guidance office informally with questions or for visits. Many of my evenings are involved with school activities; it is important to the students to have their counselors attend sports, social, and cultural events." Counselors are responsible for helping students with their educational and career development. They supply information that students can use in making their educational choices. In this way, counselors provide students with a basis for sound educational decision making. Counselors also consult and work with parents, teachers, administrators, school psychologists, school nurses, and social workers. It's a teamwork job, centered on the individual student.

What Education and Skills Will I Need?

High School Preparation for college. Most school counselors teach a subject before going into counseling.

College A master's degree in guidance and one to five years of teaching are required by most states to be a certified school counselor. A doctorate is required for big-city administrative careers in guidance.

Personal Skills Successful counselors have an interest in helping students take responsibility for themselves; they also have the ability to work with other educators, parents, and students.

How Many Counselors Are There and Where Do They Work?

There are 154,000 counselors; 70 percent of them are women, 13 percent are black, and 4 percent are Hispanic. They work mostly in public schools (61 percent) and also in social service agencies (18 percent) and in state governments (13 percent).

How Much Money Will I Make?

Salaries vary with the school system, but counselors are usually paid more than classroom teachers and less than administrators. In 1993 salaries started at $24,000; the average was $30,000; the top 10 percent made $51,900

What Are the Job Opportunities?

There are more student personnel graduates than job openings at the high school level. A large number of school counselors are expected to retire in the mid-1990s, providing new job openings through 2005.

Related Careers

Psychologist   Teacher

School administrator   Rehabilitation counselor

Where Can I Get More Information?

American School Counselor Association
c/o American Counseling Association
5999 Stevenson Avenue
Alexandria, VA 22304

National Association of College Admission Counselors
1631 Prince Street
Alexandria, VA 22314-2818

Special Education Teacher

Teaches disabled children who require part- or full-time separate, small-group instruction

What's It Like to Be a Special Education Teacher?

Special education teachers spend the day assessing students who have been referred for special education by classroom teachers, instructing small groups of children with disabilities, tutoring some children on a one-to-one basis, and supervising teachers' aides. They spend a lot of time consulting with classroom teachers about the students who leave their classrooms for tutoring but return to class and are mainstreamed most of the school day. A special education teacher also evaluates testing results and is a regular team member in developing Individualized Educational Programs (IEP) for children with disabilities. Pete Sinot, a special education teacher in Minnesota and the father of a mentally retarded child, says, "Once I learned to expect small accomplishments from the children, to slow down and let the activities of the day proceed at a natural pace for them, I was fine. Until then, I was uptight about achievement, which caused anxiety and strife in the classroom." Sinot finds his work very rewarding. He has learned to give what the student needs rather than what he thinks the student needs.

What Education and Skills Will I Need?

High School Preparation for college, with an emphasis on subjects that interest you.

College Major in any subject, including education, elementary education, or special education, and prepare for a master's degree. Most states require a master's degree for certification, although you can begin teaching with a bachelor's degree.

Personal Skills Patience with slow progress, the ability to work with disabled children and their parents, and the ability to see accomplishment in things that might seem small to the rest of the world.

How Many Special Education Teachers Are There and Where Do They Work?

There are 358,000 special educators; 85 percent are women, 12 percent are black, and 2 percent are Hispanic. They work in every school system in the country.

How Much Money Will I Make?

Salaries vary with the community and the school system. They are about the same as other teachers' salaries within a school system, averaging $36,000 a year with experience.

What Are the Job Opportunities?

The classified ads under "Education" are loaded with job opportunities for special education teachers. Even though local school systems depend upon federal funds to pay for mandated special education, the minimum services needed are not being provided. A 40 percent increase to 467,000 jobs is expected by 2005. Federal legislation mandating education for the disabled will create more jobs than can now be filled.

Related Careers

Rehabilitation counselor
Social worker

Occupational therapist
Reading specialist

Where Can I Get More Information?

National Education Association
1201 Sixteenth Street, NW
Washington, DC 20036

Engineering and Architecture

- **Architect**
- **Engineer**
- **Landscape architect**

ABOUT ENGINEERING AND ARCHITECTURE CAREERS

Engineers hold nearly 2 million jobs. Almost one-third are electrical engineers. Even though college graduates are finding it difficult to get jobs, qualified applicants in this field are in short supply because the enrollment of engineering students has been down since the 1980s. Engineering students, who earned less than 9 percent of all bachelor's degrees in the early 1990s, received more than 40 percent of the job offers. The number of jobs in engineering has tripled in the past few years.

A bachelor's degree is usually needed to enter architecture and engineering careers. Undergraduate training for architects and engineers includes courses in their major field and in related science areas, including mathematics. Courses and skills in computer science are important for all architects and engineers.

198

Students who want to specialize in a particular area of engineering should select their college or university carefully. For example, those of you who are interested in environmental engineering should consider states like Washington or Oregon, which are active in government environmental projects.

Working conditions in scientific and technical careers such as engineering can require considerable time away from home, working outdoors in remote parts of the country. Many engineers spend time in a factory or a mine, at a construction site, or at some other outdoor location. Others work under quiet conditions in modern offices and research laboratories. New graduates begin working under the close supervision of experienced engineers.

Architects spend long hours at the drawing board in well-equipped offices. New graduates usually begin as junior drafters in architectural firms, where they are closely supervised. Until junior members of a firm have gained experience and paid their "professional beginner's dues," they are often asked to work overtime to meet deadlines and to do the routine, tedious work that experienced architects prefer not to do.

To determine the specialties for which graduates are best suited, many companies have special programs to acquaint new engineers with industrial practices. Experienced engineers may advance to positions of greater responsibility; those with proven ability often become managers, and in increasingly large numbers they are being promoted to top management jobs. Some engineers go after a Master of Business Administration (M.B.A.) to improve their advancement opportunities, while others get law degrees and become patent attorneys or consultants.

Engineering and architecture are fields with a bright job outlook. If you want to have the best job opportunities, think seriously about these fields. Women tend to shy away from engineering, a career that pays more for less schooling than health or education, and less than 10 percent of engineers are women. Add some technical skills to your credentials so that you can translate the arts, business, or social sciences into engineering or architectural opportunities.

Architect

Plans and designs buildings and other structures

What's It Like to Be an Architect?

Architects meet and discuss with clients the purpose, costs, style preferences, and plan of the structure to be built. They consider the local building and zoning laws and make preliminary drawings of the building to show the client. The final design is a working one, including details of the plumbing, electrical, and heating systems. Architects help their clients select a building contractor and continue to represent the client until the structure is completed and all tests have been done. Self-employed architects work on a variety of projects from homes, churches, and office buildings to renewal projects, college campuses, new towns, and urban planning. When working for large architectural firms, architects often specialize in one phase of the work, such as design or construction contracts. This often requires working with engineers, city planners, and landscape architects.

Architect Jonathan Felsman was a political science major in college. After a year with VISTA on a city planning project, Felsman took a two-year master's in architecture. He then returned to his hometown of Philadelphia to work at several different jobs, including designing free playground spaces in the city. His wife, a filmmaker, needed to move to New York City to further her career, so Felsman pounded the pavement, talked to his friends, and landed his first job in New York, designing skyscrapers. He stayed in that job for three years. Next, Felsman worked for an architectural and planning firm with offices at the top of New York's Chrysler Building. He designed townhouses and renovated office buildings. Finally, Felsman is happily working for himself in his own business. He is interested in urban development and restoration of townhouses, although to become established, he takes any job he can get. He loves his work because he gets to begin and complete a whole project. When he and a coworker start a project, they spend about six months at the drawing board and then continue working on the same project another year and a half until it is completed. Felsman says that many architects work in large groups on one project, each person specializing and doing a small part of the job. What he likes is the opportunity to work on the details of his plans and the control he has over the complete assignment.

What Education and Skills Will I Need?

High School Preparation for college, with an emphasis on mathematics, physics, computer design, and art.

College Any major can lead to a career in architecture. There are two basic programs: one is a five-year plan that starts in the freshman year; the other is a two-year master's program designed for liberal arts graduates. There are 96 accredited schools of architecture offering such programs. After three years of experience, an architect takes a state license examination. A knowledge of computer-aided design and drafting (CADD) is essential.

Personal Skills Capacity to solve technical problems and to work independently, artistic skills, computer skills, and competitive business abilities are necessary for architects.

How Many Architects Are There and Where Do They Work?

There are 96,000 licensed architects. About 18 percent are women, 1 percent are black, and 4 percent are Hispanic. Thirty percent are self-employed. The great majority (71 percent) work for engineering, architectural, and surveying companies; and 6 percent work for the federal government. Most architects are employed in cities where many large architectural firms are located—New York, Chicago, Los Angeles, Boston, and Washington. Increasing numbers of architects are finding employment in areas of the South and Southwest that are attracting new business and residential construction. Examples are Arizona, New Mexico, and Florida.

How Much Money Will I Make?

In 1992 interns averaged $24,500, architects with 8 to 10 years of experience averaged 36,700, and partners averaged $50,000. The top 10 percent made over $100,000.

What Are the Job Opportunities?

Architecture is a very competitive field because there are many more graduates than jobs. The demand for architects is highly dependent on the economy. The demand for U.S. architects in Europe is down because an increasing number of architects are being trained in Europe.

Related Careers

Civil engineer   Urban planner
Building contractor   Landscape architect

Where Can I Get More Information?

American Institute of Architects
1735 New York Avenue, NW
Washington, DC 20006

Engineer

Applies the theories of mathematics and other sciences to practical problems at a reasonable cost in time and money

What's It Like to Be an Engineer?

Engineers develop systems for electric power, water supply, and waste disposal to meet the problems of urban living. They design machines and artificial organs as well as industrial equipment used to manufacture heating, air-conditioning, and ventilating units. Engineers also develop scientific equipment to probe outer space and the ocean depths. They design, plan, and supervise the construction of buildings, highways, and transit systems. They design and develop consumer products such as cars, television sets, video games, and systems for control and automation of business and manufacturing processes.

Most engineers study one of the more than 25 branches or specialties in the field. Within the basic specialties are over 85 subdivisions. For example, structural engineering as well as environmental, hydraulic, and highway engineering are subdivisions of civil engineering. Engineers within each of the branches may apply their specialized knowledge to many fields. For instance, electrical engineers work in medicine, computers, missile guidance, and electric power distribution. Since a knowledge of basic engineering principles is required for all areas of engineering, it is possible for engineers to shift from one branch or field of specialization to another, especially during the early stages of their careers.

There are 10 major branches of engineering in which most engineers work:

Aerospace Engineers (73,000—7 percent women, 5 percent black, 2 percent Hispanic) Design, develop, test, and help produce commercial and military aircraft, missiles, and spacecraft. They develop aerospace products from initial planning and design to final assembly and testing. Current job opportunities are affected by a major cutback in defense jobs, a downswing in aircraft construction, and expected new competition in aircraft construction from Japan. These factors will create a very competitive situation for jobs through 2005.

Chemical Engineers (52,000—11 percent women, 2 percent black, 2 percent Hispanic) Design equipment for chemical plants and determine methods of manufacturing chemical products. They often design and operate pilot plans to test their work, and develop chemical processes such as those for removing chemical contaminants from waste materials. The drop in oil prices has reduced opportunities in petroleum and energy-related industries as well as in energy research. The best opportunities will be in service industries.

Civil Engineers (173,000—5 percent women, 4 percent black, 3 percent Hispanic) Design and supervise the construction of roads, harbors, airports, tunnels, bridges, water supply systems, sewage systems, and buildings. This is the oldest branch of engineering. A growing population will produce a need for more civil engineers to develop water resource and waste disposal systems, to build large buildings, and to repair deteriorating roads and bridges.

Electrical Engineers (370,000—9 percent women, 4 percent black, 3 percent Hispanic) Design, develop, and supervise the manufacture of electrical and electronic equipment, including electric motors, generators, communications equipment, cardiac pace-makers, pollution-measuring instruments, radar devices, computers, lasers, missile guidance systems, and electrical appliances of all kinds. This is the largest branch of engineering. Although defense jobs will be down, engineers who keep up with the rapid changes in technology will have good opportunities for jobs in electronics and in computer research and development.

Industrial Engineers (119,000—12 percent women, 4 percent black, 3 percent Hispanic) Determine the most effective ways for an organization to use the basic factors of production—people, machines, materials, information, and energy. They bridge the gap between management and operations and are more concerned with people and business methods than most engineers. They also develop management control systems to aid in financial planning and cost analysis; they design production planning and control systems; and they design or improve systems to distribute goods and services. With manufacturing at an all-time low, job opportunities will be down through 2005.

Mechanical Engineers (227,000—5 percent women, 4 percent black, 2 percent Hispanic) Concerned with the production, transmission, and use of mechanical power and heat. They design and develop a great variety of machines that use power, such as rockets and refrigeration and air-conditioning equipment. Because defense spending and manufacturing are down, the job market is expected to be tough through 2005.

Metallurgical and Ceramic Engineers (19,000—7 percent women, less than 1 percent black and Hispanic) Develop new types of metals and other materials and tailor them to meet specific requirements—for example, materials that are heat-resistant, strong but lightweight, or highly malleable. Job prospects are good for ceramic and materials engineers, who are needed to develop new ways to recycle solid waste and process low-grade ores now regarded as unprofitable to mine. Jobs are expected to increase as the search for new materials and processes to produce environmentally friendly cars and other products intensifies.

Mining Engineers (3,600—2 percent women, less than 1 percent black and Hispanic) Find, extract, and prepare minerals for manufacturing industries to use. They design open-pit and underground mines, supervise the construction of mine shafts and tunnels in underground operations, and devise methods for transporting minerals to processing plants. Job opportunities are not expected to be good because the price of coal and other minerals is projected to remain low.

Nuclear Engineers (17,000—5 percent women, 6 percent black, 1 percent Hispanic) Design, develop, monitor, and operate nuclear power plants used to generate electricity and to power Navy ships. They also conduct research in nuclear energy and radiation. Public opposition to nuclear power plants and a reduction in defense spending will severely limit job opportunities through 2005.

Petroleum Engineers (14,000—13 percent women, 2 percent black, less than 1 percent Hispanic) Explore and drill for oil and gas. They develop the most efficient recovery methods for production. With the drop in oil prices, jobs are very competitive and opportunities are expected to be down through 2005.

Other engineering specialties include agricultural engineers (12,000) and biomedical engineers (3,000 and increasing).

What Education and Skills Will I Need?

High School Preparation for college, with an emphasis on science, mathematics, and computer science.

College Major in engineering at one of 290 colleges.

Personal Skills Ability to think analytically and creatively, capacity for detail, and ability to work as a team member are necessary skills.

How Many Engineers Are There and Where Do They Work?

Over half the engineers are employed by manufacturing industries; one-fourth are in construction, public utilities, and building services; and the remainder work in government and educational institutions. New job opportunities are emerging in nonmanufacturing industries, especially in engineering and architectural services and business and management consulting services, where firms design construction projects or do other engineering work on a contract basis. Some new jobs will be available in communications and utilities.

How Much Money Will I Make?

In 1992 experienced engineers averaged $52,500 a year and managers made an average of $87,000. The average starting salaries for engineers with a bachelor's degree, by branch, were:

Mechanical	$34,462
Nuclear	$34,447
Electrical	$33,754
Metallurgical	$33,502
Industrial	$32,348
Aeronautical	$31,826
Mining	$31,177
Civil	$29,376

What Are the Job Opportunities?

The opportunities in engineering will continue to be good through 2005. Engineering students, who make up about 9 percent of the total number of college graduates, receive 40 percent of the job offers. See the individual engineering entries for job opportunities in each specialty. The best job opportunities will be in civil engineering, where more engineers will be needed to restore deteriorating roads, bridges, and water and pollution control systems. There will also be very good job opportunities in electrical and electronic engineering, which focus on the computer industry. Even though only 8 percent of all engineers are women, 20 to 30 percent of engineering students are female. Purdue University, one of the most active recruiters of women, enrolls 20 percent in engineering; likewise at Princeton the number of women in engineering is increasing. Women must take the required mathematics and physics courses in high school to qualify for an engineering career. Engineering is one of the few professions that does not require a graduate degree. Young women should get in on the advantages of this high-paying career that has plenty of job opportunities. It takes the same number of years of college as a teaching career does, and pays double the money!

Related Careers

Environmental scientist

Mathematician

Physical scientist

Architect

Where Can I Get More Information?

Junior Engineering Technical Society (JETS)
1420 King Street, Suite 405
Alexandria, VA 22314

Society of Women Engineers
United Engineering Center
345 East 47th Street, Room 305
New York, NY l0017

American Institute of Aeronautics and Astronautics
Attn: Michael Lewis
The Aerospace Center
370 L'Enfant Promenade, SW
Washington, DC 20024

American Institute of Chemical Engineers
345 East 47th Street
New York, NY 10017

American Society of Civil Engineers
1015 15th Street NW, Suite 600
Washington, DC 20005

Engineering Management Society (EMS)
c/o Institute of Electrical and Electronics Engineers
345 East 47th Street
New York, NY 10017

American Society of Mechanical Engineers
345 East 47th Street
New York, NY 10017

Minerals, Metals, and Materials Society
420 Commonwealth Drive
Warrendale, PA 15086

Society for Mining, Metallurgy, and Exploration
P.O. Box 625005
Littleton, CO 80162

Society of Petroleum Engineers
P.O. Box 833836
Richardson, TX 75083

Landscape Architect

Designs areas to be functional, beautiful, and environmentally appropriate

What's It Like to Be a Landscape Architect?

College campuses, shopping centers, industrial parks, golf courses, parkways, and housing developments usually have a landscape architect on their design and planning team. Working with other architects and with engineers, Hilary Watkins, a landscape architect with a master's degree, is responsible for creating detailed plans indicating new topography, vegetation, and walkways.

The first step in the process is analysis of the site: climate, soil, slope of the land, where and when sunlight falls, and existing buildings and utilities. Next, Watkins prepares sketches using computers to design plans to show to the other professionals working on the team. The final proposal for the client will consist of written reports, sketches, models, photographs, land-use studies, and cost estimates.

Landscape architects use their knowledge of design theory and land-use planning to develop landscape projects. Ceramic artist Paul Davis, like many young adults, backed into his career by taking a job as an outdoor estate caretaker to earn money while pursuing his artistic goals. He enjoyed working outside, using his design ideas, and working with his hands. He accepted jobs at several more estates, started raising his own plants and trees, bought one truck and then another, worked long days, and here he is, an artist turned successful and happy small-business owner.

What Education and Skills Will I Need?

High School   Preparation for college, with emphasis on science, geometry, and art courses.

College   There are 50 colleges that offer accredited bachelor's degree programs in landscape architecture.

Personal Skills   A love of nature, creativity, and artistic talent are important for success in this field. Forty-four states require landscape architects to be licensed.

How Many Landscape Architects Are There and Where Do They Work?

There are 19,000 landscape architects and they work for architectural firms and construction contractors. Most job opportunities are concentrated in Florida, California, and Texas. About 20 percent of landscape architects are self-employed.

How Much Money Will I Make?

In 1993 graduates with a bachelor's degree in landscape architecture started at an average $20,400; those with a master's degree started at $30,600. Although there is a greater than usual variation in salaries, experienced landscape architects generally earned between $30,000 and $50,000 per year, the median at $41,900. Those who are partners in well-established firms may earn much more than that.

What Are the Job Opportunities?

Growth is expected in this field, although job opportunities are tied to the construction business and a strong economy. Keep an eye on the ups and downs of the housing construction business to best assess your job chances in landscape architecture. Many young people interested in the environment and the outdoors are attracted to this career, thus limiting the number of beginning jobs.

Related Careers

Architect   Urban planner
Industrial designer   Civil engineer

Where Can I Get More Information?

American Society of Landscape Architects
4401 Connecticut Avenue, NW, Fifth Floor
Washington, DC 20008

Government

- City manager
- Civil service employee
- Community planner
- Elected government official
- Foreign service officer
- Lawyer
- Military personnel
- Peace Corps volunteer

ABOUT GOVERNMENT CAREERS

The most security and the fewest risks are offered by government jobs. The federal government is the nation's largest single employer. And even more people work for state and local governments. Altogether, one worker in every six is employed by the government, which translates into about 18 million jobs. About 7 million of those workers are college graduates. The largest group of federal government workers is employed in defense; the next-largest group of employees works for the postal service. Cleaning up the environment is an up-and-coming area of employment in government. Workers in local governments include those in education, fire protection, hospitals, street and highway departments, and water and transit services. Security in the form of police protection is the fastest-growing local government career. State government workers are employed in hospitals, on highways, and in corrections, security, and public welfare.

Preparing for a career with the government is different from preparing for most career clusters, because the government hires workers for just about every career described in this book. Therefore, accountants, physicians, teachers, nurses, and purchasing agents all can pursue government careers. These positions require a great variety of educational backgrounds.

Most of the government-related careers described in this section, such as city manager, community planner, and lawyer, require graduate work. Volunteer jobs in the Peace Corps are limited to two years and do not necessarily lead to paying jobs directly related to that experience. Unless you are the top manager in your department, it is very difficult to bring about change through government employment. Rather than personal profit or the chance to change the world, many people choose government jobs to serve the public and to have a direct impact on others. And all government workers enjoy good fringe benefits, including the best pension plan in the country.

City Manager

Administers and coordinates day-to-day operations of a city

What's It Like to Be a City Manager?

Planning for future growth, cleaning up air and water pollution, and reducing crime rates demand the services of a good city manager. City managers are also in charge of tax collection, law enforcement, public works, and preparation of the city's budget. They are responsible to the community's council of elected officials, which hires them. Besides attending to the daily activities of the city, city managers study long-range problems such as traffic, housing, crime, urban renewal, pollution, and waste disposal, and they report their findings to the elected council. They often work with citizens' groups and give reports to special city committees. Many citizens' groups hold their meetings after regular work hours.

What Education and Skills Will I Need?

High School   Preparation for college, with leadership experience in as many school activities as possible.

College   Major in business, engineering, recreation, or political science. A master's degree in public or municipal administration is necessary for the better jobs.

Personal Skills   This job demands the ability to quickly isolate problems, identify their causes, and find solutions; also required are good judgment, self-confidence, and the ability to work well with others.

How Many City Managers Are There and Where Do They Work?

There are 11,216 city managers, assistant city managers, and department heads. This is a new and growing career. Over three-quarters of the city managers work for small cities with fewer than 25,000 inhabitants. Almost 40 percent of the public administrators are women, 6 percent are black, and 4 percent are Hispanic; the number of women who hold the top job in a city is on the rise. It's only in the past few years that women and blacks have been elected mayor in major cities.

How Much Money Will I Make?

In 1993 the starting salary for new college graduates was $22,000 a year as assistant city managers. Average salaries for experienced managers ranged from $33,000 a year in small cities to $125,000 in cities with populations of over one million.

What Are the Job Opportunities?

Jobs will be competitive through 2005, with towns and cities cutting their budgets and with many more graduates than jobs. The best opportunities are in the South and the West.

Related Careers

Business manager   Hospital administrator
School administrator   Operations manager

Where Can I Get More Information?

International City Management Association
777 North Capitol Street, NE, Suite 500
Washington, DC 20002

Civil Service Employee

Works for the federal government in every kind of job found in private employment

What's It Like to Be a Civil Service Employee?

Graduates of four-year colleges can enter career management, administrative and personnel management, and technical and professional jobs with the government. Graduates of two-year programs can enter at the technical assistance level in economics, administration, writing, data processing, finance, accounting, law, library science, and physical science.

There are two ways to get a federal job. The first and most common is by taking the civil service examination and being placed on a civil service register. Whenever a job opening occurs in a federal agency, the registers are scanned and the names of the best-qualified applicants are sent to the agency. You can increase your chances of getting a federal job by filling in more than one category and by agreeing to move anywhere in the country. The biggest barrier for women who have not served in the armed forces is the veterans' preference policy, which under law gives special consideration to qualified veterans on a civil service exam.

The second way to get a federal job is by political appointment. By law, there are over 3,000 high-level jobs that are filled in this way. If you are well known in your field, get in touch with your senator for a recommendation or with your company to enter the President's Program for Executive Exchange. If you have not yet made a name for yourself in your career, you can work long and hard on a successful presidential campaign to gain access to a political appointment.

After three years of work in government, a civil service employee has career status. This means, for example, that a parent who leaves her or his job to raise children can return to the same job level rather than having to compete again.

What Education and Skills Will I Need?

High School   Preparation for community college, business college, health training, or four-year college in any field that interests you.

College   The more education you have, the higher the career level open to you. Two-year college graduates take the Junior Federal Assistant Examination or the Junior Engineer and Science Assistant Examination to qualify for trainee-level positions.

Personal Skills   Skills needed vary according to the career you select.

How Many Civil Service Employees Are There and Where Do They Work?

Each year 10,000 federal jobs requiring college degrees are filled, and two-thirds of them go to men. In 1991 the federal government employed nearly 2 million white-collar workers. About 113,000 of them work in engineering and 74,000 in accounting; 47,000 are registered nurses, 35,000 are physicians, 32,000 are tax examiners and collectors, and 50,000 are systems analysts and computer scientists. Only 15 percent of federal employees work in Washington, D.C.; the remainder work all over the United States and abroad. The civil service is employing more temporary staff as it downsizes. There are now 50,000 temps—7.2 percent of all federal workers—and the number is growing.

How Much Money Will I Make?

Salaries are paid according to the General Schedule (GS) and are set by Congress. The pay scale is set for all government employees in the professions, administrative jobs, and technical and clerical jobs. There are raises within each grade and increases are periodic for each grade. Employees who advance to managerial positions are paid according to the General Management (GM) or merit pay system, which means that pay increments are based on work performance. Managers at the highest levels belong to the Senior Executive Service (SES), and their compensation, ranging from $92,900 to $115,700, is even more heavily performance-based. In 1994, graduates of a four-year college started at $19,116 (GS-

5) or $23,678 (GS-7) a year; a person with a master's degree began at $25,256. In 1994 average annual salaries for experienced professionals were $56,000 for an attorney, $42,100 for an intelligence agent, and $34,900 for a nurse. The top of the GS scale before work performance becomes relevant to salary is $90,252.

What Are the Job Opportunities?

President Clinton has promised to reduce the number of federal jobs. With the huge national deficit and attempted budget-cutting, good professional jobs in the U.S. government are competitive. Be sure to check into civil service if that's what you want; the chances for a job depend a lot on which career field interests you. Hiring will be down in defense, agriculture, and housing. The best opportunities will be with the Veterans Administration and the departments of Health and Human Services, Interior, and Education. The biggest growth area will be systems analysis, which is expected to increase 34 percent by 2005. The next highest growth area will be in inspection and compliance jobs, with a 20 percent increase predicted.

Related Careers

State government   Local government
Postal worker   Military personnel

Where Can I Get More Information?

Federal Job Information Center
1900 E Street, NW, Room 1416
Washington, DC 20415

Community Planner

Develops plans and programs for orderly growth and improvement of urban and rural communities

What's It Like to Be a Community Planner?

Alfred Lima has a bachelor's degree in landscape architecture and a master's degree in community planning. He started his own planning firm in Boston and spends a lot of time getting projects for his firm. Right now his biggest project is with the federal government—fire prevention in urban areas. Lima likes being his own boss and doing something useful and creative like preserving the urban environment. His usual work includes preparing master plans of the city, reviewing work completed by other staff members, and reading professional journals and publications. In addition he works on basic studies such as data collection, economic base and regional analysis, population studies, and map preparation; makes recommendations for land-use allocation, utilities, municipal facilities, housing, open spaces, and recreation and beautification programs; and plans implementation of budgets, subdivision regulations, and citizen information programs. Lima is a new step-father to three young children but still must devote several evenings a week to meetings with planning boards and civic groups concerned with planning and to professional meetings. He suggests that students learn the practical skills of graphics, drafting, and writing so that they can do everything necessary to run a business.

What Education and Skills Will I Need?

High School Preparation for college, with an emphasis on mathematics, computer science, and social sciences.

College A beginning job requires a master's degree in community or regional planning, which is offered in 80 colleges and universities. To prepare for graduate school, major in architecture, engineering, economics, social science, or public administration.

Personal Skills Ability to think in terms of spatial relationships and to visualize plans and designs, flexibility in solving problems, and ability to cooperate with others who may have different ideas are necessary qualities for planners.

How Many Community Planners Are There and Where Do They Work?

There are 23,000 community planners; 34 percent are women, 6 percent are black, and 1 percent are Hispanic. They work mostly for the government—73 percent for local government and 13 percent for state government. There has been an increase in management jobs in cities with populations of fewer than 50,000.

How Much Money Will I Make?

In 1993 the median annual salary for a community planner in city government was $40,000; in county governments, $36,700; in state governments, $42,000; in private consulting firms, $45,000; and in nonprofit foundations, $41,500. Consultants are paid on a fee basis, which is related to their regional or national reputation. Directors of planning can earn more than $65,000.

What Are the Job Opportunities?

The employment outlook is very good whether taxpayers like it or not. Communities must spend money to regulate water and air pollution and to protect the environment. Federal money and programs will be forthcoming. Florida and Maine have legislated planning and more states are expected to follow, creating a new job market for community planners.

Related Careers

Architect

Civil engineer

City manager

Geographer

Where Can I Get More Information?

American Planning Association
1776 Massachusetts Avenue, NW, Suite 400
Washington, DC 20036

Elected Government Official

Strives to meet the needs of constituents with an effective and efficient government

What's It Like to Be an Elected Government Official?

Chief executives and legislators at the federal, state, and local levels have overall responsibility for government functioning. In coordination with legislators, chief executives establish goals, then organize programs and formulate policies to attain those goals. They appoint people to head departments, such as highways, health, police, recreation, economic development, and finance. They prepare budgets, ensure that resources are being used efficiently, and make sure that programs are carried out as planned.

Elected government officials include the president and vice-president of the United States, state governors, commissioners, mayors, and state and federal legislators. Legislators make laws or amend existing ones to remedy problems and to regulate government activities. Legislators introduce bills and review and vote on bills introduced by others. In preparing legislation, they read reports and work with their constituents, representatives of interest groups, members of boards and commissions, the chief executive, and department heads and legislators in other units of government. Both chief executives and legislators also perform ceremonial duties—they inaugurate new structures and businesses, make proclamations, welcome visitors, and lead celebrations. They also spend considerable time and resources trying to get reelected.

What Education and Skills Will I Need?

High School   Preparation for college, with as much liberal arts and experience in communication as possible.

College   Elected government officials come from every college (American to Yale) and every major imaginable. Leadership experience in sports, publications, clubs, and other activities is as important as classroom experiences. Many elected officials come from a law background, which is best prepared for through a major in English literature, history, economics, philosophy, or social sciences.

Personal Skills   Perseverance and reasoning ability are essential to analyze complex problems and reach sound conclusions. Confidence and creativity are necessary to handle unique social and economic problems.

How Many Elected Government Officials Are There and Where Do They Work?

There are approximately 71,000 chief executives and legislators. Most of them work in local government. There are about 7,500 state legislators. Many state legislators hold second jobs. Women have always done well in nonpaid local positions and as town clerks and local legislators, but until 1992 it had been tough to get women in Washington. For the first time, four new women were elected to the United States Senate, where previously there were just two. (Joining Nancy Kassebaum of Kansas and Barbara Mikulski of Maryland are Barbara Boxer and Dianne Feinstein of California, Patty Murray of Washington, and the first African-American woman to serve in the Senate—Carol Moseley Braun of Illinois.) Forty-eight women were elected to the House of Representatives in 1992, up from 29 in the previous Congress. Women and minorities are finally moving closer to center stage in politics.

How Much Money Will I Make?

Salaries range from little or nothing for a small-town council member to $200,000 a year for the President of the United States. Salaries for appointed White House officials go up to $125,000. The average salary for state legislators was $24,000 in 1993. Gubernatorial salaries range from $37,000 in Arkansas to $135,000 in New York.

What Are the Job Opportunities?

Little change is expected through 2005. Elections provide the opportunity for newcomers to unseat incumbents or to fill vacated positions. The level of competition varies from state to state and from year to year.

Related Careers

Business manager   Social scientist
Lawyer   Educator

Where Can I Get More Information?

Council of State Governments
Iron Works Pike
P.O. Box 11910
Lexington, KY 40578

Contact your state or national political party.

Foreign Service Officer

Represents the government of the United States and conducts relations with foreign countries and international organizations

What's It Like to Be a Foreign Service Officer?

Foreign service officers protect and promote the welfare and the interests of the United States and its people. Working in the Department of State, they are responsible for advising the president on matters of foreign policy; for conducting relations with foreign countries; for protecting the political, economic, and commercial interests of the United States overseas; and for offering services to U.S. citizens abroad and to foreign nationals traveling to the United States. Ambassador Genta A. Hawkins, a career foreign service officer appointed by the president and confirmed by the U.S. Senate, writes about her first assignment to an embassy. "As consular officer, I issued visas to tourists, diplomats, and business people coming to the United States; helped U.S. citizens in distress; witnessed marriages; signed birth certificates; and renewed passports. When I was a member of the economic section, I traveled extensively throughout the Ivory Coast to identify worthwhile projects and to assess their progress. I served as escort officer for a group of U.S. journalists and for a U.S. rock group that toured the country. Most evenings were filled with official obligations. Dinners and diplomatic receptions were held at the presidential palace. My current assignment in Washington consists of writing speeches and articles, planning conferences, and acting as a liaison with private agencies. The evening responsibilities of a young foreign service officer in Washington are not as rigorous as in the field, but there are occasional receptions at the embassies and welcoming ceremonies for visiting heads of state on the White House lawn."

What Education and Skills Will I Need?

High School   Preparation for college, with emphasis on the social sciences, history, government, English, and foreign languages.

College   Almost all candidates for the foreign service have a bachelor's degree in the liberal arts. More than half have a master's degree, a law degree, or a doctorate. All are expected to have a broad knowledge of foreign and domestic affairs and to be well-informed on U.S. foreign policy and history, government, culture, basic economic theory, literature, business administration, and international affairs. Appointees need not be proficient in a foreign language, as they may receive instruction in a language before assignment to designated posts. Everyone applying for an appointment must take the written examination, which is given annually in November in about 200 cities in the United States and at U.S. embassies and consulates overseas. Application deadlines vary from year to year and are usually in mid-October. To take the examination, you must be at least 20 years old, a U.S. citizen, and available for worldwide assignment.

Personal Skills   Career foreign service officers should have a dedication to public service and a willingness to work anywhere in the world. They should be able to adapt to occasional hardships as well as change of culture and languages.

How Many Foreign Service Officers Are There and Where Do They Work?

There are 4,400 foreign service officers in the Department of State, serving overseas and in Washington, D.C. Foreign service officers serve as administrative, consular, economic, and political officers in more than 250 U.S. embassies and consulates in over 150 nations.

How Much Money Will I Make?

In 1993 entry-level salaries ranged from $26,000 to $42,000 a year. Exact figures depend on education, experience, and other qualifications. Senior officers may earn up to $108,300 a year.

What Are the Job Opportunities?

The number of openings for officers remains more or less constant, and competition for these positions is intense. Each year approximately 12,000 to 13,000 applicants take the foreign service written examination. Of this number, about 140 entry-level officers will receive a five-year probationary appointment.

Related Careers

Public relations worker

International affairs
 administrator

Environmental affairs worker

Economist

Where Can I Get More Information?

Recruitment Division
U.S. Department of State
P.O. Box 12226
Arlington, VA 22219

Lawyer

Interprets laws, rulings, and regulations for individuals and businesses

What's It Like to Be a Lawyer?

Lawyers, also called attorneys, define rights as well as obligations and restrictions, covering such diverse activities as defending or prosecuting accused criminals, applying for patents, drawing up business contracts, giving tax advice, settling labor disputes, complying with real estate codes, and administering wills. Whether acting as advocates or advisers, they are all involved with in-depth research into the purposes behind certain laws. They study judicial decisions that have applied those laws to circumstances similar to those currently faced by the client. Lawyers write reports, or briefs, which must communicate clearly and precisely. As laws grow more complex, lawyers are taking on regulatory tasks in areas such as transportation, energy conservation, consumer protection, and social welfare.

Carol Irish, a Stanford graduate who went to the University of Virginia Law School, started her career in New York City at a major law firm, where she specializes in business mergers and takeovers. A team member working in corporate law, she finds this job very different from the TV image of a trial lawyer in a small city.

Bill McDermit, married to his law partner, says there are

certain activities performed by most lawyers. Whether representing the defendant in a divorce case or the suing party (plaintiff) in a lawsuit, a lawyer has to know the relevant laws and the facts in the case to determine how the law affects the facts. Based on this determination, the lawyer decides what action is in the best interest of the client. Lawyers must be familiar with both legal and nonlegal matters. For example, divorce lawyers read about the changing role of the family in modern society, the different yet acceptable living arrangements, and the great variety of patterns of living and loving together. Most lawyers consult with clients to determine the details of problems, to advise them of the law, and to suggest action that may be taken. "Working in a husband and wife practice," reports McDermit, "gives us the kind of work and lifestyle we want together. We will not have children until we get this practice going, and maybe not even then. We work hard, and when we're finished, we really love to take off and have time for sports and sun with no other worries or commitments."

What Education and Skills Will I Need?

High School   Preparation for college, with as much liberal arts and training in language skills as possible.

College   College graduates aiming for a law career go to one of the 177 approved three-year law schools; then they must pass the bar examination in the state in which they will practice. Don't look for a "prelaw major" in college. Literature, history, government, economics, philosophy, and social sciences are all useful majors that will qualify you for law school. An understanding of society and its institutions is required for law. About one-fifth of all law students are enrolled part time, usually in night school.

Personal Skills   Integrity and honesty are vital. Perseverance and reasoning ability are essential to analyze complex cases and reach sound conclusions. Creativity is also necessary to handle unique problems.

How Many Lawyers Are There and Where Do They Work?

There are 716,000 lawyers; 21 percent are women, 3 percent are black, and 3 percent are Hispanic. Most (60 percent) work for law firms or are in corporate business; 12 percent work for local government and 7 percent for the federal government. In 1981 Sandra Day O'Connor became the first female lawyer ever to serve as a justice of the United States Supreme Court. Twelve years later, in 1993, Janet Reno was appointed U.S. Attorney General, the first woman to even be seriously considered for that position. Their presence enables young women to aspire to such esteemed and prestigious positions in law. There are 90,000 judges, all employed by the government (half by the federal government).

How Much Money Will I Make?

In 1993 the beginning salary for a new graduate hired by a law firm was from $36,600 to $80,000 a year. The average salary of the most experienced lawyers in private industry was $134,000, making law one of the top 10 highest-paid careers in the country. The big money for beginning lawyers is with the five most prestigious law firms in New York City, which start their new law school graduates at $70,000 with an increase to $90,000 within the first year. An assistant district attorney in Brooklyn, however, will start at less than half that figure. Note that 27 percent of the men and only 9 percent of the women made $100,000 or more.

What Are the Job Opportunities?

Competitive! The first hurdle is getting into law school, which is highly competitive because of the recent increase in applicants. Many law school graduates go into other jobs and use their legal education as a background for new career directions. Still others study law to help in human rights activities—to protect the rights of women and minorities, litigate environmental and consumer cases, provide legal aid, and test compliance with existing civil rights laws. And don't forget that nonprofits—museums, universities, libraries—also hire lawyers.

Related Careers

Legislator
Judge

FBI special agent
Lobbyist

Where Can I Get More Information?

The American Bar Association
750 North Lake Shore Drive
Chicago, IL 60611

Association of American Law Schools
1201 Connecticut Avenue, NW, Suite 800
Washington, DC 20036

Military Personnel

Serve in armed forces

What's It Like to Be a Member of the Military?

In peacetime, it's like getting paid for job training and work experience. In the U.S. Army there are over 200 training courses for technical, medical, communications, and electronics jobs that you can choose before you enter the service. There are more than 1,600 basic and advanced military occupation specialties for college graduates. Most of them have civilian counterparts. The job you get depends on your present level of education and achievement. Each service has its own jobs, its own job training, and its own educational programs. Check with the Army, the Air Force, the Navy, the Coast Guard, and the Marine Corps for specific details. You can enlist in a variety of combinations of active and reserve duty. Active duty ranges from two to six years; three-year and four-year enlistments are most common.

What Education and Skills Will I Need?

High School A diploma is now required for enlisted personnel. Prepare for any college major to qualify for officers' training programs. In 1993, 84 percent of all military personnel were high school graduates.

College Your major in college qualifies you for the job you wish to select in the service. The military can use any and all types of skills and educational achievement.

Personal Skills The skills required depend on your career choice. Other qualifications: You must be between 18 and 27 years old, a U.S. citizen, and in good physical condition. There is no restriction on marital status, but you cannot have dependents under 18 at the time you enlist.

Many Military Personnel Are There and re Do They Work?

There are 1.8 million people in the armed forces and the number will decrease until 1997. Twelve percent are women; blacks and Hispanics represent a larger percentage in the armed forces than in the population. Women were first accepted into military academies in 1976. The only jobs closed to women, by act of Congress, are those in actual combat and those related to combat (flying in the Air Force). The rights of women in the military have changed in the last few years. Women can now be married, have dependents, get maternity leave whether married or not, and have benefits equal to those for men for themselves and their dependents. The Army has 606,000 men and women, the Air Force 466,000, the Navy 537,000, the Marines 184,000, and the Coast Guard 38,000. They are stationed in the United States, primarily in California, Texas, North Carolina, Virginia, Georgia, and Florida; in Europe, primarily in Germany; and in the western Pacific. In addition there are 3 million men and women in reserve units. A reduction from 90,000 in the Army to 25,000 in the Marines is expected by 1997.

How Much Money Will I Make?

In 1993 basic pay and allowances for food and quarters for a second lieutenant equaled $1,650.60 a month; a captain received $2,061.00 a month. In addition, cash allowances amount to 18 percent of that figure. People in the military also receive medical and dental benefits, 30 days of paid vacation a year, and allowances for living expenses and travel.

What Are the Job Opportunities?

Because the military is now a volunteer rather than a conscription organization, it makes its offers as attractive as it can to recruit the number of personnel it needs. Many young people are interested in military education and training, which will continue to be exceptionally good for learning a skill and getting paid for it. Peacetime is a good time to find opportunities for work in the military. Participation in ROTC is a good way to pay for your college education; the scholarships for young men and women are worth checking out. The more education you have before you join the service, the higher the job level at which you will begin. Defense spending is never predictable, and the world is changing fast, which will keep military job opportunities open for the young, especially the well educated.

Where Can I Get More Information?

Write to or visit your local recruiting station for the latest official information. Local stations are listed in your phone book. Or write to the following addresses:

U.S. Army Recruiting Command
Fort Sheridan, IL 60037

USAF Recruiting Service
Randolph Air Force Base
Randolph, TX 78150

Commandant of the Marine Corps
Washington, DC 20380

Commander Naval Recruiting Command
801 North Randolph Street
Arlington, VA 22203

When you are selecting your college, ask about ROTC programs. There are 1,000 Army, 65 Navy and Marine, and 600 Air Force ROTC units in colleges across the country.

Peace Corps Volunteer

Promotes world peace and friendship by providing trained assistance to developing countries, creating a better understanding of American people among others, and creating a better understanding of other peoples among Americans

What's It Like to Be a Peace Corps Volunteer?

Judy Daloz, Peace Corps teacher for two years in Nepal, says, "Living alone and working in a foreign culture helped me realize who I am, what I can do, and what I want to do with my life. The ices I had gave me a perspective on being a woman, on being an American, on being a human being, which I doubt I could have gotten otherwise. Although in the beginning I saw it as an exciting challenge to have two years in which to affect people's lives in a positive way, in the end I realized my life had been far more affected than had the lives of the people I was living with."

Ricardo Campbell, a volunteer in Sao Mateus, Brazil, says there are many reasons for spending two years of your life in the Peace Corps, but a common theme is "the willingness to serve, to step beyond ourselves and our immediate comfort to help, in some small way, other people to help themselves." The daily living of Peace Corps volunteers is on the same economic level and in the same style practiced by the people who have invited them. The Peace Corps has been in Ghana for 32 years. Currently there are 69 trainees there, involved in raising rabbits and keeping bees. They glaze pottery, patch dams, and teach family planning to medicine men and plowing with a bullock to farmers who have traditionally used hoes. Volunteers have served in Guatemala for 30 years. Currently there are 117 trainees who are working in agriculture: leading 4-H clubs, improving grain seed, and improving storage of grain. Papua New Guinea has invited the Corps for the past 12 years, mostly for health and secondary education volunteers. There are currently 50 trainees there, many working in the high schools, which are often administered by Catholic missionaries.

The newest and hottest area of interest is Central Europe, where 45 volunteers are currently training in the Czech Republic. Most of them will advise small, private businesses on start-up and management.

What Education and Skills Will I Need?

High School Preparation for college. You can use any skill or professional achievement to become a volunteer in the Peace Corps. The world is not waiting for an uneducated and unskilled person—not even the Third World.

College Most of the volunteers are liberal arts graduates. The Peace Corps is a temporary (two-year) work experience, and many volunteers go to graduate school after service. A 13-week training program in the United States is required before the volunteer leaves the country.

Personal Skills   Skills needed depend on your job and responsibilities.

How Many Volunteers Are There and Where Do They Work?

There are 6,500 volunteers in the Peace Corps. Most are college graduates; 8 percent are married. They work in the 95 countries that have invited them, including sub-Saharan Africa, Latin America, North Africa, the Near East, South Asia, and the Pacific Rim. The average age of the volunteers is 30. Jane and Gus Root from Vermont joined the Peace Corps after they retired from college teaching. They sold their home along with most of their worldly possessions and took off to volunteer in the Third World. The Peace Corps attracts, and therefore you will meet, many creative people.

How Much Money Will I Make?

Travel and living allowances are paid. The living allowance is based on the local conditions where the volunteer is working. In Ghana, volunteers earn more than those in most other countries because of the high cost of living. Most volunteers accumulate from $1,800 to $2,000 while in the Peace Corps. They usually spend it traveling before their return to the United States.

What Are the Job Opportunities?

The Peace Corps is on the rise again and there will continue to be a need for volunteers of all ages. Peace Corps workers return from overseas with an interest in another area of the world. They have had the opportunity to learn and use a foreign language and to know the culture and traditions of the country in which they worked. Many of the volunteers return home to take advanced work in college. Of those who do not return to school, most enter public service. The following skills are needed and are scarce among applicants: diesel mechanics, foresters, nurses, math and science teachers, and engineers.

Related Careers

Foreign service officer
Missionary

International business
  executive
International health worker

Can I Get More Information?

Peace Corps
806 Connecticut Avenue, NW
Washington, DC 20525

Call the Peace Corps toll free at 1-800-424-8580.

Health

Manager
- Health service manager
- Medical records manager

Practitioner
- Chiropractor
- Dental hygienist
- Dentist
- Dietitian
- Doctor
- Nurse
- Optometrist
- Osteopathic physician
- Pharmacist
- Physician assistant
- Podiatrist
- Veterinarian

Therapist
- Occupational therapist
- Physical therapist
- Recreation therapist

- **Respiratory therapist**
- **Speech therapist, hearing therapist**

Allied Health

- **Medical illustrator**
- **Medical technologist**
- **Nuclear medicine technologist**

ABOUT HEALTH CAREERS

Health services is the second largest industry in the United States, with over 8.9 million jobs. One out of every six new salaried jobs created between 1990 and 2005 will be in health services. Half of the 30 occupations projected to grow the fastest are concentrated in health services. There is a critical need for nurses and allied health specialists. An unprecedented labor shortage is predicted for the mid-1990s. The need is so great that there is no other career with more options and opportunities than health services.

The health industry provides an estimated 400 individual health-care careers, and the options within each category have never been greater. Government, insurance companies, and unions are working to cut costs. Hospitals are closing; funds are tight. The trend is to get as many people as possible into outpatient care, where costs are less. The jobs go with the patients from hospitals to surgical centers, home health agencies, hospices, special AIDS centers, and freestanding emergency centers. Doctors are beginning to work for health maintenance organizations (HMOs), taking salaried jobs, and nurses and therapists are doing just the opposite and entering private practice.

Hospitals employ about half of all workers in the health field, although that figure is predicted to go down. Others work in clinics, home health agencies, private practice, laboratories, pharmacies, public health agencies, and mental health centers.

Most of the jobs described here require a number of years of preprofessional and professional college work and a passing grade on a state licensing examination. Only the jobs of dental hygienist and nurse require less than a four-year program to start in an entry-level position.

Working conditions usually involve long hours. Because health facilities such as nursing homes and hospitals operate around the clock, administrators in these institutions may be called at all hours to handle emergencies.

There is a major change in the use of computers in the health-care field. No longer used just to manage accounts and medical records, computers are now being used to monitor patients and diagnose disease. Health is catching up with other industries in the use of computers. The innovations in the utilization of computers for patient care include monitoring blood pressure, heart rate, temperature, and brain pressure; delivering controlled amounts of heat to treat tumors in cancer patients; measuring stomach acid; and analyzing all the data to determine a patient's condition.

The nursing field is the largest employer of health-care workers—one-third of the total, or over 2 million jobs. The demand for nurses will continue to provide an increasing number of jobs, giving nurses more negotiating power as they plan their time and tasks.

The critical demand for health care will increase as the population grows older and the public becomes increasingly health-conscious. Expansion of coverage under prepayment medical programs that make it easier for persons to cover hospitalization and medical care costs is also contributing to growth in the health-care field. In addition to jobs created by this growth, many new jobs will open as a result of turnover and retirement.

Where are there more health workers than jobs? Besides an oversupply of doctors in private practice in many parts of the country, there is an oversupply of people with master's degrees in public health and in hospital administration, and there are more general medical technologists than jobs.

And where are the job opportunities? In all areas of nursing. There are also positions available in occupational, respiratory, and physical therapy; in home health care; in nuclear medicine and the use of radioisotopes; and in emergency room care. Unprecedented shortages have resulted in secure and meaningful employment, opportunities for advancement, jobs in every and any setting you want to choose, and a chance to serve people who need your help.

"And don't forget the many related health-care jobs," says Hardwick Health Clinic office manager Jocelyne Lussier. "As a college student I wanted to be in the health field but didn't like the hospital and emergency room setting. As clinic manager I get the versatility that I want in a job. I help patients by answering their questions on the phone, doing the billing, and making the clinic run as smoothly as possible. Keeping patients informed and calm often helps them deal more adequately with their illness."

The Clinton administration promises a new focus on health care for the elderly, the applications of sophisticated technology in medical procedures, the prevention of disease, research for cures for AIDS and cancer, and containing costs. The United States in the late 1990s can expect to see more change in the health industry than in its entire history.

MANAGER

Health Service Manager

Plans programs, sets policies, and makes decisions for hospitals, medical clinics, nursing homes, HMOs, home health-care agencies, and other health facilities

What's It Like to Be a Health Service Manager?

"Health service managers need the same skills that any management career requires plus the ability to handle the ever-present funding needs of a nonprofit business," says Elizabeth J. Davis, vice-president of operations for VNS Homecare, a subsidiary of the Visiting Nurse Service of New York, the biggest nonprofit home health agency in the world. "What I like most about managing the VNS is that it fits into my value system. Providing health care in the home is different because it's in the patient's own environment. It's easier to involve the patient in the healing process. Something special can be worked out, no matter how intensive the care, to ensure the best possible conditions for the patient. The difficulties of clerical and paperwork are even worse than other fields because we have so many regulatory agencies monitoring everything we do. The challenge of a private health service is to find the funding for the comprehensive care we provide our patients, regardless of their incomes.

"Medicaid and Medicare never cover the cost; we have to get out and do our own fund-raising and think of creative ways to cut costs without cutting services. The VNS has a credible public image, which makes city, state, and national politicians accessible. It gives me an opportunity to be in on doing something political about the gaps I see in health care. In Vermont I often met with U.S. Senators Patrick Leahy and Robert Stafford to provide them with information, to testify, to lobby, and to help write health legislation. I've been in New York City for three years, and I met with U.S. Senator Patrick Moynihan the first year I got there. It is important to build political access in New York, so that once again, my experience in home health care serves to effect badly needed change in our nation's health policy."

Edward H. Noroian, executive vice-president of the Presbyterian Hospital of New York City, says, "A management job in a hospital is different from other management jobs in that a hospital contains many divisive elements. For the most part the primary providers of care, the physicians, are not employed by the hospital. There are different groups of highly technical employees, a complex physical plant with high energy demands, and a need for fast transfer of information. Furthermore, hospitals are highly regulated. In New York State, more than 160 different regulatory bodies inspect our affairs."

What Education and Skills Will I Need?

High School   Preparation for college, nursing school, or business college.

College   Major in the social sciences, nursing, or business. There are 60 U.S. colleges and universities that offer a master's degree in health service administration. Health administrators usually have a master's degree in business, public health, or health administration.

Personal Skills   Dealing with millions of dollars worth of facilities and equipment, you will need a command of business and communication skills that allow you to make good decisions and to motivate your employees to implement those decisions. Administrators need to be self-starters. They must enjoy working with people and be able to deal effectively with them. Public speaking is also important.

How Many Health Service Managers Are There and Where Do They Work?

There are 302,000 managers; 60 percent are women, 6 percent are black, and 2 percent are Hispanic. Most (46 percent) work in hospitals, 19 percent in offices of physicians, and 14 percent in nursing, home health, and personal care facilities.

How Much Money Will I Make?

In 1993 health service managers' median salary was $45,200; the highest 10 percent earned $96,000. Health service managers are paid according to the size and location of the hospital. In 1993 hospital CEOs earned from $77,000 to $223,600 a year. Nursing home administrators averaged $36,500 in homes with fewer than 50 beds and $68,200 in those with more than 400 beds.

What Are the Job Opportunities?

Health facilities are in a crisis because of the increasing needs of an older population and the skyrocketing costs of health care. Hospital care is decreasing while home health care is increasing. The jobs are competitive because enrollment in public health programs is high, and there are more graduates than jobs.

Related Careers

Business administrator
Professional health
  association worker
Social welfare administrator
College administrator

Where Can I Get More Information?

American College of Health Care Executives
840 North Lake Shore Drive, Suite 1103 W
Chicago, IL 60611

Association of University Programs in Health Administration
1911 North Fort Myer Drive, Suite 503
Arlington, VA 22209

Medical Records Manager

Manages health information systems consistent with the medical, administrative, ethical, and legal requirements of the health-care deliverer

What's It Like to Be a Medical Records Manager?

Medical records managers compile statistics and write summaries for reports required by state and health agencies. Medical records include case histories of illnesses, doctors' notes, and X-ray and lab reports. Administrators hold meetings with hospital department heads and medical records committees and plan research projects for the medical team treating the patient. Raj Nashabandi, a Rutgers University graduate, earned his certification at the University of Miami. He works at Boston's Deaconess Hospital, where he trains and supervises workers who verify, transcribe, code, and maintain files on patients' medical histories; he also develops systems for documenting, storing, and retrieving medical information. Nashabandi says he thinks he had to get a lot of education for the responsibilities of his job, and he plans to look for a general health management position as soon as he's put in a couple of years in medical records.

What Education and Skills Will I Need?

High School   Preparation for college, with emphasis on biological science and computer science.

College   Two or three years of college are usually required before entering one of the 80 approved training programs. High school graduates can enter a one-year or two-year college program for medical records technicians. A college degree is required from one of the 85 approved college programs. Programs include anatomy, physiology, hospital administration, and computer science.

Personal Skills   Accuracy, interest in detail, ability to write and speak clearly, and ability to be discreet in handling confidential information are needed by medical records managers.

How Many Medical Records Managers Are There and Where Do They Work?

There are 76,000 medical records technicians; 87 percent are women, 15 percent are black, and 8 percent are Hispanic. Technicians must get a college degree before they can advance to management. Most (62 percent) work in hospitals, 13 percent in nursing homes, and 11 percent for the federal government.

How Much Money Will I Make?

In 1993 the average starting salary for registered medical records managers was $18,000 a year. Supervising jobs averaged $29,599, and a department head averaged $41,700 a year.

What Are the Job Opportunities?

Opportunities will be very good for trained medical records personnel as the number of older people increases and medical records become more complex.

Related Careers

Hospital insurance
   representative
Health service manager

Medical librarian

Where Can I Get More Information?

American Health Information Management Association
919 North Michigan Avenue, Suite 1400
Chicago, IL 60690

PRACTITIONER

Chiropractor

Treats patients by manual manipulation of the body, especially the spinal column

What's It Like to Be a Chiropractor?

Chiropractic is a system of healing based on the principle that a person's health is determined by the nervous system. Chiropractors treat their patients by massage; by using water, light, and heat therapy; and by prescribing diet, exercise, and rest. They do not use drugs or surgery. Howard Riley, a chiropractor in a small city, sees about 50 patients a week, ranging in age from 6 months to 90 years old. He likes the great variety of patients he works with. Riley doesn't like the necessary insurance forms, the X-ray forms, and the business operations in general. He advises young people to visit and observe a chiropractor at work to see what the job is like.

Grace Johnson has opened a new practice in northern New England. She says that the chiropractic approach to health is gaining in popularity because it is holistic, stressing the patient's overall well-being. Johnson points out that chiropractic recognizes that many factors affect health, including exercise, diet, rest, environment, and heredity. Chiropractors use natural, nondrug, nonsurgical health treatments and rely on the body's inherent recuperative abilities. They also recommend lifestyle changes—in eating and sleeping habits, for example.

What Education and Skills will I Need?

High School Preparation for college, with as much science as possible.

College Two years of college are required for admission to the 17 chiropractic colleges (14 are fully approved by the American Chiropractic Association). The degree of Doctor of Chiropractic (D.C.) is awarded after four years of chiropractic college (a total of six years of training after high school).

Personal Skills   Sharp observation powers and hand dexterity, together with sympathetic understanding of patients.

How Many Chiropractors Are There and Where Do They Work?

There are 46,000 chiropractors, and even though most are men, the number of women has increased in the past four years. Ninety-five percent of chiropractors are in private practice and three-fourths practice alone. Half of all chiropractors work in California, New York, Texas, Missouri, Pennsylvania, and Michigan.

How Much Money Will I Make?

In 1993 experienced chiropractors averaged $74,000 a year. The lowest 10 percent had incomes of $24,000 and the highest 10 percent earned $190,000 or more.

What Are the Job Opportunities?

The number of graduates is keeping up with the need, giving everyone a job. Much of the demand depends on whether the treatment meets the requirements of insurance companies. The outlook for jobs is good because the elderly population is increasing and chiropractic medicine is gaining the approval of a wider range of people.

Related Careers

Optometrist   Audiologist
Podiatrist   Osteopath

Where Can I Get More Information?

American Chiropractic Association
1701 Clarendon Boulevard
Arlington, VA 22209

Dental Hygienist

Cleans teeth, charts tooth conditions, X-rays teeth, and teaches patients how to maintain good oral health

What's It Like to Be a Dental Hygienist?

Dental hygienists perform preventive services for patients and teach dental health. Hygienists who work in public school systems promote dental health by examining students and reporting the dental treatment required to their parents. "I work in a county health department quite independently with my patients in the mornings and in elementary schools in a dental-health program in the afternoons," writes Gail Brochu from Louisiana, wife and mother of three young children. She likes working with educators in the community and is frustrated by the poor care most people give their teeth and gums. She enjoys the variety of working for the government and for the public school system. Brochu wanted a job in which she could arrange her schedule so she could be home after school with her children.

What Education and Skills Will I Need?

High School Preparation for a two-year dental program, with emphasis on science. Most university programs require the Dental Aptitude Test for admission. The requirements for admission are usually the same as the requirements for the university's four-year program.

College Four-year dental hygienist degree programs are available for those who want to go into research or teaching. Each state has its own licensing examination. Most students take a two-year program.

Personal Skills Manual dexterity, ability to help people relax under stress, and neatness are necessary in dental hygiene.

How Many Dental Hygienists Are There and Where Do They Work?

There are 108,000 dental hygienists; 98 percent are women, 3 percent are black, and 3 percent are Hispanic. Most (96 percent) work in a dentist's office. Fifty percent are employed part time.

How Much Money Will I Make?

As in any career dominated by women, the pay is very low. In 1993 salaries for experienced dental hygienists were $22,500 to $38,000 a year.

What Are the Job Opportunities?

Opportunities will be good through 2005, especially for part-time work and in rural areas. Young dentists want to work with hygienists, creating job opportunities for today's graduates.

Related Careers

Nurse

Nurse anesthetist

Radiologic technologist

Medical technologist

Where Can I Get More Information?

American Dental Hygienists Association
444 North Michigan Avenue, Suite 3400
Chicago, IL 60611

Dentist

Examines, diagnoses, and treats various oral diseases and abnormalities

What's It Like to Be a Dentist?

Dentists fill cavities, straighten teeth, take X-rays, and treat gums. They clean and examine teeth and mouths as part of preventive dentistry. Most of their time is spent with patients, and usually their laboratory work is sent out to dental technicians. Orthodontist Suzanne Rothenberg's mother and father were dentists. She finds dentistry an exciting career because she can adapt her work to whatever interests her most—patients, research, or teaching. Dentists are independent and can work the hours and days they want. Rothenberg urges young women to major in science so that they are prepared to choose dentistry and get in on a high-paying job with flexible hours that allow for family life.

What Education and Skills Will I Need?

High School   Preparation for a predental program in college, with as much science and mathematics as possible.

College   Two years of college are required for admission to one of the 20 approved four-year dental schools. Nearly half of the dental schools now require three years of college, and most dental students have a college degree. Predental work includes chemistry, English, biology, and physics.

Personal Skills   A good visual memory, excellent judgment of space and shape, a delicate touch, and a high degree of manual dexterity are necessary for dentists.

How Many Dentists Are There and Where Do They Work?

There are 183,000 dentists; 9 percent are women, 5 percent are black, and 4 percent are Hispanic. Most (55 percent) are self-employed; others work for the federal government, in hospitals and clinics, and in industry. About 13 percent work part time.

How Much Money Will I Make?

In 1993 the average income for dentists was $85,000 a year for generalists and $130,000 for specialists. The median salary for all dentists was $90,000.

What Are the Job Opportunities?

There has been a sharp drop in dental school graduates, creating improved job opportunities through 2005. The oversupply of dentists in the early 1990s has balanced out, and new jobs are expected to be available in the next five years.

Related Careers

Optometrist   Veterinarian
Podiatrist   Physician

Where Can I Get More Information?

American Dental Association
211 East Chicago Avenue
Chicago, IL 60611

Dietitian

Plans nutritious meals to help people maintain or recover good health by promoting healthy eating habits

What's It Like to Be a Dietitian?

Administrative dietitians apply the principles of nutrition and management to large-scale meal planning and preparation, such as that done in hospitals, prisons, company cafeterias, and schools. *Hospital dietitians* plan modified meals, teach special diets to hospital patients and outpatients, and consult with doctors and nurses concerning the special needs of patients who must also take prescribed drugs. The primary responsibility of the dietitian is to teach other professionals in the hospital the value of nutrition for patients trying to recover good health. Because a hospital functions 24 hours a day, 365 days a year, a dietitian's schedule includes all hours and all days. *Research dietitians* work in academic medical settings conducting studies on subjects that link diet and health.

What Education and Skills Will I Need?

High School   Preparation for college, with an emphasis on science and mathematics.

College   Preparation for a degree in foods and nutrition or in institutional management in one of the 301 approved college programs. To qualify for professional recognition, take one of the 73 approved one-year internships in a hospital. Most of the top jobs are offered to students who have completed the internship, which provides further education and on-the-job experience under supervision.

Personal Skills   An aptitude for science and organizational and administrative abilities are needed as well as the ability to work well with other people.

How Many Dietitians Are There and Where Do They Work?

There are 50,000 dietitians; 15 percent are men, 19 percent are black, and 5 percent are Hispanic. Most (38 percent) work in hospitals, 20 percent in government jobs in prisons and health departments, 17 percent in nursing homes, and 14 percent for social service agencies.

How Much Money Will I Make?

In 1991 beginning salaries of new graduates of an internship program averaged $28,500 a year. Experienced dietitians in hospitals made from $32,000 to $42,000 a year.

What Are the Job Opportunities?

Job opportunities will be good through 2005. There are fewer industry and hospital jobs due to the recession, but there are more nursing home jobs because the proportion of elderly people is increasing.

Related Careers

Food technologist   Home economist
Food service manager   Nurse

Where Can I Get More Information?

The American Dietetic Association
216 West Jackson Boulevard, Suite 800
Chicago, IL 60606

Doctor

Diagnoses diseases and treats people who are ill; also works in research, in rehabilitation, and in preventive medicine

What's It Like to Be a Doctor?

"Very exciting, fatiguing, satisfying. It pays better than most careers do. The hours are long, but there is a high degree of independence," says Mary Jane Gray, M.D., who combines private practice, research, and teaching at Duke University's Medical Center in North Carolina. Dr. Gray describes her day as follows; "Mornings begin with a lecture or conference, rounds and consultations in the hospital, and laboratory work or operating all morning. Afternoons consist of office hours once a week and/or research lab four days a week. Evenings include one or two professional meetings a week, a few hours of work at home, and deliveries of babies as they occur."

Resident Julius Boenello tells us that residents work an average of 100 to 110 hours a week for three to five years. He stresses that young people will need the ambition to put the necessary time into the training. "You really have to give up your personal life for most of this time. If you're married, you never see your family. If you're single, you don't have a chance to be with friends. But the training is all a means to an end. Brighter days are ahead when you practice on your own."

What Education and Skills Will I Need?

High School　Preparation for college by taking as much science and mathematics as possible. A strong B average in the sciences and high motivation for staying in premed and medical school are the main requirements. You don't have to be a genius to go into medicine, as many students are led to believe.

College　Premedicine or biology is the usual major to prepare for one of the 127 accredited medical colleges. In addition to the physical sciences, behavioral and computer sciences are becoming more important in medical education. Changes in the curriculum include a broader education for clinical work as well as for the classroom. After graduation from a four-year medical school, one year of internship is required to be licensed to practice. Interns are paid by the hospital, and a paid year (or more) of residency or specialization in a field of medicine follows the internship.

Personal Skills　A strong interest and desire to care for the sick and injured are needed, as are persistence in continued study and the ability to make fast decisions in emergencies.

How Many Doctors Are There and Where Do They Work?

There are 556,000 doctors; 20 percent are women, 3 percent are black, and 5 percent are Hispanic. The percentage of black medical students (5.6 percent) is down from 6.3 percent 10 years ago. A third of the black students are concentrated in three predominantly black medical schools: Howard University in Washington, D.C., Morehouse College in Atlanta, and Meharry Medical College in Nashville. Only 24 percent of doctors are self-employed, a big change from the days when almost all doctors were in independent practice. Most doctors (approximately two-thirds) are in group practice, 20 percent are on hospital staff, and 8 percent work for the federal government. Even though only 20 percent of doctors are women, there are double that number of women in medical school who will soon be out and practicing.

How Much Money Will I Make?

Doctors are among the dozen biggest money-makers. They averaged $170,000 in 1993; pediatric and family medicine practitioners earned less ($105,000 and $98,000 respectively), while radiologists and surgeons averaged more (over $200,000). In 1993, medical school graduates who had completed three years of residency received $52,200 at Veterans Administration hospitals, in addition to other cash benefits. Residents make from $28,618 to $36,258 annually through six years of residency, and in addition get their board and room in hospital housing.

What Are the Job Opportunities?

There is a surplus of doctors on the market, and competition for postgraduate residencies is stiff. Enrollment in medical schools is increasing after a sharp drop in the 1980s, and the increase in foreign medical students continues. The costs of starting a private practice and paying malpractice insurance have stayed the same. The best chances for jobs are in inner-city and rural areas and in the fields of public health, medical research, industrial medicine, and rehabilitation.

Related Careers

Dentist   Optometrist
Veterinarian   Audiologist

Where Can I Get More Information?

American Medical Association
Council on Medical Education
515 North State Street
Chicago, IL 60610

Nurse

Observes, assesses, and records symptoms, reactions, and progress of patients; administers medications; helps rehabilitate patients; instructs patients and family members in proper health care; and helps maintain a physical and emotional environment that promotes recovery

What's It Like to Be a Nurse?

Nurses work with patients and families in a variety of settings. They provide direct care to patients in hospitals and nursing homes. They teach patients how to prevent complications and promote good health practices at home. Within the hospital setting, there are areas of specialization, such as psychiatric nursing, coronary care, intensive care, pediatric nursing, and obstetrics nursing. Nurses who provide direct care to patients are called staff nurses, or *primary care nurses*. Administrators who provide indirect care to patients are *head nurses* or *coordinators, team leaders*, and *supervisors*. Nurses also provide care to clients and families in the community. *Public health* and *home health nurses* provide direct care to patients who have been discharged from the hospital or who do not need hospitalization. They also teach health and health practices, provide immunizations, and work with teachers, parents, and doctors in the community, home, and school. *Office nurses* help physicians care for patients in private practices or clinics. *Private duty nurses* work in patients' homes or in hospitals to take care of individual patients who need special and constant attention. After advanced training, *nurse practitioners* provide primary health care as independent decision makers. They often establish a joint practice with a physician or run their own clinics.

"You seldom see a male nurse on television," says Kenneth Zwolski, a former science teacher who is enrolled in nursing school. "Now that I'm right where the action is, I'm amazed at what's available in terms of future career opportunities. I can do a great variety of jobs as a nurse."

What Education and Skills Will I Need?

High School Preparation for nursing education in a college preparatory program, with an emphasis on science.

College   A bachelor's degree is required to become a professional nurse; all others are considered technical nurses. There are, however, three types of registered nurse (RN) education: a three-year diploma program conducted by a hospital, a bachelor's degree program at a college, and an associate degree program offered in a two-year junior or community college. Nurses who plan a career in teaching and research will need to have a doctorate in nursing. There are many opportunities for specialization through a master's degree program, including a master's in public health leading to careers in administration.

Personal Skills   Ability to accept responsibility, initiative, good judgment, mental and physical stamina, and the ability to make reasoned decisions.

How Many Nurses Are There and Where Do They Work?

There are 1,835,000 registered nurses; 95 percent are women, 7 percent are black, and 3 percent are Hispanic. Most (66 percent) work in hospitals. Others are employed by agencies, nursing homes, the government, and families for private duty. Twenty-five percent work part time.

How Much Money Will I Make?

In 1993 the minimum median income for nurses was $27,476 a year; those with experience earned $33,278, while the top 10 percent made more than $41,563. Those working in nursing homes made less; the median was $22,300 a year. Nurse anesthetists averaged $66,622 and nurse practitioners $43,680.

What Are the Job Opportunities?

The number of nurses has sharply declined in the past five years. Nursing school enrollments are up for the first time in 20 years. There is projected growth of 44 percent by 2005, bringing the numbers of nurses to 2,494,000. Opportunities for all nursing jobs will be excellent though 2005. Nursing may be one of the most exciting, expansive, developing professions in the next decade. Salaries, advancement opportunities, and fringe benefits are increasing rapidly. The shortage of nurses provides diverse opportunities. Increasing numbers of men are entering nursing as they learn that the 1.5 percent unemployment rate for nurses is one of the lowest in the entire work force.

Related Careers

Occupational therapist	Health service manager
Doctor	Physical therapist

Where Can I Get More Information?

American Nurses' Association
600 Maryland Avenue, SW
Suite 100 W
Washington, DC 20024

National League for Nursing
350 Hudson Street
New York, NY 10014

Optometrist

Examines people's eyes for vision problems and disease, and tests eyes for depth, color, and focus perceptions

What's It Like to Be an Optometrist?

"I work with young adults who want their first contact lenses. Contacts change the client's looks completely, and when a client is happy with the results, it makes my day," says optometrist Geno Grattini, father of three preschool children. "I work from 8 a.m. until 6 p.m. and I like every aspect of my work. I'm my own boss and I make all the decisions. The most exciting part of the work is when I hold up different lenses for children and ask them what they can see, and they give me a cat-ate-the-canary grin, suddenly realizing the things they haven't seen clearly before."

Optometrists use instrumentation and observation to examine eye health and to correct patients' visual problems. Optometrists have a doctor's degree in optometry, but unlike ophthalmologists, they do not have a medical degree. They often provide postoperative care to cataract and other patients of ophthalmologists.

What Education and Skills Will I Need?

High School   Preparation for college, emphasizing science.

College   Two years of college are required for admission to the four-year program of a college of optometry, which grants a Doctor of Optometry (O.D.) degree. Subjects required in college are English, mathematics, biology, physics, and chemistry. There are 16 accredited schools of optometry in the United States. Optometrists must be licensed in the state in which they work.

Personal Skills   Business ability (most optometrists are self-employed), self-discipline, and tact with patients are needed.

How Many Optometrists Are There and Where Do They Work?

There are 31,000 optometrists; only 2 percent are women, 1 percent are black, and 1 percent are Hispanic. Thirty-two percent are self-employed; others work in group practice and for retail optical goods businesses.

How Much Money Will I Make?

In 1992 beginning optometrists averaged $45,000 a year. Experienced optometrists averaged $75,000 a year.

What Are the Job Opportunities?

The increasing age of the population with an accompanying need for glasses, the value of good vision for all ages, and health insurance coverage of vision problems will continue to contribute to good opportunities for jobs.

Related Careers

Chiropractor   Podiatrist
Dentist   Nurse

Where Can I Get More Information?

American Optometric Student Association
243 North Lindbergh
St. Louis, MO 63141

Osteopathic Physician

Diagnoses and treats diseases, with special emphasis on the musculoskeletal system—bones, muscles, ligaments, and nerves

What's It Like to Be an Osteopathic Physician?

One of the basic treatments used by an osteopathic physician (D.O.) centers on manipulating the musculoskeletal system with the hands. The D.O. also uses surgery, drugs, and all other accepted methods of medical care. Most osteopathic physicians are in family practice and engage in general medicine. These physicians usually see patients in their offices, make house calls, and treat patients in one of the 200 osteopathic hospitals.

What Education and Skills Will I Need?

High School Preparation for college, with an emphasis on science and mathematics.

College Most osteopathic students have a college degree, with courses that include biology, chemistry, physics, and English, to qualify for a three- or four-year program in one of the 16 colleges of osteopathy. They are awarded the degree of Doctor of Osteopathy (D.O.).

Personal Skills A strong interest in osteopathic principles of healing, a keen sense of touch, and self-confidence are needed.

How Many Osteopathic Physicians Are There and Where Do They Work?

There are 20,000 D.O.'s; 87 percent of them are men. Almost 85 percent are in private practice, chiefly in states with osteopathic hospitals. Four-fifths of all osteopathic physicians practice in Michigan, Pennsylvania, Ohio, Florida, Texas, and New Jersey. More than half practice in towns with fewer than 50,000 people.

How Much Money Will I Make?

In 1991 the average salary for family physicians, including D.O.'s, was $98,000 a year.

What Are the Job Opportunities?

Chances for work will be very good through 2005, especially in states with osteopathic hospitals.

Related Careers

Chiropractor   Optometrist
Dentist   Doctor (M.D.)

Where Can I Get More Information?

American Association of Colleges of Osteopathic Medicine
6110 Executive Building
No. 405
Rockville, MD 20852

Pharmacist

Selects, compounds, dispenses, and preserves drugs and medicines to fill prescriptions written by physicians and dentists

What's It Like to Be a Pharmacist?

"I dispense medication to hospital patients and staff, write up orders to pharmaceutical houses, compound and manufacture pharmaceuticals, and answer questions about drugs from nurses and physicians," says June Marie Jones, assistant director of the pharmacy in a university hospital. "In addition, I meet with nursing staff to discuss patient care and medication, meet with physicians, and write the Pharmacy Bulletin, which gives doctors and nurses the latest information on drugs. After gaining experience, I plan to go into business for myself. Most women in pharmacy work for others. I've decided I want to be the owner of a drugstore—where the money is."

Pharmacists often develop computerized records of patients, drug therapies, and medical profiles to help patients choose over-the-counter medicines and to check the compatibility of prescriptions from different doctors. *Pharmacotherapists* specialize in drug therapy and work closely with physicians, talk to patients, and monitor pharmaceutical use.

What Education and Skills Will I Need?

High School   Preparation for college, with an emphasis on biology, chemistry, mathematics and computer science.

College   Seventy-four U.S. colleges and universities offer an accredited five-year degree program in pharmacy. The program includes chemistry, physics, mathematics, computer science, zoology, and physiology. Each state has its own licensing requirements.

Personal Skills   Business ability, interest in medicine, orderliness, accuracy, and the ability to build customers' confidence are needed for success in pharmacy.

How Many Pharmacists Are There and Where Do They Work?

There are 163,000 pharmacists; 37 percent are women, 4 percent are black, and 4 percent are Hispanic. They work in drugstores (65 percent) and hospitals (25 percent). Approximately 14 percent are employed part time.

How Much Money Will I Make?

Pharmacy pays better than do most health-related careers that require the same level of education. In 1992, the median salary for those working in chain pharmacies was $45,000 a year. In hospitals, experienced pharmacists earned a median of $50,300. Those working for HMO's averaged $52,300 a year. Independent pharmacists made much more than that if they owned their own drugstore.

What Are the Job Opportunities?

Job opportunities are excellent. The number of pharmacy graduates went down in the 1980s, creating a shortage of pharmacists through 2003. The increased age of the population and health insurance coverage of prescriptions will lead to a strong demand for pharmacists.

Related Careers

Pharmaceutical chemist
Dietitian
Nurse

Pharmaceutical sales
representative

Where Can I Get More Information?

American Association of Colleges of Pharmacy
1426 Prince Street
Alexandria, VA 22314

American Society of Hospital Pharmacists
4630 Montgomery Avenue
Bethesda, MD 20814

Physician Assistant

Provides primary care to medical patients and assists doctors with medical and surgical procedures

What's It Like to Be a Physician Assistant?

Physician assistants (PAs) take medical histories, perform physical examinations, order laboratory tests, make preliminary diagnoses, and give inoculations. They also treat minor injuries by suturing, splinting, and casting. In some states, physician assistants prescribe medications. They may also have managerial duties. Physician assistants always work under the supervision of a doctor. In some rural areas and inner-city clinics where doctors are scarce, they may treat patients all week and see a doctor for consultation once a week. This job emerged in part because of the shortage of health-care workers and because men often hesitate to go into nursing, viewing it as a woman's job. Physician assistant positions have helped draw men into "helping" jobs in health care.

What Education and Skills Will I Need?

High School Preparation for college, with an emphasis on science.

College All physician assistant programs require at least two years of college and some experience in health care. Thirty-seven colleges offer degree programs, and there are 55 two-year programs offered by medical schools, schools of allied health, and community colleges.

Personal Skills   Self-confidence, emotional stability, and a desire to care for the sick are necessary to be successful in this career.

How Many Physician Assistants Are There and Where Do They Work?

There are 58,000 physician assistants, most of whom work in physicians' offices and in clinics. Others work in hospitals and in public health clinics, nursing homes, and prisons. The majority are men.

How Much Money Will I Make?

In 1993 the starting salary for physician assistants working in hospitals and medical schools was $32,466. The average salary for all physician assistants was between $50,000 and $55,000. Most physician assistants are men and therefore make more money than women in comparable jobs. Young women should consider this health field.

What Are the Job Opportunities?

Job opportunities are expected to be excellent for physician assistants, especially in rural and inner-city clinics. With good pay and minimum educational requirements, this is the job for health-care workers who want to take on a lot of responsibility.

Related Careers

Nurse practitioner   Physical therapist
Occupational therapist

Where Can I Get More Information?

American Academy of Physician Assistants
950 North Washington Street
Alexandria, VA 22314

Podiatrist

Prevents, diagnoses, and treats foot diseases and injuries

What's It Like to Be a Podiatrist?

Podiatrists take X-rays and perform tests to diagnose diseases, injuries, and other disorders of the foot. Depending on the condition, they perform surgery, fit corrective devices or proper shoes, and prescribe drugs and physical therapy. Many young podiatrists specialize in sports injuries of the foot and the lower leg. Others are generalists and treat corns, bunions, calluses, ingrown toenails, skin and nail diseases, deformed toes, and arch disabilities. Most podiatrists are generalists and provide all types of foot care.

What Education and Skills Will I Need?

High School   Preparation for college, with strong emphasis on science and mathematics.

College   Most students of podiatric medicine are college graduates and go on to one of the six podiatric colleges for four years.

Personal Skills   Manual dexterity, scientific interest, ability to perform detailed work, and a pleasant personality are all important for success in podiatry.

How Many Podiatrists Are There and Where Do They Work?

There are 14,700 podiatrists; about 12 percent are women, 1 percent are black, and less than 1 percent are Hispanic. Fifty-one percent are self-employed, others (16 percent) work in hospitals, and 10 percent work in nursing homes.

How Much Money Will I Make?

In 1993 beginning podiatrists averaged $35,578 a year. Established podiatrists averaged $100,287 a year.

What Are the Job Opportunities?

Opportunities are very good because of the growing elderly population; because of the continued popularity of jogging and other fast-moving sports that often result in foot and lower-leg injuries; and because podiatry is well covered by health insurance.

Related Careers

Chiropractor   Dentist

Optometrist   Nurse

Where Can I Get More Information?

American Association of Colleges of Podiatric Medicine
1350 Piccard Drive, Suite 322
Rockville, MD 20850

American Podiatric Medical Association
9312 Old Georgetown Road
Bethesda, MD 20814

Veterinarian

Prevents, diagnoses, treats, and controls diseases and injuries of animals

What's It Like to Be a Veterinarian?

Veterinarians treat animals in hospitals and clinics or on farms and ranches. They perform surgery on sick and injured animals and prescribe and administer drugs, medicine, and vaccines. A large number of vets specialize in the health and breeding of cattle, poultry, sheep, swine, or horses. Their work is important for the nation's food production and also for public health. Amy Merrit, D.V.M., is a partner in a Kansas veterinary clinic. She likes the physical and intellectual challenge of her career. She says that a vet must really have an inquiring mind. "So much of veterinary medicine is a puzzle, and there is no book of treatments to cover all diseases or solve most of the problems." Specialties in veterinary medicine include research, federal health services, teaching, hospital staff service, self-employment, and working in a partner-ship or clinic.

What Education and Skills Will I Need?

High School   Preparation for college, with emphasis on biologi-cal sciences.

College   Two years of preveterinary medicine are required for ad-mission into one of the 27 accredited four-year veterinary col-leges.

Personal Skills   Manual dexterity and the ability to calm ani-mals that are upset, to communicate with animal owners, and to make decisions in emergencies are important qualities for success as a vet. Since many animals live outside, a love of the outdoors is helpful.

How Many Veterinarians Are There and Where Do They Work?

There are 44,000 veterinarians and veterinary inspectors; 24 per-cent are women. Most (43 percent) are self-employed; others work for agricultural services and the federal government.

How Much Money Will I Make?

In 1991 veterinarians started at an average of $27,857 a year in private practice. Experienced vets averaged $63,069 a year.

What Are the Job Opportunities?

Job opportunities are expected to be very good through 2005. The rise in pet ownership among 34- to 59-year-olds, who are able to spend money on their pets, will increase job opportunities. Other good opportunities are for those who specialize in small-animal practice, toxicology, and pathology. Jobs in rural areas are plen-tiful because most young graduates want to live and work in met-ropolitan areas.

Related Careers

Dentist
Chiropractor

Doctor
Podiatrist

Where Can I Get More Information?

American Veterinary Medical Association
930 North Meacham Road
Schaumburg, IL 60196

Association of American Veterinary Medical Colleges
1101 Vermont Avenue, Suite 710
Washington, DC 20005

THERAPIST

Occupational Therapist

Plans and directs activities to help patients return to work; aids patients to adjust to their disabilities

What's It Like to Be an Occupational Therapist?

An occupational therapist works as a member of a medical team with a doctor, physical therapist, vocational counselor, nurse, and social worker. Therapists teach skills that range from office procedures to the use of power tools. The goals of the therapist are to help patients gain physical stability, combat boredom during long illnesses, and develop independence in performing routine daily skills such as eating, dressing, and writing. "The biggest problem of being a man in a woman's world, as most occupational therapists are women," explains Julio Gigetti, "is that the money isn't there. For the time being, I'll stay in occupational therapy until I can't afford the luxury of a job I love so much." Rod Whalen has a master's degree from the University of Illinois and has worked for a year on the design, construction, and application of splints. He guides his patients in the selection of adaptive equipment used in his clinic at the Illinois Medical Center.

What Education and Skills Will I Need?

High School   Preparation for college, with emphasis on science, crafts, and social science.

College   Sixty-five colleges and universities offer a degree in occupational therapy. Many college graduates go into occupational therapy from a variety of majors—often biology or physical education—and get a master's degree in occupational therapy in one year.

Personal Skills   An advocate's attitude toward the sick and disabled, manual skills, maturity, patience, and imagination are needed.

How Many Occupational Therapists Are There and Where Do They Work?

There are 40,000 occupational therapists; 95 percent are women, 1 percent are black, and 4 percent are Hispanic. Most (43 percent) work in hospitals, 17 percent work in educational services, and 11 percent work for state and local governments. Twenty-one percent work part time.

How Much Money Will I Make?

In 1992 salaries ranged from $30,470 to $44,958 a year. Managers earned more than $45,000 a year, and beginners working for the federal government started at $26,900 a year.

What Are the Job Opportunities?

The future is expected to be excellent through 2005, with over 2,000 new job openings each year. Occupational therapy is one of the 20 fastest-growing occupations. The expanding older population, the saving of children with birth defects, and the reduced enrollment in occupational therapy degree programs will result in more jobs than graduates. The number of occupational therapists in private practice is increasing, and their salaries are higher because they can bill Medicare and get contracts through home health-care agencies.

Related Careers

Physical therapist	Nurse
Rehabilitation counselor	Recreation therapist

Where Can I Get More Information?

American Occupational Therapy Association
1383 Piccard Drive
P.O. Box 1725
Rockville, MD 20849

Physical Therapist

Uses exercise, massage, heat, water, and electricity to treat and rehabilitate people with disabilities

What's It Like to Be a Physical Therapist?

Physical therapists perform and interpret tests and measurements for muscle strength, motor development, functioning capacity, and respiratory and circulatory efficiency. They plan a program of therapy to include the following: exercises for increasing strength, endurance, and coordination; stimuli to make motor activity and learning easier; instructions to carry out everyday activities; and applications of massage, heat and cold, light, water, or electricity to relieve pain or improve the condition of muscles. Ernie Natlette says what he likes best about being a physical therapist is the great variety of patients he deals with—accident victims, crippled children, disabled older persons, cardiac rehabilitation patients, pulmonary patients, and more. He also likes the interaction with other health-care professionals who are working with his patients.

What Education and Skills Will I Need?

High School Preparation for college, with emphasis on science.

College There are 78 bachelor's degree programs and 44 master's degree programs. A physical therapy major begins in the freshman year, and the class fills up fast. In many cases you must apply for college by October of your senior year to get into one of these very competitive programs; many are closed by Thanksgiving. It's very difficult to transfer into physical therapy because few students leave the program.

Personal Skills Resourcefulness, patience, manual dexterity, physical stamina, and the ability to work with disabled people and their families are needed to be a good physical therapist.

How Many Physical Therapists Are There and Where Do They Work?

One-fourth of the 90,000 therapists are men, 4 percent are black, and 3 percent are Hispanic. About half work in hospitals, and 18 percent are in private practice. The government and the armed forces also employ many physical therapists. Twenty-seven percent work part time.

How Much Money Will I Make?

In 1993 physical therapists averaged $35,464 a year. Experienced therapists earned $45,300, and the top 10 percent made around $52,468.

What Are the Job Opportunities?

The opportunities will remain excellent through 2005. One of the 20 fastest-growing careers, physical therapy is expected to provide 155,000 jobs by 2005, a growth rate of 76 percent. New graduates are not keeping up with the number of jobs available. Advances in medical technology and an aging population are contributing to increased job opportunities.

Related Careers

Occupational therapist   Recreation therapist
Speech therapist   Nurse

Where Can I Get More Information?

American Physical Therapy Association
1111 North Fairfax Street
Alexandria, VA 22314

Recreation Therapist

Designs activities to help people with disabilities lead ful-filling and independent lives

What's It Like to Be a Recreation Therapist?

Jan Woodward, a recreation therapist in Norwalk, Connecticut, found out about this career after being a physical education teacher for eight years. She took a master's degree while teaching, and has now turned her sports, games, dance, drama, arts and crafts, music, and field trips school program into a community mental health program. Woodward says she plans medically approved activities to treat the physical and emotional needs of her patients. She rehabilitates people with specific medical problems, working in cooperation with doctors, nurses, psychologists, social workers, and occupational therapists. Woodward encourages group activities to improve general health and well-being. Sometimes she is called upon to plan programs for area nursing homes, for a residential facility for adolescents, and for the Norwalk Community Recreation Department.

What Education and Skills Will I Need?

High School   Preparation for college, with as many leadership and sports activities as possible, plus an emphasis on science.

College   Sixty-two degree programs for recreation therapists are accredited by the National Council on Accreditation.

Personal Skills   Patience, tact, and a persuasive personality are necessary for success in this field. Imagination and physical fitness are also important.

How Many Recreation Therapists Are There and Where Do They Work?

There are 30,000 recreation therapists and most of them are women. Forty percent work in hospitals; another third work in nursing homes. Others are employed in community mental health centers, adult day-care programs, correctional facilities, and substance abuse centers.

How Much Money Will I Make?

In 1991 the average salary for recreation therapists working in nursing homes was between $15,000 and $25,000. Salaries remain low; part-time opportunities are good.

What Are the Job Opportunities?

Job prospects are expected to be good through 2005. The expansion of long-term care, provision of more services for the disabled, and the fact that few graduates are coming out of recreation therapist programs will assure jobs in this interesting, but poorly paid, career.

Related Careers

Occupational therapist   Music therapist
Physical education teacher   Nurse

Where Can I Get More Information?

National Therapeutic Recreation Society
2775 South Quincy Street
Suite 300
Arlington, VA 22206

Respiratory Therapist

Evaluates, treats, and cares for patients with breathing disorders

What's It Like to Be a Respiratory Therapist?

"A person may live without water for a few days and without food for a few weeks. But without oxygen, a person will suffer serious brain damage within a few minutes and death after nine minutes or so," warns respiratory therapist Paul Graff. In evaluating patients, respiratory therapists test lung capacity and analyze oxygen and carbon dioxide concentrations and hydrogen potential, a measure of the acidity or alkalinity of the blood. To measure lung capacity, respiratory therapists have patients breathe into an instrument that measures the volume and flow of air during inhalation and exhalation. By comparing the reading with the norm for the patient's age, height, weight, and sex, respiratory therapists can determine whether lung deficiencies exist. Respiratory therapists relay the results of their tests to the doctors on the case. They treat all kinds of patients—premature babies whose lungs are not fully developed as well as elderly people whose lungs are diseased. Graff says that his job also includes giving temporary relief to patients with chronic asthma or emphysema and emergency care to heart failure, stroke, drowning, or shock victims.

What Education and Skills Will I Need?

High School   Preparation for college, with an emphasis on science and mathematics; volunteering for community emergency medical service or firefighter programs.

College   Qualify as a Certified Respiratory Therapy Technician (C.R.T.T.) and a Registered Respiratory Therapist (R.R.T.) by completing a two- or four-year program.

Personal Skills   Sensitivity to patients' physical and psychological needs; ability to pay attention to detail, follow instructions, and work as part of a team are necessary skills.

How Many Respiratory Therapists Are There and Where Do They Work?

There are 74,000 respiratory therapists; 60 percent are women, 12 percent are black, and 3 percent are Hispanic. Most (90 percent) work in hospitals.

How Much Money Will I Make?

In 1993 hospital salaries for respiratory therapists ranged from $24,770 to $36,553 a year. The top 10 percent earned over $48,000.

What Are the Job Opportunities?

Like most health-care jobs, respiratory therapy is expected to provide very good opportunities through 2005. The growth in the elderly population and increases in the numbers of premature babies and in patients with AIDS will all boost the demand for respiratory therapists.

Related Careers

Occupational therapist
Physical therapist

Nurse
Radiation therapist

Where Can I Get More Information?

American Association for Respiratory Care
11030 Ables Lane
Dallas, TX 75229

Speech Therapist, Hearing Therapist

Diagnoses and treats people who are unable to speak or hear clearly

What's It Like to Be a Speech Therapist or a Hearing Therapist?

Speech and hearing therapists, also called speech pathologists and audiologists, work with children and adults who have communication disorders (speech, hearing, language, learning). This work may be with one person or with small groups. Lessons vary from one-half hour in length to group classes of two hours and deal with problems of stuttering, defective articulation, brain damage, mental retardation, or emotional disturbance. The responsibility of the therapist is to identify and evaluate the disorder; consult with the other specialists involved, such as the physician, psychologist, social worker, or counselor; and organize a program of therapy.

What Education and Skills Will I Need?

High School Preparation for college, with a strong science program.

College Most students major in speech pathology and audiology, or in any related field such as education, psychology, or education for the blind or deaf, to prepare for graduate school. A master's degree from one of the 230 programs offered is required for professional certification in most states. Many scholarships and fellowships are available from graduate schools through the United States Vocational Rehabilitation Administration.

Personal Skills Patience with slow progress, a sense of responsibility, objectivity, ability to work with detail, and concern for the needs of others are important for therapists.

How Many Speech and Hearing Therapists Are There and Where Do They Work?

Of the 73,000 speech and hearing therapists, 12 percent are men, 3 percent are black, and 3 percent are Hispanic. Most (91 percent) work in special education programs in public schools and in hospitals.

How Much Money Will I Make?

In 1993 salaries in hospitals and medical centers ranged from $29,050 to $41,300 a year. Audiologists earned up to $45,000. Public school therapists earned the same salary as other teachers.

What Are the Job Opportunities?

Job opportunities will be excellent. The number of positions is expected to increase by 34 percent to 91,000 jobs by 2005. The federal government is committed to special education, where most of these jobs are. Increased numbers of young school children will mean more jobs for graduates.

Related Careers

Occupational therapist   Physical therapist
Teacher   Optometrist

Where Can I Get More Information?

American Speech-Language-Hearing Association
10801 Rockville Pike
Rockville, MD 20852

ALLIED HEALTH

Medical Illustrator

Creates graphics designed to communicate medical information through a variety of media

What's It Like to Be a Medical Illustrator?

Medical illustrators draw illustrations of parts of the human body, animals, plants, surgical procedures, and patient-care techniques. These illustrations are used in medical textbooks and in slide and video presentations for teaching purposes. Medical illustrators also work for doctors and lawyers, producing exhibits for court cases.

Emery Elrod has been involved in drawing, painting, sculpting, layout design, typography, computer graphics, and electronic imaging in the past three years on the job. He has never specialized—although many of his classmates have—because he enjoys handling a great variety of ever-changing assignments. Elrod has been a member of many medical illustration teams that provide the highly accurate medical illustrations used in medical books, journals, films, videotapes, exhibits, posters, wall charts, and computer programs. After a few more years, Elrod hopes to manage a biomedical communications center or direct the illustration services of a major teaching hospital.

What Education and Skills Will I Need?

High School Preparation for college, with biological science, chemistry, and art and drawing courses.

College Preparation for one of the six accredited master's programs in medical illustration, with a balance of art, premedical biology, and the humanities. Applicants for a master's program must submit a portfolio of their artwork.

Personal Skills Artistic and drawing skills, knowledge of anatomy and physiology, and draftsmanship are all required.

How Many Medical Illustrators Are There and Where Do They Work?

There are 50,000 medical illustrators, including those who free-lance. They work mostly for medical schools, large medical centers, and medical publishers. Free-lancers get much of their work from pharmaceutical houses and advertising agencies.

How Much Money Will I Make?

In 1993 medical illustrators averaged between $28,000 and $40,000 per year. Most free-lancers had other jobs as well.

What Are the Job Opportunities?

Like all art-related jobs, illustration opportunities will be competitive through the late 1990s.

Related Careers

Architect

Biologist

Publications illustrator

Visual artist

Where Can I Get More Information?

Association of Medical Illustrators
1819 Peachtree Street, NE, Suite 560
Atlanta, GA 30309

Medical Technologist

Performs chemical, microscopic, and bacteriological tests under the supervision of a pathologist to diagnose the causes and nature of diseases

What's It Like to Be a Medical Technologist?

Medical technologists perform tests, ordered by the physician, to determine blood count, blood cholesterol level, and so forth. They also do skin tests and examine other body fluids and tissues microscopically for bacteria, fungi, and other organisms. In small hospitals the medical technologists do all procedures; in larger hospitals they specialize in an area such as the study of blood cells or tissue preparation and examination. Medical technologists are usually assisted by medical and laboratory technicians who perform simple tests. The routine tasks of medical technologists are performed by computer, so more specialization is now required of the technologist.

What Education and Skills Will I Need?

High School Preparation for college, with emphasis on science and mathematics.

College A college degree or one year of special training after three years of college is required. Chemistry, biology, mathematics, and computer science are required courses.

Personal Skills Manual dexterity and good eyesight, accuracy, and ability to work under pressure are essential.

How Many Medical Technologists Are There and Where Do They Work?

There are 268,000 medical technicians and technologists. About 50,000 of these are technologists with a college degree. Seventy-six percent are women, 5 percent are black, and 4 percent are Hispanic. Most (70 percent) work in hospitals, 12 percent in doctors' offices, and 11 percent for medical and dental laboratories.

How Much Money Will I Make?

In 1993 the average starting salary was $24,888 a year. Experienced technologists averaged $36,844 a year. Chief technologists made more than $45,000.

What Are the Job Opportunities?

Chances for a job will be excellent through 2005. Increased use of laboratory tests for chemotherapy patients, for example, has created more jobs. The number of graduates in medical technology declined during the 1980s, resulting in a shortage in this field. The demands are for those with advanced technological skills, because computer systems do the routine work.

Related Careers

Chemistry technologist   Dietitian
Food tester   Nurse

Where Can I Get More Information?

American Medical Technologists
710 Higgins Road
Park Ridge, IL 60068

Nuclear Medicine Technologist

Utilizes the properties of radioactive and stable nuclides for diagnostic evaluation and radioactive therapy

What's It Like to Be a Nuclear Medicine Technologist?

Joan Guilford, a nuclear medicine technologist, greets the patient coming into the nuclear medicine unit at Memorial Sloan-Kettering Cancer Center in New York City and describes the procedure for bone and liver scans. She explains to the patient that the injection to be received is a radioisotope. An isotope is a radioactive tracer material that will enable technologists to get "pictures," or scans, of the area of interest. For a bone scan, the injection is given two hours before scanning. During this time the patient may eat and should drink an extra two glasses of liquid. The scan itself will take about 30 minutes. When the scan is finished, it will be developed, and physicians will read it (much the same way as X rays are read) and send the results to the patient's doctor, who informs the patient.

In addition to its diagnostic purposes, nuclear medicine is also used as a treatment for cancer to reduce the size of tumors and in place of surgery to eliminate cancer cells. Nuclear medicine technologists work with radiologists, who are M.D.'s in this field.

What Education and Skills Will I Need?

High School   Preparation for college, with an emphasis on mathematics, biology, physics, chemistry, and computer science.

College   The nuclear medicine technology curriculum includes patient care, nuclear physics, health physics, biochemistry, radiation biology, clinical nuclear medicine, and computer science.

Personal Skills   Manual dexterity and good eyesight are essential, as well as accuracy and the ability to work under pressure and to help patients remain calm.

How Many Nuclear Medicine Technologists Are There and Where Do They Work?

There are 12,000 nuclear medicine technicians; 76 percent are women, 13 percent are black, and 5 percent are Hispanic. Nine-tenths work in hospitals and major medical centers. Others work in clinical research, education, and administration.

How Much Money Will I Make?

In 1993 entry-level salaries averaged $26,402 a year. The size and location of the hospital determine salaries and promotions. Technicians with experience averaged $38,840.

What Are the Job Opportunities?

Projections estimate 268,000 jobs in this field by 2005, a 68 percent increase.

Related Careers

Cardiovascular technologist   Respiratory therapist
Clinical laboratory
  technologist

Where Can I Get More Information?

Society of Nuclear Medicine
136 Madison Avenue, 8th Floor
New York, NY 10016

Science

- **Agricultural scientist**
- **Biologist**
- **Chemist**
- **Conservationist**
- **Environmentalist**
- **Geoscientist**
- **Physicist**

ABOUT SCIENCE CAREERS

Science will be the career opportunity for the late 1990s, when the whole world changes its focus from defense to cleaning up the environment. Many science jobs that required a Ph.D. are now open to science graduates, right out of college, who know anything at all about conservation, biology, chemistry, or environmental studies.

A bachelor's degree is usually needed to enter scientific and engineering careers. In mathematics and in physical and biological sciences, more emphasis is placed on advanced degrees. For some careers, such as astronomy, a doctorate is required for full professional status. Undergraduate training for scientists includes courses in their major field and in related science areas, including mathematics. Courses and skills in computer science are important for all scientists.

Students who want to specialize in a particular area of science should select their colleges carefully. For example, those who plan to become biomedical engineers or biochemists and work in medicine should study at a university affiliated with a research hospital. Those who want to be agricultural scientists can get the best practical training at state universities with agricultural research and development programs.

Working conditions in scientific careers, such as forestry, range management, engineering, geology, and meteorology, can involve considerable time away from home, working outdoors in remote parts of the country. Foresters may also work extra hours on emergency duty, such as in firefighting or on search-and-rescue missions.

Exploration geologists often work overseas. They travel to remote sites by helicopter and jeep and cover large areas by foot, often working in teams. Geologists in mining sometimes work underground. Meteorologists in small weather stations generally work alone; those in large stations work as part of a team.

New science graduates begin working under the close supervision of experienced scientists. To determine the specialties for which graduates are best suited, many companies have special programs to acquaint new engineers with industrial practices. Experienced scientists may advance to positions of greater responsibility; those with proven ability often become managers and in increasingly large numbers are being promoted to top management jobs. Some scientists take a Master of Business Administration (M.B.A.) to improve their advancement opportunities, while others take law degrees and become patent attorneys or consultants.

Science is the field with the most jobs. If you want to have the best job opportunities, think seriously about science. Whatever your career choice, add some technical skills to your credentials so that you can translate the arts, business, or social sciences into science opportunities.

Agricultural Scientist

Uses the principles of biology, chemistry, and other sciences to solve problems in agriculture

What's It Like to Be an Agricultural Scientist?

Agricultural scientists study farm crops and animals and develop ways of improving their quality and quantity. They usually specialize in one of the following areas: Food scientists discover new food sources; analyze food content to determine levels of vitamins, fat, sugar, or protein; and search for substitutes for harmful or undesirable additives. Animal scientists do research on the breeding, feeding, and diseases of domestic farm animals. They study genetics, nutrition, reproduction, growth, and development. Plant scientists study plants to develop ways to feed a growing population while conserving natural resources. Horticulturists work with orchard and garden plants such as fruit and nut trees, vegetables, and flowers. They also seek to improve plant cultivation methods for cleaning the environment and for beautifying communities, homes, and parks. Soil scientists provide information and recommendations to farmers and other landowners regarding the best use of land and how to avoid or correct problems.

What Education and Skills Will I Need?

High School   Preparation for college, with an emphasis on science.

College   Each state has at least one land-grant college that offers agricultural science. Many students major in biology, chemistry, or physics and get a graduate degree in agriculture.

Personal Skills   Ability to work independently or as part of a team and the ability to communicate findings clearly and concisely, both orally and in writing.

How Many Agricultural Scientists Are There and Where Do They Work?

There are 29,000 agricultural scientists, including college professors; 20 percent are women, less than 1 percent are black, and 4 percent are Hispanic. Many work for universities (21 percent), others work for local government (16 percent) or federal government (14 percent), and still others for agricultural businesses and services (11 percent).

How Much Money Will I Make?

In 1992 the average starting salary with a bachelor's degree was $20,189 in animal science and $22,150 in plant science. The federal government started agricultural scientists with a master's degree at $23,678 or $25,256. Experienced agricultural scientists working for the federal government averaged $44,802.

What Are the Job Opportunities?

Jobs opportunities will be good through 2005 because government spending on the environment will increase. The best jobs will go to those with a background in molecular biology, microbiology, genetics, or biotechnology and to soil scientists with an interest in the environment.

Related Careers

Chemist

Extension service worker

Conservationist

Veterinarian

Where Can I Get More Information?

Soil Science Society of America
677 South Segoe Road
Madison, WI 53711

Soil and Water Conservation Society
7515 Northeast Arkeny Road
Arkeny, IA 50021-9764

Biologist

Studies the structure, evolution, behavior, and life processes of living organisms

What's It Like to Be a Biologist?

Major industry is just beginning to find applications for the new biology—that is, genetic engineering to manufacture living materials. For example, bacteria are being used to convert sunlight into electrochemical energy, and new forms of bacteria are being bred to replace nuclear power plants. More traditional biologists are working to improve medicine, to increase crop yields, and to improve our natural environment. The biological sciences include many branches, such as botany, in which all aspects of plant life are studied, and zoology, which deals with animal life. Zoologists usually specialize in birds, insects, or mammals. Other fields of biological specialization are genetics, horticulture, nutrition, and pharmacology. Biologists usually work in the field or in a laboratory with a team of scientists, publish their findings, and also teach. Sometimes called life scientists, they study all aspects of living organisms, emphasizing the relationship of animals and plants to their environment. Creating entirely new foods and fibers by cheap and simple methods will be the biologists' work of the late 1990s. Biologists will also be major players on the science teams for cleaning up the environment.

What Education and Skills Will I Need?

High School   Preparation for college and graduate school, with as much science, mathematics, and computer science as possible.

College   Major in any biological science and get as broad an understanding as possible of all sciences, including chemistry, physics, mathematics, and computer science.

Personal Skills   Ability to work independently or with a team, curiosity, and good communication skills are necessary for the biologist.

How Many Biologists Are There and Where Do They Work?

There are 117,000 biologists; 41 percent are women, 3 percent are black, and 3 percent are Hispanic. Many of them work for the federal government (26 percent); others work for state governments (14 percent), for chemical manufacturers (12 percent), and for research and development companies (11 percent).

How Much Money Will I Make?

In 1992 private industry offered an average starting salary of $21,850 a year for biologists with a bachelors' degree. Biologists with a master's degree made from $26,000 to $46,800 a year.

What Are the Job Opportunities?

Opportunities are expected to be very good through 2005, especially in private industry, in research, and in the genetic, cellular, and biochemical areas of biology. While federal cuts are expected in long-term science projects, a bachelor's degree in biology is all it takes to get one of the many jobs focusing on the environment or on health care.

Related Careers

Forester
Biochemist
Agricultural scientist
Geologist

Where Can I Get More Information?

American Institute of Biological Sciences
730 Eleventh Street, NW
Washington, DC 20001

American Society for Microbiology
Office of Scientific Affairs
1325 Massachusetts Avenue, NW
Washington, DC 20005

Chemist

Studies the properties and composition of substances and organisms

What's It Like to Be a Chemist?

In basic research, a chemist investigates ways to create or improve new products. The process of developing a product begins with descriptions of needed items. If similar products exist, the chemist tests samples to determine their ingredients. If no such product exists, the chemist experiments with various substances until a product is found with the required specifications. Chemists usually specialize: An analytical chemist determines the composition and nature of substances; an organic chemist studies the chemistry of carbon compounds; an inorganic chemist studies compounds other than carbon; a physical chemist studies energy; a biochemist studies living matter. Some biochemists go into biotechnology (applied biological science) and become genetic engineers; there are now over 6,000 of them. Genetic engineers design or alter the genetic material of animals and plants to enable them to do things they cannot do naturally. In medicine, biotechnology will lead to new, better, and cheaper drugs.

What Education and Skills Will I Need?

High School   Preparation for college, with as much science, mathematics, and computer science as possible.

College   Almost 600 colleges offer a bachelor's degree in chemistry. Mathematics and physics are required for all chemists. The top jobs in research require a Ph.D. as well as computer skills.

Personal Skills   Interest in studying math and science, good hand coordination for building scientific apparatus, and ability to concentrate on detail are essential for the chemist.

How Many Chemists Are There and Where Do They Work?

There are 92,000 chemists; 24 percent are women, 4 percent are black, and 2 percent are Hispanic. Chemists work for chemical product manufacturers (37 percent), research and development labs

(11 percent), durable goods manufacturers (10 percent), and the federal government (10 percent).

How Much Money Will I Make?

In 1992 private industry started college graduates at $24,000, holders of master's degrees at $32,000, and Ph.D.'s at $48,000 a year. Experienced chemists with Ph.D.'s averaged $58,000 a year.

What Are the Job Opportunities?

Manufacturing is slowing down in the United States. The best job opportunities will be for chemists specializing in polymers and synthetics, analytical chemistry, and food chemistry. Jobs are expected to be competitive through 2005.

Related Careers

Agricultural scientist   Biological scientist
Chemical engineer   Physicist

Where Can I Get More Information?

American Chemical Society
1155 Sixteenth Street, NW
Washington, DC 20036

Conservationist

Manages, develops, and protects forest, rangelands, wildlife, soil, water, and energy resources

What's It Like to Be a Conservationist?

Foresters often specialize in timber management, outdoor recreation, or forest economics. They deal with one of our most important natural resources, trees, which are fast becoming scarce because of unconstrained timber production. Range managers—sometimes called range conservationists, range scientists, or range ecologists—determine the number and kind of animals to be grazed, the grazing system to be used, and the best grazing season in order to obtain high livestock production. At the same time they must conserve soil and vegetation for other uses, such as wildlife grazing and outdoor recreation, and for the protection of the environment. Soil conservationists help farmers and ranchers to conserve soil and water. They prepare maps with soil, water, and vegetation plans for land, recommend ways land can best be used, and help estimate costs and returns on land use. Chip Williams, graduate student in forestry economics, has enjoyed his college studies since committing himself to a specific career. Williams says, "Now all of my course work has a purpose and falls into place. What excites me about forestry is the scientific knowledge. I thought it was a little more woodsy than it is. I spend most of my study hours figuring out things related to forestry." Vermont Public Utilities specialist Sue Hudson states that "energy conservation has to be concerned with three dimensions of energy: (1) existing sources of power, (2) production of power as it affects the environment, and (3) how to reduce energy demands." State government takes lead responsibility for conserving energy in our nation.

What Education and Skills Will I Need?

High School Preparation for college, with as much science as possible.

College Major in one of the 45 approved forestry programs or attend one of the 31 universities with a range science or an agricultural science major.

Personal Skills A love of the outdoors, physical hardiness, and scientific curiosity are required for this career.

How Many Conservationists Are There and Where Do They Work?

There are 35,000 conservationists and foresters; 11 percent are women, 1 percent is black, and 4 percent are Hispanic. Conservationists work for the federal government (46 percent), for state governments (20 percent), and in the forestry industry (15 percent).

How Much Money Will I Make?

In 1993 a conservation scientist with a bachelor's degree started with the federal government at $22,717 a year; those with a master's degree started at $27,789.

What Are the Job Opportunities?

The national deficit and budget cuts have led to decreases in the number of jobs in conservation and forestry. Private industry offers the best job opportunities.

Related Careers

Agricultural scientist   Agricultural engineer
Wildlife manager   Biologist

Where Can I Get More Information?

American Forestry Association
1516 P Street, NW
Washington, DC 20005

Society for Range Management
1839 York Street
Denver, CO 80206

U.S. Forest Service
U.S. Department of Agriculture
14th Street and Independence Avenue, SW
Washington, DC 20250

Professional Organization of Employees of the
        U.S. Department of Agriculture
South Building, Room 1414
Washington, DC 20250

Environmentalist

Studies the earth's water, interior, and atmosphere as well as the environment in space

What's It Like to Be an Environmentalist?

"The environmentalists," writes a geologist, "share many methods with other fields of science—the collection of evidence leading to new conclusions, the application of all available techniques to test a hypothesis, and the thrill of discovery. In addition, they have certain satisfactions peculiar to themselves—the immediacy of using the earth and the sea as a laboratory, the healthful exercise of fieldwork, and the unusual perspective one gets from dealing with the immensity of geological time." *Geophysicists* study the size and shape, interior, surface, and atmosphere of the earth; the land and bodies of water on its surface and underground; and the atmosphere surrounding it. They often use satellites to conduct tests from outer space and computers to collect and analyze data. *Meteorologists* study the air that surrounds the earth, including weather patterns. Besides weather forecasting, they work to understand and solve air pollution problems. *Oceanographers* study the ocean—its characteristics, movements, plant life, and animal life.

Oceanographer and diver James Leichter majored in English at Stanford University, then went to Northeastern for a master's degree in marine biology before winning a fellowship back at Stanford in the Ph.D. program in marine biology. Leichter says he learned to write by majoring in English, and now he can turn his attention to what he loves, diving and studying the ocean depths. Since he is especially interested in plant life, Leichter finds and tags plants and returns to them later to measure their growth.

What Education and Skills Will I Need?

High School   Preparation for college, with emphasis on science and computer science.

College   Major in environmental science at one of the 160 colleges that offer it or in a related science to prepare for graduate work, which is necessary for many sciences. Or, like Leichter, major in English and hone your writing skills before going on to a graduate degree in science.

Personal Skills   Interest in doing new research, an analytic mind, and the physical stamina to lead an outdoor life are necessary.

How Many Environmentalists Are There and Where Do They Work?

There are 48,000 geologists and related majors; 14 percent are women, fewer than one percent are black and Hispanic. There are 5,500 meteorologists; 18 percent are women. Most environmentalists work for private industry, oil and gas producers in the

Southwest, and agencies of the federal government. Few are in academics or in research and development.

How Much Money Will I Make?

In 1992 beginners with a bachelor's degree made $31,000; with a master's degree environmentalists started at $37,300 a year in private industry. The median salary for experienced environmentalists with the federal government was $65,000 a year. Private industry will pay $55,000 for experienced scientists, and the top 10 percent will make over $100,000.

What Are the Job Opportunities?

There are 10,000 environmental engineers available for 22,500 jobs that need to be filled right now—5,000 in waste cleanup alone. At least 1,200 more environmentalists will be needed each year for the next five years, and 2,300 a year for the following five years. The competition for academic positions, however, is extremely keen.

Related Careers

Engineer   Geologist
Conservationist   Biologist

Where Can I Get More Information?

Marine Technology Society
1828 L Street, NW, No. 900
Washington, DC 20036

American Meteorological Society
45 Beacon Street
Boston, MA 02108

American Geophysical Union
2000 Florida Avenue, NW
Washington, DC 20009

Geoscientist

Studies the composition, structure, and history of the earth's crust

What's It Like to Be a Geoscientist?

Geologists and geophysicists are playing an increasing role in preserving and cleaning up the environment. Many design and monitor waste disposal sites and determine how to preserve water supplies and reclaim contaminated land and water to comply with stricter federal environmental rules. They also help locate safe sites for hazardous waste facilities, nuclear power plants, and landfills.

Geoscientists analyze information collected by bouncing sound waves off deeply buried rock layers; examine surface rocks and samples of buried rocks recovered by drilling; and study information collected by satellites. They also identify rocks and minerals, conduct geoscientific surveys, construct maps, and use instruments such as a gravimeter and a magnetometer to measure the earth's gravity and magnetic field. Besides locating oil and minerals, geoscientists also advise construction companies and government agencies on the suitability of proposed locations for buildings, dams, and highways.

What Education and Skills Will I Need?

High School Preparation for college, with an emphasis on science and mathematics.

College More than 270 universities award advanced degrees in geology and about 70 award them in geophysics.

Personal Skills Curiosity and the ability to analyze and communicate effectively are important skills. Those involved in fieldwork must have physical stamina.

How Many Geoscientists Are There and Where Do They Work?

There are 48,000 geologists and geophysicists; 14 percent are women, fewer than 1 percent are black and Hispanic. Most work for oil and gas companies (44 percent); the federal government employs 16 percent, and oil and gas field services employ 14 percent. Fourteen percent are self-employed.

How Much Money Will I Make?

In 1992 private industry started geologists with a master's degree at $25,704 a year. Experienced geologists with the federal government had a median income of $65,000.

What Are the Job Opportunities?

The best job opportunities are expected to be in hydrology and geochemistry. The number of geology graduates is down because oil production is down. Environmental problems will create most of the new job opportunities because geoscientists will be needed to evaluate and enforce environmental regulations.

Related Careers

Petroleum engineer   Meteorologist
Environmentalist   Oceanographer

Where Can I Get More Information?

American Geological Institute
4220 King Street
Alexandria, VA 22302

Marine Technology Society
1825 L Street, NW, No. 900
Washington, DC 20036

Physicist

Describes in mathematical terms the fundamental forces and laws of nature and the interaction of matter and energy

What's It Like to Be a Physicist?

Through systematic observation and experimentation, physicists use mathematics to describe the basic forces and laws of nature, such as gravity, electromagnetism, and nuclear interaction. Most physicists work in research and development for private industry and the government. They often specialize in areas such as nuclear energy, electronics, communications, aerospace, or medical instrumentation. The flight of the space shuttle and the safety of the family car are dependent upon research by physicists.

Physicists have developed lasers (devices that amplify light and emit it in a highly directional, intense beam) that are used in surgery, microwave devices that are used for ovens, and measuring instruments that can detect the kind and number of cells in blood or the amount of lead in foods. Tom Kepler, research physicist at Brandeis University, works with his wife, Grace, whom he met when they were working on their Ph.D. degrees in physics. They emphasize that increasingly physicists work in combined fields such as biophysics, chemical physics, and geophysics. And, more and more physics graduates are taking jobs with engineering firms.

What Education and Skills Will I Need?

High School   Preparation for college, with as much mathematics and computer science as possible.

College   Major in physics or mathematics in college to prepare for graduate school. There are 170 colleges that offer a Ph.D. in physics and 72 colleges that offer one in astronomy. A career as a physicist requires a Ph.D.

Personal Skills   Mathematical ability, an inquisitive mind and imagination, plus the ability to think in abstract terms, are needed to be a physicist.

How Many Physicists Are There and Where Do They Work?

There are 21,000 physicists, including college professors; 7 percent are women, 1 percent are black, and 3 percent are Hispanic. Most of them work for the federal government (30 percent); others work for private research labs (21 percent), as consultants for engineering and architectural firms (15 percent), and for electronics manufacturers (12 percent). Twelve percent are self-employed.

How Much Money Will I Make?

In 1992 beginning physicists with a master's degree started at $30,000 a year in private industry, and with a Ph.D. degree at $41,000. The median salary with the federal government for Ph.D.'s with experience was $65,000; industry paid $75,000.

What Are the Job Opportunities?

Job opportunities in physics are expected to be limited because money for research and defense and space budgets are down.

Related Careers

Engineer   Chemist
Mathematician   Geoscientist

Where Can I Get More Information?

American Institute of Physics
335 East 45th Street
New York, NY 10017

Social Science

- **Anthropologist**
- **Economist**
- **Geographer**
- **Historian**
- **Political scientist**
- **Psychologist**
- **Sociologist**

ABOUT SOCIAL SCIENCE CAREERS

It's important to know that most social science majors in college do not go into a social science career. What do they do? Like many liberal arts students, they go into business, into sales, into management. They go into the arts, into education, and many go into government. See the chapter "What Becomes of All Those History Majors?"

The trend in the financial industry is to hire increasing numbers of social science majors as trainees for management positions. Research councils and other nonprofit organizations provide an important source of employment for economists, political scientists, and sociologists.

Every liberal arts college in the country offers majors in most of the social sciences. The choice of a graduate school is important for those who want to become social scientists. Students interested in research should select graduate programs that emphasize training in research, statistics, and computers.

Social science is a career field in which a Ph.D. is needed for many entry-level positions and for almost all the top jobs. Other than economists, most social scientists are employed in colleges and universities, where the job market for Ph.D.'s has crashed.

Working conditions in the social sciences are very good because colleges provide excellent benefits with sabbatical leaves of absence, life and health insurance, and retirement plans. Working hours for professors are generally flexible, with few teaching hours when a professor must actually "be there." Professors with tenure have a low-stress job with prestige. The biggest problem is finding employment. In other words, it's nice work—if you can get it. Clinical and counseling psychologists often work in the evenings, since their patients are sometimes unable to leave their jobs or school during the workday.

Social science is one of the most overcrowded career groups. If social science is where you want to be, prepare for jobs in the applied sciences by acquiring computer and management skills.

Anthropologist

Studies people—their origins, physical characteristics, customs, languages, traditions, material possessions, structured social relationships, and value systems

What's It Like to Be an Anthropologist?

Anthropologists usually specialize in cultural anthropology (sometimes called ethnology), archaeology, linguistics, or physical anthropology. *Ethnologists* may spend long periods (up to two years) living in primitive villages to learn about a people's way of life. Sometimes their studies include complex urban societies as well. *Archaeologists* dig for past civilizations. They excavate and study the remains of homes, tools, ornaments, and evidence of activity in order to reconstruct the people's history and customs. *Linguists* scientifically study the sounds and structures of languages and the relationship between language and behavior. *Physical anthro-*

pologists study human evolution by comparing the physical characteristics of different races or groups of people. Related to these basic areas of study are subfields of applied, urban, and medical anthropology. Anthropologist William E. Mitchell, specialist in ethnology, took his family, including two preschool children, to the bush of New Guinea for two years. Mitchell encourages young people to be anthropologists if they "have an insatiable curiosity about people and the patience and tact to study firsthand the different ways—often strange to us—in which human groups have arranged to live their lives. What delights me most about being an anthropologist," says Mitchell, "is that the problems are so immense and the factors so complex for understanding human behavior that it will always elude my grasp. I may sometimes be frustrated but *never* bored with my work."

What Education and Skills Will I Need?

High School   Strong preparatory courses for a competitive liberal arts program in college.

College   Liberal arts degree to prepare for graduate work. Most anthropologists major in a social science, although you don't have to take an anthropology major as an undergraduate. A Ph.D. in anthropology is required for a professional career in a university or in research.

Personal Skills   Reading, research, and writing skills are essential, as well as an interest in detail and an ability to work independently.

How Many Anthropologists Are There and Where Do They Work?

There are 12,200 anthropologists and half of them are women. Almost all work in universities, although some are employed by museums and the government.

How Much Money Will I Make?

In 1993–94 starting salaries for college instructors with a Ph.D. averaged $27,200 a year. Full professors averaged $59,500. Many anthropologists supplement their teaching salaries with summer research grants or sponsored field trips for students.

What Are the Job Opportunities?

There are virtually no jobs for anthropologists. All college teaching jobs are competitive because student enrollments are decreasing. Very limited opportunities will be available in museums and research programs because federal and university spending is down and there has been an oversupply of Ph.D.'s in anthropology.

Related Careers

Sociologist   Psychologist
Community planner   Reporter

Where Can I Get More Information?

American Anthropological Association
1703 New Hampshire Avenue, NW
Washington, DC 20009

Economist

Studies how a society uses scarce resources such as land, labor, and raw materials to produce goods and services

What's It Like to Be an Economist?

An economist deals with the relationship between supply and demand for goods and services. Most economists are concerned with the practical applications of economic policy in a particular area, such as finance, labor, agriculture, transportation, real estate, energy, or health. They use their understanding of economic relationships to advise business firms, insurance companies, banks, securities firms, industry associations, labor unions, and government agencies. Some economists work in specific fields, such as control of inflation, prevention of depression, and development of farm, wage, and tax policies. Others develop theories to explain causes of employment and unemployment, international trade influences, and world economic conditions.

Economist Anne Kahl, who works for the United States Department of Labor, collects data and assesses economic trends regarding employment in the United States. She specializes in the analysis of women and older workers in the work force. Her analyses include data on prices, wages, employment, and productivity. Kahl keeps up with current economic theory through ongoing graduate studies at George Washington University.

What Education and Skills Will I Need?

High School   Preparation for a liberal arts major in college, with as much mathematics as possible.

College   Major in economics or a related social science, or mathematics with computer science or statistics, to prepare for an advanced degree in economics. A Ph.D. is required for the top teaching and research jobs.

Personal Skills   Ability to do detailed, accurate research is needed. Economists must also be able to express themselves well in writing.

How Many Economists Are There and Where Do They Work?

There are 51,000 economists; 43 percent are women, 4 percent are black, and 3 percent are Hispanic. Almost half work for the federal government (45 percent), 20 percent teach in universities and colleges, and 10 percent are employed in business. Most are employed in New York, Chicago, and Washington. Thirty percent are self-employed.

How Much Money Will I Make?

In 1993 new graduates started at $25,200 a year. Economists with experience averaged $65,000 a year in business. Ph.D.'s in business had a median income of $78,000. Economics professors earn the same as other college professors.

What Are the Job Opportunities?

Jobs will be very competitive through 2005. The best chances will be for those who are skilled in econometrics and statistics, who will find positions in financial services and consulting firms.

Related Careers

Actuary   Sociologist
Bank officer   Financial manager

Where Can I Get More Information?

American Economic Association
2014 Broadway
Suite 305
Nashville, TN 37203

American Marketing Association
250 South Wacker Drive, Suite 200
Chicago, IL 60606

Geographer

Studies the distribution of both physical and cultural phenomena at local, regional, continental, and global scales

What's It Like to Be a Geographer?

Geographers specialize. *Economic geographers* study the distribution of resources and economic activities. *Political geographers* are concerned with the relationship of geography to political phenomena. *Physical geographers* study climate, vegetation, soil, and land forms. *Urban geographers* study cities and metropolitan areas. *Medical geographers* study health-care delivery systems, epidemiology, and the effect of the environment on health. Mike Taupier, a 30-year-old graduate student in geography, is looking for a job in the ecological sciences. "Geography," says Taupier, "isn't as popular as many other sciences, and the job market is better. It fits into work with both the physical and social sciences and is often related to work in botany, geology, political science, and history."

Geography is often an overlooked field in U.S. universities, in contrast to its popularity in European universities. For example, Günter Eisebith, a graduate student in geography at Aachen

University in Germany, spent a year studying the steel industry in India. He married geographer Martina Fromhold, an industrial geographer specializing in Central Europe who works with a university consulting team. Both are interested in geography careers in the Third World.

What Education and Skills Will I Need?

High School Preparation for college, with emphasis on all social and biological sciences.

College Graduate work is required for a career in geography. There are 56 universities offering a Ph.D. in geography.

Personal Skills Reading, studying, computing, and research skills are needed, along with an interest in working independently.

How Many Geographers Are There and Where Do They Work?

There are 21,000 geographers; 21 percent are women. Most of them teach in universities and colleges; the remainder are with the government, primarily in the Department of Defense and the Department of the Interior.

How Much Money Will I Make?

In 1992 a graduate with a master's degree started at $28,400 and those with a Ph.D. started at $30,000. Salaries range from $24,700 to $51,300; geography professors earn the same as other college professors.

What Are the Job Opportunities?

The outlook for work is better than for most social scientists through 2005. Those with computer skills and training in cartography, satellite data interpretation, or planning will have the best chances for jobs.

Related Careers

Anthropologist
Oceanographer

Geologist
Meteorologist

Where Can I Get More Information?

Association of American Geographers
1710 Sixteenth Street, NW
Washington, DC 20009

Historian

Studies the records of the past and analyzes events, institutions, ideas, and people

What's It Like to Be a Historian?

Historians relate their knowledge of the past to current events in an effort to explain the present. They may specialize in the history of a specific country or area, or a particular period of time such as ancient, medieval, or modern. They may also specialize in the history of a field, such as economics, culture, the labor movement, art, or architecture. The number of specialties in history is constantly growing. Newer specialties are concerned with business archives, quantitative analysis, and the relationship between technological and other aspects of historical development. A growing number of historians now specialize in African, Latin American, Chinese, Asian, or Near Eastern history. For example, Harvey J. Spalding, a black Ph.D., majored in African history in college. He now works for a historical society that is seeking new understanding of minorities in the United States. Other specialties include archivists, who are associated with museums, specialized libraries, and historical societies. Oral history is another speciality that is growing in importance.

What Education and Skills Will I Need?

High School   Preparation for college, with an emphasis on social sciences.

College   Most historians major in history, with minors in government, economics, sociology, or anthropology. A doctorate is necessary for a career in college teaching and for the better government jobs.

Personal Skills   An interest in reading, studying, and research and the ability to write papers and reports are necessary.

How Many Historians Are There and Where Do They Work?

There are about 31,000 historians and 20 percent of them are women. Seventy percent of all historians work in colleges and universities; others are employed by the government, archives, libraries, museums, and historical societies.

How Much Money Will I Make?

In 1993 college instructors averaged $27,200 a year, and full professors averaged $59,500. Other historians made from $24,700 to $51,300 a year in 1992.

What Are the Job Opportunities?

Historians will find stiff job competition through 2005. But there are all kinds of other jobs for history majors. Be sure to read "What Becomes of All Those History Majors?" There are many more Ph.D.'s in history than there are jobs. Historians with computer skills are expected to have the best chances for jobs in business and research.

Related Careers

Political scientist   Economist
Sociologist   Journalist

Where Can I Get More Information?

American Historical Association
400 A Street, SE
Washington, DC 20003

Political Scientist

Studies how political power is organized, distributed, and used

What's It Like to Be a Political Scientist?

Political scientists study a wide range of subjects such as Mexican-American relations, the beliefs and institutions of nations in Asia and Africa, the politics of a New England town or a major metropolis, and the decisions of the U.S. Supreme Court. Studying topics such as public opinion, political discrimination, and ideology, they analyze the structure and operation of governments as well as of informal political entities. Most political scientists teach in colleges and universities, where they combine research, consultation, or administration with teaching. Many of them specialize in a general area of political science, such as political theory, U.S. political institutions and processes, comparative political processes, or international relations. Joseph and Maria Manelli are graduate students in political science. They plan to work together at a private firm surveying public opinion on political questions. They can also use their research skills to evaluate proposed legislation for reference bureaus and congressional committees. Manelli and Manelli eventually hope to start their own legislative research service.

What Education and Skills Will I Need?

High School Preparation for college, with an emphasis on history, government, and other social sciences.

College Major in political science or in a related major, such as government, history, or economics, to prepare for graduate work. A master's degree is usually required for a beginning job, and a Ph.D. is required for a career in political science. Law school is an alternative to a Ph.D.

Personal Skills Political scientists must have an interest in details, be objective in their thinking, and have good oral and writing skills.

How Many Political Scientists Are There and Where Do They Work?

There are about 18,000 political scientists; three-fourths of them teach in colleges and universities. Others are employed by government agencies, political organizations, public interest groups, labor unions, and research institutes.

How Much Money Will I Make?

In 1993–94 a political scientist with a Ph.D. averaged $46,300 a year as a college professor. Other political scientists earned from $41,700 to $51,000 a year in 1992.

What Are the Job Opportunities?

Employment opportunities are very competitive in college teaching, business, and government. A political science degree is helpful for a career in journalism, foreign affairs, law, or other related work. Well-qualified political scientists with computer skills will find that the best opportunities are in applied fields.

Related Careers

Politician   Historian
Lawyer   Sociologist

Where Can I Get More Information?

American Political Science Association
1527 New Hampshire Avenue, NW
Washington, DC 20036

Psychologist

Evaluates, counsels, and advises individuals and groups

What's It Like to Be a Psychologist?

Clinical psychologists help the emotionally or mentally disturbed to adjust to life and to life stresses that many people encounter, such as divorce and aging. Those working in mental health clinics spend most of their time administering and scoring individual psychological tests. The psychologist meets with a clinical team of social worker, psychiatrist, and educator to interpret the test scores and determine ways to help the individual. Psychologists often do group therapy with young parents, adolescents, children, or whatever group needs therapy in the particular community or agency. They have conferences with parents, community leaders, and educators about clients and encourage joint efforts to help individuals with problems. Specializations include counseling, developmental, industrial, and health psychology.

What Education and Skills Will I Need?

High School Preparation for college, with emphasis on science, computer science, and social science.

College Major in psychology, although many students major in a related field such as sociology, anthropology, or education, to prepare for graduate work in psychology. A master's degree is required for most practical work in psychology in schools and government or mental health agencies. A Ph.D. is required for research, college and university teaching, and for promotions in many jobs.

Personal Skills Sensitivity to others and a genuine interest in people are important for counseling. Research jobs require an interest in detail and accuracy as well as writing skills.

How Many Psychologists Are There and Where Do They Work?

There are 144,000 psychologists; 58 percent are women, 7 percent are black, and 4 percent are Hispanic. Most (41 percent) work for schools, 15 percent work for hospitals, and 12 percent work for state and federal government agencies. Thirty-three percent are self-employed and 21 percent work part time.

How Much Money Will I Make?

In 1991 the average annual salary for a psychologist with a doctoral degree was $48,000 a year in counseling, $50,000 in research, $53,000 in clinical practice, $55,000 in public schools, and $76,000 in industry.

What Are the Job Opportunities?

There will be many more Ph.D.'s than jobs in psychology through 2005. Tight school and government budgets and an overload of Ph.D.'s make jobs almost impossible to find with only a bachelor's or a master's degree. But the demand for psychologists with Ph.D.'s will remain high because dysfunctional families and violence continue to grow in our society. Psychologists will be needed in programs designed to combat increases in alcohol abuse, drug dependency, marital strife, sexual harassment, and sexual abuse of children.

Related Careers

Psychiatrist

Social worker

School counselor

Clergy

Where Can I Get More Information?

American Psychological Association
750 First Street, NE
Washington, DC 20002

Sociologist

Studies the behavior and interaction of people in groups

What's It Like to Be a Sociologist?

Sociologist Hope Jensen Leichter, a professor at Columbia University, says, "My interest in sociology is to provide the significant theory about how people are affected by their families, by their schools, and by their work, so that professionals in the helping careers, such as social workers, educators, and nurses, will have some idea of what makes people behave as they do."

Sociologists study human groups and social institutions. These include families, tribes, communities, and governments, as well as a variety of social, religious, political, business, and other organizations. Sociologists study social groups, tracing their origins and growth and analyzing the influence of group activities on individual members. While some sociologists are concerned primarily with the characteristics of groups, others are more interested in the ways individuals are affected by each other and by the groups to which they belong. Still others focus on social traits such as gender, age, or race, that make an important difference in how a person experiences life. Some sociologists study the causes of social problems such as crime and poverty, patterns of family relations, or different living patterns in communities of varying types and sizes. Others are working in prison systems, education, industrial public relations, and regional and community planning.

What Education and Skills Will I Need?

High School Preparation for college, with a strong academic program and computer skills.

College Major in any social science and prepare for graduate work in sociology. A Ph.D. is required for a career in sociology.

Personal Skills Analytic and research skills are required, as well as an inquiring mind, intellectual curiosity, and communication skills, especially writing.

How Many Sociologists Are There and Where Do They Work?

There are 22,600 sociologists (including college professors); about half of them are women. Many (20 percent) work for state governments, and another 20 percent work in hospitals; 12 percent are professors, and 14 percent work for local governments.

How Much Money Will I Make?

In 1993 the median annual salary for a sociologist with a doctorate working for the federal government was $33,600. College instructors started at $27,200 and averaged $59,500 as full professors.

What Are the Job Opportunities?

College jobs will be very scarce because there will be thousands of Ph.D.'s in sociology without jobs through 2005. Many sociologists go into another career area. Don't forget that sociology majors can do anything. See "What Becomes of All Those History Majors?"

Related Careers

Anthropologist	Historian
Political scientist	Community planner

Where Can I Get More Information?

American Sociological Association
1722 N Street, NW
Washington, DC 20036

Social Service

- Clergy
- Human service worker
- Recreation worker
- Rehabilitation counselor
- Social worker

ABOUT SOCIAL SERVICE CAREERS

Social service jobs require more education for less pay than any other field of work except education. There are over a million jobs represented in this career group, and it is projected to be among the fastest growing in the late-1990s. Job opportunities should remain plentiful as the population increases in size and age. Concern for people, not desire for money, is needed to be satisfied with a career in the social services. Patience, tact, sensitivity, and compassion are necessary personal qualities.

Social service careers offer a great variety of settings and tasks. Depending on their specific occupation, workers may advise consumers on how to get the most for their money; help people with disabilities to achieve satisfactory lifestyles; provide religious services; counsel people who have problems in their job, home, school, or social relationships; or treat people with emotional problems.

Although social services are provided in different settings, workers in these careers require many of the same skills. In general, a knowledge of the field is gained through a college degree. One to three years of graduate work in a professional school are required for many social service careers such as counseling, clergy, and social work.

Beginning counselors and social workers who have little experience are assigned the less difficult cases. As they gain experience, their caseloads are increased and they are assigned clients with more complex problems. After getting experience and more graduate education, rehabilitation counselors and social workers may advance to supervisory positions or top administrative jobs.

After a few years of experience, recreation workers may become supervisors. Although promotions to administrative jobs may come more easily after graduate training, advancement is still possible through a combination of education and experience.

Social service jobs usually involve irregular hours because social service workers provide a wide range of services to people in many different circumstances. For example, the clergy must assist people whenever a crisis occurs, as well as visit parishoners regularly. Recreation workers can expect night work and irregular hours, because they often have to work while others are enjoying leisure time.

Social service jobs often depend on government spending because so many of the programs are tied to federal budgets. When money is tight and budgets are cut, the job market gets tight.

Clergy

Serves within Jewish, Roman Catholic, or Protestant religious institutions

What's It Like to Be a Member of the Clergy?

Young people who choose to enter the ministry, priesthood, or rabbinate do so mainly because they have a strong religious faith and a desire to help others. Deciding on a career in the clergy involves considerations different from those in other career choices. In addition to the clergy who serve in congregations and parishes, there are teachers and administrators in education; chaplains in the military, prisons, hospitals, and on college campuses; and missionaries and those who serve in social welfare agencies.

Protestant ministers lead their congregations in worship services and administer the rites of baptism, confirmation, and Holy Communion. They prepare and deliver sermons and give religious instruction to new members of the church.

Rabbis are the spiritual leaders of their congregations and the teachers and interpreters of Jewish law and tradition. They conduct religious services and deliver sermons on the Sabbath and on Jewish holidays. Rabbis serve either Orthodox, Conservative, or Reform congregations. They differ in the extent to which they follow the traditional form of worship—for example, in wearing head coverings, in using Hebrew as the language of prayer, or in using music and a choir.

Roman Catholic priests attend to the spiritual, pastoral, moral, and educational needs of the members of their church. Their duties include presiding at liturgical functions, delivering sermons, hearing confessions, administering the sacraments, and conducting funeral services. There are two main classifications of priests—diocesan (secular) and religious. Diocesan priests generally work in parishes assigned to them by the bishop of their diocese. Religious priests generally work as part of a religious order, such as Jesuits, Dominicans, or Franciscans. They engage in specialized work assigned to them by superiors in their order, such as teaching or social work.

All clergy conduct weddings and funeral services, visit the sick, help the poor, comfort the bereaved, supervise religious education programs, engage in interfaith activities, and involve themselves in community affairs. Clergy serving smaller churches or synagogues usually work on a personal basis with their parishioners. Those serving large congregations have greater administrative responsibilities. They spend a lot of time working with committees, church officers, and staff, in addition to performing many community duties. They often have one or more associates who share specific aspects of the ministry and help them meet the individual needs of parishioners.

What Education and Skills Will I Need?

High School   Preparation for a strong college liberal arts program.

College Major in religion or theology, or any related field that involves understanding people, as preparation for a master's degree in divinity for Protestants, a three- to five-year seminary program for Jews, and a four-year seminary program for Roman Catholics.

Personal Skills Religious careers require a deep conviction about the religious and spiritual needs of people and the ability to meet those needs by providing spiritual leadership.

How Many Clergy Are There and Where Do They Work?

There are 348,000 clergy and another 62,000 professional religious workers. In the clergy, 10 percent are women, 9 percent are black, and 3 percent are Hispanic. Women account for 50 percent of the enrollment in Protestant seminaries. Some 290,000 Protestant ministers are in churches serving 72 million people. There are an estimated 5,500 practicing rabbis. About 850 Orthodox, 1,300 Conservative, and 1,600 Reform rabbis serve 6 million Jews. There are 53,000 priests and an additional 9,500 lay deacons serving 49 million Catholics. Every community in the United States has at least one Protestant church with a full-time minister. Most ministers work for the five largest churches—Baptist, Methodist, Lutheran, Presbyterian, and Pentecostal. Rabbis are concentrated in the major cities of the United States that have large Jewish populations. There are priests in nearly every city and town in the country, although the majority are in metropolitan areas where most Catholics live.

How Much Money Will I Make?

In 1992 the average salary for Protestant ministers was about $27,000 a year plus housing and other benefits valued at $44,000; $38,000 to $60,000 plus housing and gifts for rabbis; and an average stipend of $9,000 plus all maintenance expenses for priests, who take a vow of poverty.

What Are the Job Opportunities?

Jobs for Protestant and Jewish clergy will continue to be competitive through 2005 as congregations decrease in size and the number of seminarians goes up. Conservative and Reform rabbis will have the best chance for jobs. Catholic priests are in demand because of a sharp drop in seminary enrollment and the need to replace priests who leave or retire. Jobs for women continue to be very difficult to get because of discrimination against women in the church. In the past 20 years, fewer than 125 Reformed women rabbis have been ordained, and the first Conservative Jewish woman, Rabbi Amy Eilberg, was ordained in 1985. It was less than 20 years ago that Episcopalians ordained women. Catholics have yet to admit women to their clergy.

Related Careers

Social worker   Counselor

Human service worker   Missionary

Where Can I Get More Information?

For career information, your local church or synagogue can give you the name and address of the headquarters of your religious group.

Hebrew Union College—Jewish Institute of Religion
     [Reform Jewish]
3101 Clifton Avenue
Cincinnati, OH 45220

The Rabbi Isaac Elchanan Theological Seminary
     [Orthodox Jewish]
2540 Amsterdam Avenue
New York, NY 10033

National Ramah Commission [Conservative Jewish]
3080 Broadway
New York, NY 10027

National Council of Churches [Protestant]
Professional Church Leadership
475 Riverside Drive
New York, NY 10115

Human Service Worker

Serves as a paraprofessional in group homes and halfway houses, in correctional programs, programs for the mentally retarded, and community health centers and agencies

What's It Like to Be a Human Service Worker?

In a mental health center, mental health technicians work directly with clients. They may help them to master the practical aspects of everyday living and to get along better with others. They may be on a team with a social worker, a psychologist, and an educator, working with families, or they may work in music, art, or dance therapy. Some supervise halfway houses and group homes.

Residential counselors take a close interest in each member of a group home. Some counselors supervise beginning human service workers, depending on their level of education and experience. Many human service workers learn on the job, after getting a general college education. For example, when Steve Delbanco graduated from Earlham College in Richmond, Indiana, he went west to find an interesting job in Seattle. He took a position in a residential home for adolescents, where he learned what he needed to know on the job. After two years, he returned to graduate school for his master's degree.

In group homes and halfway houses, human service workers oversee residents who need some supervision or support on a daily basis, but who do not need to live in an institution. They review clients' records, talk with their families, and confer with medical personnel in order to gain better insight into their clients' backgrounds and needs. Human service workers may teach residents to prepare their own meals and handle other housekeeping activities. They also provide emotional support, lead recreation activities, and make oral and written reports on the condition and progress of residents.

What Education and Skills Will I Need?

High School   Prepare for college, with an emphasis on the social sciences.

College   Major in one of the social sciences to be in a position for graduate school in social work or psychology if you want to advance in human services.

Personal Skills   A strong desire to help others is important. Patience, understanding, and a strong sense of responsibility are required for these jobs.

How Many Human Service Workers Are There and Where Do They Work?

There are 189,000 human service workers; about one-fourth are employed by state and local governments, usually in mental health centers, programs for the mentally retarded and developmentally disabled, and public welfare agencies.

How Much Money Will I Make?

In 1992 the starting salary for a human service worker with a bachelor's degree ranged from $12,000 to $20,000 a year. Experienced workers averaged from $15,000 to $25,000.

What Are the Job Opportunities?

Chances of getting a job will be excellent through 2005 because adult day-care needs are increasing. Poor pay for an emotionally draining job results in high turnover and means that there are job openings most of the time.

Related Careers

Social worker   Religious worker
Occupational therapist   Recreation worker

Where Can I Get More Information?

National Organization for Human Service Education
P.O. Box 6257
Fitchburg State College
Fitchburg, MA 01420

Recreation Worker

Helps people develop good physical and mental health through recreation and group activity within an organization

What's It Like to Be a Recreation Worker?

Recreation workers organize activities for all ages and interests at local recreation programs, community centers, churches, hospitals, camps, and playgrounds. The major youth agencies are the Boy Scouts and Girl Scouts, YWCA, YMCA, 4-H Clubs, Red Cross, and American Youth Hostels. These organizations help people use and enjoy their leisure time constructively in physical, social, and cultural programs. Recreation directors lead classes and discussions, teach skills, take charge of hikes and trips, and direct programs and camps. They operate recreational facilities and study the recreational needs of individuals and communities. Garcia and Pam Rodriguez are the directors of a coed camp for sailing. They met as camp counselors, married, and went into the recreation business. They have developed a year-round business promoting, recruiting for, and operating their camp for teenagers. Both worked for several agencies before they decided to go into business for themselves. They are both physical education majors; Garcia is working on his master's in recreation, and Pam is getting her advanced degree in business administration.

What Education and Skills Will I Need?

High School   Preparation for a two-year or four-year college program.

College   Half the professional recreation workers are college graduates. Community college graduates also have good employment opportunities in recreation work. A major in physical education, recreation, or social sciences and a master's degree are necessary for many administrative jobs.

Personal Skills   Skill in sports, music, and crafts; creativity; enthusiasm about activities; and good judgment are necessary for success in a recreation career.

How Many Recreation Workers Are There and Where Do They Work?

There are 204,000 recreation workers; 71 percent are women, 15 percent are black, and 6 percent are Hispanic. About 21 percent are employed part time. Most of them work for local government (38 percent), others for major recreational organizations (22 percent), and still others for social services (13 percent) and nursing homes (10 percent).

How Much Money Will I Make?

In 1993 the median salary for those with a college degree was $14,900 a year. The top 10 percent made $27,000. Community supervisors of recreation earned from $22,000 to $95,000.

What Are the Job Opportunities?

Recreation will continue to be a competitive career because there are more graduates and interested people than jobs. However, there are part-time opportunities in the public schools, and jobs are increasing in nursing homes, community centers offering adult day care, athletic clubs, and sports clinics.

Related Careers

Club manager   Physical education teacher
Camp director   Psychologist

Where Can I Get More Information?

National Recreation and Park Association
2775 South Quincy Street
Suite 300
Arlington, VA 22206

American Camping Association
5000 State Road 67 North
Martinsville, IN 46151

Rehabilitation Counselor

Helps people deal with the personal, social, and vocational impact of their disabilities

What's It Like to Be a Rehabilitation Counselor?

Rehabilitation counselors evaluate their clients' potential for employment and arrange medical care, rehabilitation programs, occupational training, and job placement. Norma McNall of Ardmore, Oklahoma, says, "I work out a plan of rehabilitation after consulting with the person's social worker, medical doctor, and sometimes the family. Most of my work is with alcohol abusers, although some of my co-workers specialize in working with the mentally ill or the retarded, and others help any person who can't adjust to a job. I keep in touch with my clients' employers and look for more employers who will hire the disabled. The amount of direct counseling varies with each person, but we try to involve family members and other agencies in helping the person as she or he tries to get back to work on a regular basis."

What Education and Skills Will I Need?

High School   Preparation for college, with emphasis on the social sciences.

College   Major in education, psychology, guidance, or sociology to prepare for graduate school. A master's degree in psychology, student personnel, vocational counseling, or rehabilitation counseling is usually required.

Personal Skills   Ability to accept responsibility, to work independently, and to motivate others who may progress very slowly are all necessary to be successful in rehabilitation.

How Many Rehabilitation Counselors Are There and Where Do They Work?

There are about 30,000 rehabilitation counselors; about half are women and 10 percent are black. Most work for state or local rehabilitation agencies. The rest work in hospitals and for labor unions, insurance companies, and sheltered workshops.

How Much Money Will I Make?

In 1993 schools paid an average of $34,000 a year for rehabilitation counselors; other agencies paid slightly less.

What Are the Job Opportunities?

Rehabilitation counselors with a master's degree are expected to have good job opportunities through 2005. As job and family stress increase, the need for rehabilitation, especially for alcohol and drug abuse, will grow. Insurance is more frequently paying for rehabilitation counselors, increasing the numbers that human service agencies can hire.

Related Careers

School counselor   Social worker
Occupational therapist   Clergy

Where Can I Get More Information?

National Rehabilitation Counseling Association
1910 Association Drive
Suite 206
Reston, VA 22091

Social Worker

Helps individuals, families, and groups solve their problems

What's It Like to Be a Social Worker?

Social workers plan and conduct activities for children, adolescents, families, and older people in settings such as settlement houses, hospitals, and correctional institutions. They try to strengthen family life and improve its functioning. They work to improve the physical and emotional well-being of deprived and troubled children. They advise parents on child care and work with school social workers and community leaders. School social workers are employed in the public schools; medical social workers work in hospitals; and psychiatric social workers work in mental health centers and clinics. Cy Abdelnour, a 30-year-old social worker for a state agency, prefers working with children. He believes that chances are better for changes in attitudes and behavior in a child's life than in an adult's. Abdelnour works with children in school, in courts, and in child centers. His lunches are usually with children at the nearest McDonald's. He often visits children at their homes after school, and his evenings may be spent taking clients to sports events and school plays.

What Education and Skills Will I Need?

High School   Preparation for college, with as broad an education as possible.

College   Major in one of the social sciences to prepare for graduate school, or take a bachelor's degree in social work (B.S.W.). A master's degree (M.S.W.), offered by 113 colleges, is required for professional membership in the National Association of Social Workers.

Personal Skills   To be happy in social work you must be sensitive to others, be as objective as possible, and have a basic concern for people and their problems.

How Many Social Workers Are There and Where Do They Work?

There are 484,000 social workers; 68 percent are women, 22 percent are black, and 6 percent are Hispanic. Most work for local (25 percent) or state (24 percent) governments or for private social service agencies (22 percent).

How Much Money Will I Make?

In 1992 the median starting salary for a social worker with a bachelor's degree in social work was $20,000 a year. A social worker with a master's degree and one year's experience earned $30,000 a year. Hospital social workers made from $25,600 to $38,700.

What Are the Job Opportunities?

Chances for jobs are expected to be very good through 2005 because of the decrease in social work graduates, the increasing demand for services by the elderly, higher unemployment, and fewer government programs. As the government cuts its budget, most job opportunities will be with private agencies, nursing homes, hospices, rehabilitation programs, HMOs, and home health programs.

Related Careers

Clergy

Counselor

Rehabilitation counselor

Psychologist

Where Can I Get More Information?

National Association of Social Workers
7981 Eastern Avenue
Silver Spring, MD 20910

Career Day

A PLAN FOR HIGH SCHOOL GUIDANCE COUNSELORS

The most successful Career Day programs are usually those that include students, teachers, and parents in both planning and implementation. Even though teachers are not always eager to relate their discipline to career possibilities, they will feel much more confident about Career Day if they have a copy of *The College Board's Guide to Jobs and Career Planning*. The book will make it easier for teachers to develop a list of job titles with their own subject in mind. Teachers can ask students to respond to the jobs that appeal to them and, at the same time, get a feeling for information students need as a planning tool for organizing Career Day. A student-interest list is a good source for selecting guest speakers. The Career Day committee will want to create a parent-community file for potential speakers based on student interest.

Careful coordination among the school staff and guests will ensure success. For example, the speakers must know the kind of information to present as well as when and where to meet. Some of the speakers will not be familiar with teenagers; you can help by spelling out your expectations for them. Don't forget to invite members of your faculty who may also be writers or artists or former athletes. It's great for high school students to see their teachers in another career role. After Career Day is over, student evaluations will make next year's planning easier.

The academic-centered Career Day concentrates on relating high school subjects to jobs. Helping students to build on their high school academic strengths and interests in order to keep as many career options open as possible is the goal of a Career Day program. Here's the plan:

1. Survey students in the classroom to find out which careers interest them most.

2. Plan the program for all high school students. Younger students can learn how curriculum choices influence career options, while eleventh and twelfth graders will be more interested in learning about how career options relate to college choices.

3. Survey the students to find potential speakers among their parents and neighbors. Selecting parents and teachers as guest speakers always makes a more interesting Career Day for the students. The more parents involved in the program, the better.

4. Plan to begin your activities in one large group and then divide into smaller groups.

   (a) In the large group, welcome students. A short talk by the career counselor or an outside career "expert" (a personnel director or a well-known local employer or the career counselor from *another* high school) should focus on "Self-assessment," which is Step 1 in the career selection process. The students should come away from the initial meeting with some answers to the question "What kind of student am I?"

   (b) Next, the career counselor can introduce Step 2, "Researching careers," which is best presented by describing the career resources available in the guidance office, and by specifically mentioning and displaying *The College Board's Guide to Jobs and Career Planning* and *The Occupational Outlook Handbook*. At this time, the guests can be introduced, with comments on the students' interest in the particular careers these guests represent. Provide the students with the most dramatic and interesting outside speakers. As you select the speakers, be careful not to stereotype, by gender, race, or age, the guests you invite. For example, don't choose only men for science and finance careers, only women for service careers, Asians for medicine and computer careers, and blacks for sports or education careers. Mix them up! Get a woman engineer, a white male social worker, and a black bank manager or stockbroker. Break into smaller groups by classroom or career. Make sure that the leaders of the small groups have lists of students who will be in their groups.

(c) Finally, Step 3, "Educational pathways," can be presented to a reunited large group or to the individual small groups. This step focuses on educational pathways to a particular career. It's important for the teacher and the counselor to emphasize the great variety of educational possibilities open to students depending on their abilities and interests. For example, the possibile ways to train for a career in accounting range from a year of business school after high school, to a two-year associate's degree in accounting, to a B.S. degree in accounting, to a certified public accountant (CPA), which requires graduate study plus a series of examinations. Another example of the range of educational pathways to a career is nursing, in which the required study ranges from six weeks of on-the-job training to be a nurse's aide, to a one-year practical nursing program, to a two-year, three-year, or four-year degree in nursing, to six years for a master's or eight years for a doctorate.

(d) Wrap up: Emphasize curriculum and college choices rather than definite career choices for 14- to 18-year-olds. As long as students do their best in high school they will be opening their career doors. Encourage them to take the most challenging curriculum they can handle well, rather than to make curriculum choices based on the career they think they want to pursue, because their career choice will change many times before they get out of college.

Checklist

1. Plan publicity at least a month ahead of time. Use the public address system, bulletin boards, school and local press, as well as encouragement in the classroom from all teachers.
2. Send reminders of the date and time along with the small-group student lists to teachers and staff.
3. Send an informational letter to all guest speakers:

   (a) State the purpose of the program.
   (b) Be clear about your expectations for guest participation.
   (c) Enclose a copy of the program.
   (d) Request a confirmation of the speaker's participation.

4. Print name tags for all guests and speakers.
5. Display posters listing the guest speakers and the careers they represent.
6. Use the art class and the newspaper staff to print the Career Day program.
7. Place a large sign on the door of each room to be used.
8. Schedule photo opportunities for the school paper and the local press.
9. Send thank-you notes to all guest speakers and parents who helped with the Career Day. And thank yourself for a job well planned!

Index